Marx and Engels's "German ideology" Manuscripts

Marx, Engels, and Marxisms

The collapse of "communism" as a geopolitical force has liberated Marx, Engels, and all the variants of Marxism from ideologically motivated and intellectually stultifying presumptions. Running contrary to nineteenth- and twentieth-century practices of conflation and simplification, this innovative series revitalizes major figures and intellectual traditions, and its authors and editors present recent scholarly discoveries in imaginative ways, challenging twenty-first-century readers with unfamiliar perspectives.

Terrell Carver and Marcello Musto, Series Editors

A Political History of the Editions of Marx and Engels's "German ideology Manuscripts"
Terrell Carver and Daniel Blank

Marx and Engels's "German ideology" Manuscripts: Presentation and Analysis of the "Feuerbach chapter"
Terrell Carver and Daniel Blank

Marx and Engels's "German ideology" Manuscripts
Presentation and Analysis of the "Feuerbach chapter"

Terrell Carver and Daniel Blank

MARX AND ENGELS'S "GERMAN IDEOLOGY" MANUSCRIPTS
Copyright © Terrell Carver and Daniel Blank, 2014.

Softcover reprint of the hardcover 1st edition 2014 978-1-137-48543-4

All rights reserved.

First published in 2014 by
PALGRAVE MACMILLAN®
in the United States—a division of St. Martin's Press LLC,
175 Fifth Avenue, New York, NY 10010.

Where this book is distributed in the UK, Europe and the rest of the world, this is by Palgrave Macmillan, a division of Macmillan Publishers Limited, registered in England, company number 785998, of Houndmills, Basingstoke, Hampshire RG21 6XS.

Palgrave Macmillan is the global academic imprint of the above companies and has companies and representatives throughout the world.

Palgrave® and Macmillan® are registered trademarks in the United States, the United Kingdom, Europe and other countries.

ISBN 978-1-349-50369-8   ISBN 978-1-137-48545-8 (eBook)
DOI 10.1057/9781137485458

Library of Congress Cataloging-in-Publication Data is available from the Library of Congress.

A catalogue record of the book is available from the British Library.

Design by Newgen Knowledge Works (P) Ltd., Chennai, India.

First edition: December 2014

10 9 8 7 6 5 4 3 2 1

Transferred to Digital Printing in 2015

Contents

Acknowledgments — vii

Analytical Introduction — 1
Brief Apparatus Criticus — 33
New Textual Presentation and English Translation from a New German Text
Rough Notes, formerly known as "I. Feuerbach," drawn from "the German ideology" manuscripts by Karl Marx, Friedrich Engels, and Joseph Weydemeyer — 34

Abbreviation and Bibliography — 383
Index — 385

Acknowledgments

The research for this volume was supported by a grant to Terrell Carver from the Arts and Humanities Research Council, PID 122462/AID 120775, awarded July 18, 2006.

The authors would like to thank de Gruyter, Berlin, for permission to use the textual research in the following work in preparing the presentation and analysis contained in this volume:

Editors: Inge Taubert and Hans Pelger

Title: *Karl Marx, Friedrich Engels, Joseph Weydemeyer, Die Deutsche Ideologie: Artikel, Druckvorlagen, Entwürfe, Reinschriftenfragmente und Notizen zu I. Feuerbach und II. Sankt Bruno, Text und Apparat – Marx-Engels Jahrbuch 2003*

ISBN: 3-05-003837-3

Publisher: Akademie Verlag

Date of publication: 2 vols, 2004

Text pp. 6–100, Apparat pp. 163–281

Analytical Introduction

Marx and Engels's "German ideology" Manuscripts presents a completely fresh translation of the manuscript fragments misleadingly known as the "chapter" "I. Feuerbach," by far the most widely read element of the published volume named *The German Ideology*.[1] Uniquely in English the rendition of these manuscripts in this volume makes changes and corrections undertaken individually by the two authors visible within the text itself. Each opening presents a "variant-rich" text on the left (verso) page and a "smooth" text of the "last hand" for each author on the right (recto). The reader thus gains easy access to a collaborative "laboratory" in which Marx and Engels worked actively together—sometimes sparring with one another—to find a new way of answering questions such as: What should we understand by humanity, civilization, industry, politics, and society? How do we connect social change with a desirable future? What validates the truth and the politics of the answers?

The textual presentations and English translations that follow have been assembled and substantively analyzed in a uniquely recontextualized manner. These manuscript "printer's sheets," left aside by Marx and Engels in 1846, are considered here neither in relation to a supposed breakthrough of mutual "self-clarification" by the two, nor as an exposition of a joint "outlook" in a lengthy and definitive account, the twin pillars of the now traditional but in fact early-twentieth-century reception (see Carver, 2010). As shown in Carver and Blank (2014), after 1924, political attention and scholarly commentary have focused on this set of very rough, discontinuous, and hitherto unwanted manuscripts with both those purposes in mind. That approach has necessarily driven scholarship in a doctrinal direction, namely, how can these "offcuts" be assembled and interpreted so as to affirm a "conception of history" (said to be "materialist" in some sense)?[2]

While there are certainly debates about the contextual "match" between this familiar view of the authors' intentions and achievements at this point (and of their similar and different intentions and achievements later on in their careers), the textual presentation and substantive study in the remainder of this volume will simply leave those issues aside and take up a rather different question. That question is: By studying "variant-rich" manuscripts, what can be learned about the *thinking* of Marx and Engels as they worked on what was left of several very heated but narrowly focused polemics? This question thus sidelines any rush to determine the "final" content of their *thought*—which is the usual political and scholarly goal—at this point or later. A focus on "thought" usually spurs most commentators to summary accounts and a characterization of these thinkers as doctrinaires, whereas we focus here on their *thinking*.

The commentary that follows will capitalize on the roughness and unpolished character of these fragments, the crossings-out and insertions that they engaged in, just to see what happens when we look for detailed process rather than "final" view. From 1847, Marx himself advertised to the world that he had left these materials unfinished and "in the sleep of the just," thus evidently not a work in progress.[3] Yet curiously textual presentation and scholarly commentary have focused on finishing them, making them into a "text of the last hand," and squaring them (or otherwise) with the tenets of the "thought" in a broad sense on which the two were later said to have agreed. This mutual agreement was more of a scholarly trope and argumentative goal than a demonstrable fact, an ongoing puzzle with numerous solutions proffered over the years. The same is very much true of the rather narrower "materialist interpretation of history," numerous attempts to specify this—including those by Engels—notwithstanding. Whatever the virtues of these exercises, they are put to one side here, and the reader is invited to enter a kind of workspace where the two authors are writing together, making mistakes, debating corrections, spilling out their thoughts (sometimes rather literally), and from all accounts having a lively time of it.[4]

The texts and commentary that follow are thus in no way a "new edition" of the putative chapter "I. Feuerbach" of *The German Ideology* as a "book" by Marx and Engels alone (see Carver and Blank, 2014). Nor are the following materials any kind of prolegomenon to a properly complex "contextual edition," which would provide a political and substantive interpretation for the various unfinished polemical critiques on which Marx and Engels were working (together and with others) during 1845–46, as these critiques were begun, broken off, reconceived, rewritten, and ultimately abandoned (see ibid., Chapter 9 and Appendix C).

Rather this venture is much more exploratory and frankly resists a scholarship that already knows what we are supposed to be interested in, how it will "fit" (or not) with previous accounts that have made similar presuppositions, and why a readership will—so it is presumed—be interested. The *Bogen* (printer's sheets) under consideration here were rather fortunately left to us and not to the mice. (After personally examining all the manuscript sheets conserved at present, we found only one possible very small mouse-tooth excision.) These fragments represent an unusual resource among the voluminous extant papers, because these unwanted sheets (each folded and thus representing a possible four "sides" on which to write) are in a rough state, very much prior to any "fair copy" destined for a printer. There is thus more evidence here than usual of the *thinking* process involved in moving from one thought to a subsequent revision by means of word-by-word addition, deletion, substitution, reordering, and the like. But there is another, and quite underrated, reason why these pages are a particularly unusual resource.

Marx and Engels produced only three works as jointly composed endeavors (in some overt sense). These were *The Holy Family* of 1845 (by Engels and Marx in that order on the title page, with individually signed chapters, and no extant manuscript materials); the manuscript sheets of 1845–46 under consideration at this point in the present volume; and the anonymously published *Manifesto of the Communist Party* of 1848 (of which only one manuscript page survives). From the biographical information available it is likely that the physical presence of the two together as they worked was much more a feature of the polemical manuscript works of 1845–46 than of the others.[5] While there have been more or less extreme versions of putative "joint authorship" extending to some—or indeed all—of their individual productions and while the mutual correspondence between the two (and other letters involving third parties) indicates interesting and sometimes important exchanges of ideas from time to time, our conclusion here is that the "leftover" printer's sheets, which are presented and translated in the present volume, are the premier resource for considering their intellectual interaction in holographic detail. This is despite the claim—somewhat exaggerated since Engels's biographer Gustav Mayer ventured the suggestion—that "perhaps" (*vielleicht*) Engels was merely an amanuensis taking dictation (for a discussion of this point, see Carver, 2010: pp. 123–24). However, following the recontextualized methodology proposed for the present analytical study, there will be no great rush to form any conclusions about the character of an intellectual relationship that had itself only just got under way.

Analytical Introduction

The problems with reading and transcribing the manuscripts at all are very well known. Marx's handwriting was in cursive gothic and very difficult to read; rather fortunately, most of these manuscript sheets are in Engels's hand, which—though still a matter for the specialist—is easier. Nonetheless, an attempt to decipher the various editorial workings inscribed in, on, around, and over what was once a first draft presents further difficulties. The copy-text for this reading of the manuscripts is that presented in the *Deutsche-Zeitschrift für Philosophie 2003* (see Carver and Blank, 2014, especially Chapter 8). There are of course possibilities of misreading even there, and we have done some spot-checking and produced relevant notes.

However, the methodology adopted in that edition to deal with editorial "variants" not only presupposes a "smooth" text of the "last hand" as the desired result, but also renders the "variants" in a potentially useful but rather controversial manner. They are recorded in the *apparatus criticus* volume not just descriptively as single-word (or single-letter) changes[6] but rather in many cases as successive "thoughts," that is, phrased as an initial thought, followed by a rephrased thought, followed by a further thought, and so on. While this makes apparent good sense of the thinking involved as the writing (by one or the other author) progressed, it is also quite controversially "interpretive" and of course subject to revision as other readers/editors gain access to digitized images of the original sheets.[7] Thus, the present exercise is a reading of a reading, and indeed a reading of a particular sort and so subject to error or debate on that basis.

The goal of this presentation and analysis is thus to create a resource that will be useful in opening up discussions and debates in a wide-ranging way, rather than simply filling in a gap in preexisting (and very long-standing) interpretive frameworks. Readers will be free—bearing in mind the caveats listed earlier—to engage with these texts and thoughts just to see what it might say to them on subjects of current and perennial interest (rather than just about Marx and/or Engels, and/or the "materialist interpretation of history"). The present day and possible futures are of course always and already conceptualized in relation to an understanding of the past and indeed of humanity and civilization. Whether and how "we" and "it" have changed over the millennia and what the significance of this might be for the future are familiar modes of *thinking*, particularly in relation to politics.

This is just what Marx and Engels were doing when they wrote these pages, and unusually we have a record of precisely how their thinking progressed, given that this can be done only through alterations that their editorial changes—word-by-word—record for us. It may be that in these abandoned pages the thinking of Marx and of Engels won't be all that impressive and a consideration of their detailed word changes uninformative. Those judgments will depend on any given reader's engagement with the general issues involved and on their ability to empathize with Marx's and Engels's frankly argumentative and hortatory style. As explained in Carver and Blank (2014), their thinking was not merely political but self-consciously polemical, and their sarcasm inherently ungenerous and doubtless unfair to their (absent) interlocutors. On the other hand, attentive readers may find productive puzzlement and ongoing inspiration in the thinking of the two as it emerges in our presentation and analysis in the pages that follow.

Analysis in the present exercise is not intended to be in any sense definitive, but rather true—at least in spirit—to what has been made of these horrendously messy manuscripts by the latest transcription and editorial team. The substantive treatment is thus somewhat personal but we hope of interest, and the reflective discussion is organized substantively in a thematic way. The "reflective discussion" that follows is thus composed in the manner of meditations on some of the themes that two unusually inspiring and transgressive thinkers were raising between themselves.

The extant manuscript pages are presented *Bogen* by *Bogen* as Engels numbered them, separately paginated and in double-column format, with Marx's and Engels's handwriting clearly distinguished from each other (see the "Brief Apparatus Criticus" in the present volume). This ordering reflects the rough timing of initial composition, though of course it is impossible now to determine the exact chronology of further authorial changes as the two worked together, shuffling the leaves around.[8] Given that some materials are missing, and that the extant sheets are discontinuous and related to different projects anyway, the reflections that follow are—in our exploratory manner—not particularly dependent on the idea that commentary must follow a chronological order of composition anyway. Given that this reflective discussion thus violates numerous canons of contextual interpretation and bibliographical methodology, it is necessarily something of an experiment. However, the intention is not to supplant but to supplement other hermeneutic methods of investigation and scholarly methods of presentation.

Thus the reading and writing strategies deployed here are not focused on the question "where did the two get to?" but rather on the question "what do we think about the way their minds were working?"—whether we agree with any of the specifics or not. In that way, as editors and interpreters, we do not aim here to judge a finished enterprise (because it wasn't) but rather to engage, with Marx and Engels, on an inquiry—not into human understanding—but into how to understand humans. How are humans misperceived and misrepresented by historians and philosophers? How exactly can this be corrected? Why is correction important politically? How can the *language* of misperception and misrepresentation be corrected? What is the effect of this correction supposed to be? What discursive contrasts thus emerge? What epistemological contrasts are asserted? What political contrasts are drawn?

Reflective Discussion

At the time of writing, 1845–46, Marx and Engels were engaged in drawing a line between themselves and the "German ideologists," their term of abuse for certain political rivals in the philosophically coded politics of the time (see Carver and Blank, 2014, Chapter 6). The terms through which they understood their opponents and critics as "idealists" in the philosophical sense are quite well understood in political and scholarly literature, at least since the 1960s. That is, "idealists" are those who assign an ultimate reality to ideas (assumed to be nonmaterial) as opposed to material things (which are thus effects in some sense of ideas), on the presumption that ideas/matter are dichotomous and exhaustive of reality.

However, the sense in which Marx and Engels were defining themselves as "materialist"—in opposition to these idealists—has been a matter of debate and confusion since the origins of scholarly and political commentary on Marx (by Engels) in 1859 (see Carver, 2003). "Materialist" can of course refer to traditional materialism in opposition to idealism, as just mentioned, or it could—if we follow a strand of interpretive commentary very carefully (see Kitching and Pleasants, 2002)—refer to a "new" understanding of materialism, as Marx was suggesting in his "Theses on Feuerbach." These were of course written just before the present "German ideology" fragments, and in Theses 1, 9, and 10, Marx dismisses "all previous materialism" as "contemplative" and opts for a "new [one]" (CW 5: pp. 3 and 5; see also Carver and Blank, 2014, Chapters 2 and 7). The textual presentation of the manuscript sheets under consideration here shows in a number of places exactly how this position—amongst other considerations—was put into words.

Starting with the remaining two sheets of the presumed *Bogen* 1, here is Engels's hand in full polemical flow:

Naturally of
course we will not take the trouble to enlighten
~~to~~ our wise philosophers with the fact that the

"liberation" of "man" does not get a single
step further when they have dissolved
philosophy, theology, substance & all that
foolery into "self-consciousness", when they
have liberated "man" from domination by
these phrases to which he had never been in
thrall; that it is not possible to achieve actual
liberation other than in the actual world &
with actual means,

[01 Bogen, 01 Seite, L Column, pp. 34, 36]

And here is Marx's summary reduction—making the same point without the rhetorical turns of sarcastic polemic ("we will not trouble to enlighten") present in the other, left-hand column in Engels's hand. Feuerbach is throughout addressed as superior to "his rivals" (e.g., Bruno and Edgar Bauer, Max Stirner, etc.)[9] but still suffering from the same affliction, namely, being a philosopher, protestations to the contrary notwithstanding:

**Just like his rivals Feuerbach believes
{himself} to have transcended philosophy!**
~~The act{ual}~~ **The struggle against general
conceptions, which have previously
oppressed the individual, summarises the
standpoint of German philosophical
criticism. We maintain that this struggle,
pursued in this manner, is itself founded on
philosophical illusions of the sovereignty of
general conceptions.**
<u>**Feuerbach.**</u>
<u>**Philosophical and actual liberation.**</u>
Man. Individuality. The <u>Individual.</u>

| Geological, hydrographical etc. conditions. |
| The human body. Needs and labour. |

[01 Bogen, 01 Seite, R Column, p. 34]

This is not to say that Marx is here rejecting polemic (a *very* odd idea) by adverting to an independent, freestanding statement of an apparently "materialist" view, but rather that the text records a pattern of compositional dialogue (rather than successive attempts at a single authorial voice and tone—which might of course have happened later on had the two pursued these projects jointly as planned). Possibly Marx's deletion, ~~The act{ual}~~, allowed him to finish the pejorative characterization of idealism and idealists as a matter of **struggle** and then proceed to a clear contrast: **<u>Philosophical and actual liberation.</u>** And after that he advances—interestingly—to conditions conventionally understood as material and as the "external" setting for humans (**Geological, hydrographical etc. conditions**), then to humans "materially" considered (**body**) and finally to the social yet still "material" constitution of individuals and societies (**Needs and labour**). This sets out an argumentative trajectory from the speculative realm of (merely philosophical) ideas to a realm of actuality, where materiality and sociality intersect in practical (rather than abstract) ways, and where an abstraction such as "man" does not figure as a syntactical agent but rather more flesh and blood conceptualizations take his [*sic*] place.

Actuality is thus "filled in" by Marx not so much with materiality as with sociality and history, understood quite apart from a generally presumed philosophical parsing of reality into dichotomous categories of matter/mind, objects/ideas, and so on. The left-hand column draft in Engels's hand—"actual world & with actual means"—has in a sense been resolved into an agenda for specifics in Marx's right-hand column commentary. This of course is a move with (anti-)philosophical and political significance already noted, but here we have an opportunity to follow the actual vocabulary through which this is pursued—though this is not to suggest that a "resulting" and "agreed" text or even position was an intended outcome. The stance adopted in the present commentary works against such conclusions. Rather the point is to focus on the contrasting vocabularies involved and to see how they arise in making the contrast work as it is developing.

Engels's left-hand draft indeed becomes much more specific in terms of Marx's **Needs and labour** by historicizing industrializing societies:

> that it is not possible to achieve actual
> liberation other than in the actual world &
> with actual means, that slavery cannot be
> transformed {*aufheben*} without the steam-
> engine & spinning machines, serfdom without
> improved agriculture, that in any case men
> cannot be liberated so long as they are not in a
> position to obtain food & drink, shelter &
> clothing adequate sufficient in quality &
> quantity.
> [01 Bogen, 01 Seite, L Column, p. 36]

While this view of human history is not completely novel and indeed it reflects the historical mode through which political economy had been developing since the seventeenth century, the "communist" twist here is of course the view that the future offers "liberation":

> "Liberation" is a historical action,
> not a conceptual action, & it is accomplished
> through historical relations, through the state
> of industry, of trade, of agriculture, of social
> interaction {relation}s{,}
> [01 Bogen, 01 Seite, L Column, p. 36]

Analytical Introduction

Using "history" to project a future is a familiar move with considerable rhetorical value, and indeed in that way history is never simply of the past. The present is the past as far as it has got, and the future—in these conventional terms—is where the present is going (or should be going if moved along properly). History of course could be a history of concepts, or a chronologically arranged account of conceptual transformations, which was indeed the accusation that Marx and Engels were leveling against their "idealist" opponents, in this case "Saint Bruno" Bauer.

Marx and Engels are evidently working to distinguish themselves from such "idealists" by defining actuality as the developmental trajectory (past, present, future) of human productive industries. These are of course words and in some sense abstractions. Where then is the epistemological dividing line? What is it about these words that references actuality more truthfully than idealist assertions (as Marx and Engels portray them) of transformations involving "man," "self-consciousness," "substance," and "liberation"?

Reading through the following sequence as we have it, *Bogen 6–Bogen* 11, it becomes striking that the traditional interpretive strategy suggested by Engels in 1888 and later endorsed by Mehring,[10] namely, that mere polemic can be excised from substantive (and in their terms validly philosophical) content, can usefully be reversed. This is not to say that the specific points made by Marx and Engels against Bauer (and against Bauer's version of Feuerbach, and against Marx and Engels's understanding of Feuerbach independent of that) are of particular interest, but rather that Marx and Engels's substantive theses on humanity, history, modernity, and a communist future develop in these fragments as *political* points through and through. This is by way of contrast to "truths" derived abstractly that would make sense whatever the context or indeed require no context. What emerges in the manuscripts' discussions is that the two have a common position—which they are working out in some sense jointly—but one conceived preeminently as a political position, and the arguments as political ones.

Indeed the tenor of the argumentation is such that extraction of their views as "theory" (whether a philosophical one or a "theory of history") would be a regression to the very position—excoriated as both "ideological" and typically "German"—that they were at such pains to attack in their sustained critique of the "critical critics." The nub of the matter was not so much that these philosophers were thinking the wrong things because they were thinking the wrong way, but that they were doing politics the wrong way (hence thinking the wrong way) and were thus merely encouraging others to be just as wrongheaded and (so Marx and Engels were arguing) ineffectual.

This is not to say that interesting and provocative ideas cannot be extracted from these fragments of polemic but rather that there is a contextual and interpretive disjunction in doing so. Marx and Engels (in this period) can be made into methodologists of philosophy and/or history (or indeed into many other things), but doing so traps the commentator in the very critique that the two are mounting. This was a relentless critique of political posing and posturing, of self-deceiving fantasies of potency belied by evident social realities and predictable economic developments. Of course there could be spirited defenses today of Bauer and company and cynical judgments that Marx and Engels were never on to a winner with their own political strategy (and were thus self-deluding in their own ways, which were not entirely dissimilar). However, for the present exercise—making something of the "variant-rich" texts that the two have (rather accidentally) left for us—we can let the pair have it their own way on their own manuscript pages.

Here we have what might be an interesting illustration of a move from stating what is the case in very general and abstract terms—as a philosopher might do—to a more direct approach (via a strike-through), namely, stating what a "practical materialist" should be doing politically. Note the force of Marx's emphasis:

> in reality {it} ~~is a matter of~~ & for the
>
> **practical** materialists, i.e. the **communists**,[11] it

is a matter of revolutionising the existing
world
[06 Bogen, 08 Seite, L Column, p. 44]

In the pages that follow, Marx is devaluing the language of theorizing with scare quotes and excising an abstraction in favor of a concrete reference:

> Feuerbach's
> ~~theoretical conception~~ "conception" of
> ~~perceptibility~~ the perceptible world
> is limited on the one hand to
> merely viewing it, & on the
>   to merely
> other   feeling {it}
> [06 Bogen, 08 Seite, L Column, p. 44]

Here is Marx's insertion (p. 44) nailing down this contrast—between a philosopher's very general abstractions and a "concrete" reference to a politically potent alternative:

> {insertion}
> **{he} considers "<u>man</u>" instead of "actual historical man". "<u>Man</u>" is in reality "German man".** {end insertion}

In these passages that follow, the two are criticizing Feuerbach for merely hinting at what they themselves are stating directly—as opposed to more egregious "ideologists" who have not advanced even to the point that Feuerbach had reached with his hints. The critique from Marx and Engels throughout is two-fisted: German "ideologists" have the wrong philosophy and wrong practice (and indeed, they are philosophers, so the vocational and nonpractical outlooks go together), and they have the wrong history (because philosophy in general is abstractly timeless, so they really have no historical sense at all, hints and protestations notwithstanding). In the lines here, "He" is again Feuerbach:

> He does not see
> how the perceptible world surrounding him is
> not **a thing** handed down directly from
> eternity, staying always the same, **but rather**
> **the product of industry & of social**
> **conditions & to be sure in the sense that it is**
> **a historical product, the result of the**
> **activity of a whole series of generations**,
> [06 Bogen, 08 Seite, L Column, p. 44]

Analytical Introduction

From this Marx/Engels perspective there is little point in a materialism of "things" or objects of perception as such, given that things/objects are asserted to have human histories of production. Effectively, this view dissolves and transcends the most entrenched dichotomy of post-seventeenth-century philosophy, that of matter/consciousness as exclusionary categories, one (consciousness) "knowing" the other (matter).

However, as mentioned earlier, the Marx/Engels critique is a political one, rather than a contribution to other rather more academic discussions. Perhaps their position could be characterized as an epistemology of action, rather than of knowledge as such. The following "NB" in Engels's hand in the right-hand column is rather wordy and repetitious, but it gets to the point in the end, implying that "spectacles" in this case produce not just impaired vision but failure to make sense of human experience in a more politically progressive manner than merely "spectating" (as an "idealist" and "philosopher" would):

> NB. F[euerbach's] mistake is not that he
> subordinates the immediately apparent,
> <u>perception</u>, to the perceptible actuality attested
> by precise investigation of perceptible
> circumstances, but that he cannot in the end
> cope with perceptibility except by considering
> it with the "eyes", i.e. through the
> "spectacles", of the <u>philosophers</u>.
> [06 Bogen, 08 Seite, R Column, p. 46]

The following lengthy passage produces a clear if philosophically controversial (still) definition of what constitutes an empirical fact, which Marx and Engels argue is not a reference to what something "is" but rather to "what has happened" to produce it historically. This means that an empirical fact is not a linguistic representation of, and thus a conceptual reflection of, an object, which is discretely given to perception and simply "is" what it is in itself. Marx's insertions ram home the point polemically, saying that Bauer and company have not grasped the essentially and profoundly historical character of things/objects, even supposedly natural ones, because they presume an antithesis between (timeless) nature and (happenstance) history:

> Moreover in this
> conception ~~also the~~ of things as they actually
> are & have happened, every profound
> philosophical problem resolves itself quite
> simply into an empirical fact, as is shown even
> more clearly below. E.g. the important
> question of the relation of man
> to nature ~~on which~~, {*insertion*} **(or especially
> ~~the "relation between~~ as Bruno says (p.
> 110)**[12] **the "antitheses in nature and history",
> as if** {*further insertion*} **the two were quite**

separate "things", {*end further insertion*} {**as if**} **man is not always confronted with a historical nature and a natural history,**)
{*end insertion*}
[06 Bogen, 09 Seite, L Column, p. 50]

The argument here is that for humans, their world is **a historical nature and a natural history**, a chiasmus worth pondering, precisely because to be human is to be historical "all the way down" and thus to make a history of material/natural objects (not just a "perception") and to see material/natural objects within a historical perspective (not a "timeless" one). Rounding off this revolution, the two authors in the passage that follows collapse a quoted phrase linking the two abstractions "man" and "nature"—the phrase has a philosophical and quasi-religious ring to it—into an utterly mundane and everyday concept of industry (which has its ups and downs historically):

the much ~~famed~~ vaunted "unity of man with
nature" has always existed in industry & has
existed variously in every epoch depending on
the lesser or greater development of industry,
[06 Bogen, 09 Seite, L Column, p. 50]

The question of the temporal priority of "nature" over "man" arises here within a long insertion in Engels's hand, as it would in a philosophical argument that "man" and "nature" must be considered distinct because the former arose before, and independently of, the latter. But then, this conventional treatment is brusquely replaced with a different understanding, one that locates meaning in the current political setting (rather than in some timeless elsewhere):

~~For~~ In any case the {temporal}
       external
priority of   nature remains intact here,
~~& it is no accident for us &~~ & in any
case ~~this nature no distinction~~ all this has
no
[06 Bogen, 09 Seite, L Column – continuing]

application to the first men produced through
spontaneous generation; this distinction,
however, only has meaning in so far as one
considers man to be distinguished from nature.
Moreover this nature, which precedes human
history, is really not ~~Feuerbach's, in which~~ the

nature in which Feuerbach lives, not the nature
which no longer exists anywhere today except
perhaps ~~in the interior of newly f{ormed}~~ on
isolated Australian coral islands of recent
origin
[06 Bogen, 10 Seite, L Column, p. 56]

Another passage in Engels's hand much later in this set of fragments—and possibly written somewhat later in the compositional processes anyway—puts this issue with great clarity. Note also the strike-through on "proof," which might have philosophical connotations of certainty via abstract reasoning. This move further devalues Feuerbach's method that—according to Marx and Engels—was to universalize abstractly from (ever-shrinking) "examples" of supposed certainties founded on their timelessness and thus in contradistinction to human history:

> Feuerbach therefore never speaks of the
> human world but rather he flees every time
>   external
> into   nature, & to be sure into <u>the</u>
> nature which has not yet been brought under
> human control. But with each new invention,
> each advance of industry a new patch is
> detached from this terrain, & the soil, from
> which grow the ~~proof~~ examples for similar
> Feuerbachian propositions, is thus becoming
> ever smaller.
> [11 Bogen, 29 Seite, R Column, p. 160]

The historicity of the human-nature relationship could not be clearer than the way it is put in the previous passage. What is "external" is merely not yet under control and thus emphatically not a realm of timeless certainty on which human reasoning could rely. One of Marx's pithy insertions in the passage that follows also puts the conclusion unmistakably and in simple terms:

> Feuerbach has in any case a big advantage
> over the "pure" materialists because he ~~also
> realises how~~ realises how man too is "a
> perceptible object"; however, {insertion}[13]
> **apart from the fact that he only conceives of
> him as "~~perceptible~~ a "perceptible object"
> not as "perceptible activity"**
> [06 Bogen, 10 Seite, L Column, p. 56]

Or, in other words, any politically significant conception of humanity must start by conceiving of humans not as objects in any discrete or "material" sense but as always already immersed in activities, which are themselves necessarily historical and thus time- and sequence-dependent.

In the passage that follows, in Engels's hand, the critique of Feuerbach's ultimate "philosophism" (which is of course in this context a way of trouncing Bauer and company as even worse than Feuerbach) is attacked in another of Marx's insertions, where he moves from the pithy to the earthy, and in a potentially even more revolutionary way. Feuerbach, it says here in Engels's hand,

> only gets as far as
> recognising the "actual, individual, embodied
> men" in terms of emotion, i.e. he ~~arrives at~~
> knows no other "human relations" "of
> man to man" other than love & friendship,
> {insertion} **and idealised at that. There is no critique of present-day loving relations.**
> {end insertion}
> [06 Bogen, 10 Seite, L Column, p. 58]

Marx, as is well known, did not take this gender(ed) question up with much intellectual or political seriousness (though he said rather more on the subject than some have realized; see Carver, 1998, Chapter 10). But there is no doubt that he recognized a problematic zone of oppression not just in social class but also in "the woman question" (albeit in an underspecified way and always from a masculine point of view).

The following chiasmus, in Engels's hand, seems rather muddled about the two different senses of "materialism" that have been outlined in previous passages, that is, Feuerbach is said to be a philosophical materialist both when he *does* and when he *does not* consider "man" and "nature" historically, but then—see the insertion—bringing "history into consideration" would—on Engels's second thought, perhaps—make him a "new" materialist in the Marx-Engels sense just established earlier (see Marx, 1996: 118, "Theses on Feuerbach," Thesis 10):

> In so far as Feuerbach is a materialist,
> history does not register with him, & in so far
>   no
> as he brings history into consideration, he is
> materialist.
> [06 Bogen, 10 Seite, L Column, pp. 58, 60]

Due credit to the political economists for offering influential clues about history—which for Marx and Engels are producing a new politics—is given further along. In this passage in Engels's hand, "this fact" evidently refers to the man-nature merger as industry producing the perceptible world:

> The French & the English ~~at~~
> ~~least~~, even when they ~~have conceived~~
> conceived of the connection of this fact with

so-called history in a highly tendentious way,
particularly as long as they were biased by
political ideology, have ~~always~~ all the same
made the first attempts to give a materialistic
basis to the writing of history by being the first
to write histories of civil society, of trade &
of industry.
[06 Bogen, 11 Seite, L Column, p. 64]

By "materialistic" in the previous passage Marx and Engels are clearly referring to their view of the world as politically significant only insofar as its "material" aspects are conceived of historically and thus as products of human activities. In this way, philosophizing and philosophy are pushed to one side and, in political terms, soundly trounced (discursively, at least).

The following passage is a gem, well-worth foregrounding as a stinging critique of sociobiology and "evolutionary" approaches to humanity and history today. The discussion, in Engels's hand, singles out "ideological" treatments of

the "prehistoric era", not history at
all, without making clear to us how one gets
from this nonsense about "prehistory" to
proper history – although on the other hand
their historical speculation casts itself in
particular on "prehistory" because it is
believed to be safe there & from the intrusion
of "crude facts" & at the same time because
they give full rein to their speculative impulse
& {it} can set up & knock down ~~non{sense}~~
~~irre{futable}~~ hypotheses by the thousand
[07 Bogen, 12 Seite, L Column, p. 66]

While for the philosophers a timeless realm of "nature" had some rhetorical and possibly empirical utility as a repository of certainties, in the passage above Marx and Engels are arguing that prehistory is a far worse "basis" for philosophizing. In their view, there are even fewer bounds limiting what could possibly be projected into a "realm" that—unlike the ever-diminishing number of untouched coral islands—is simply inaccessible because it no longer exists at all.

The following passages in Engels's hand struggle mightily to get from the material—but also language-based—character of human activities and on to an explanation of "consciousness" as such. This raises the mind/matter dichotomy and leads to an unhelpful excursus on the materiality of language itself: it is said to comprise three "aspects" or "moments," subsequently altered to four without any clear amendment:

Only now, after we have considered four
moments, four aspects of original, historical

relations do we find that man ~~among other things also has "mind", & that this "mind" "manifests" itself~~ **also has "consciousness".** ~~as "consciousness"~~ But even this {is} not from the outset "pure" consciousness. The "mind" has from the start the curse of being "burdened" with matter, which ~~here in the form of vibrating layers of air, sounds, in short, language~~ occurs here in the form of vibrating layers of air, sounds, in short, language. Language is as old as consciousness – language i̲s̲ practical, actual consciousness existing for other men as well {*insertion*}, only therefore does it also exist for me myself {*end insertion*},

[07 Bogen, 13 Seite, L Column – 07 Bogen, 14 Seite, L Column, pp. 72, 74]

A summary comment from Marx makes short work of this apparent problem: humans-in-activity simply *are* a union of physicality and consciousness:

Men have history, because they must pro̲d̲u̲c̲e̲ their life, and indeed must do so in a s̲p̲e̲c̲i̲f̲i̲c̲ way; ~~they ha{ve}~~ this is given by their physical organisation; just the same as their consciousness.

[07 Bogen, 13 Seite, R Column, p. 72]

Here is an antiphilosophical manifesto from the text, dissolving epistemology into history:

The distinction between what is personal to the individual & what is contingent to the individual is not a conceptual distinction but rather a historical fact. This distinction has a different significance at different times, e.g. the medieval estate as something contingent to the individual in the 18th century, also the family, more or less. It is not a distinction

that we have to make for each era but rather
each era makes the distinction itself out of the
different elements that it finds to hand, & to
be sure not according to a concept but rather
forced by the material interactions of life.
[89 Bogen, 60 Seite, L Column, p. 324]

A further comment by Marx (p. 74) demarcates human activity (bearing in mind that the Marx/Engels conception refuses the mind/matter dichotomy) from animal activity. Today this would be more controversial as a hard-and-fast distinction than it was at the time. The point here is that the "constitutive outside" to the concept of human activity is neither matter nor consciousness—because it is inherently both, or rather correctly conceived, human activity makes nonsense of the distinction. Instead, the "other" to human activity—as put by Marx—is animal activity:

For the animal its relationship
to others does not exist as a relationship.
[07 Bogen, 14 Seite, R Column]

The discussion moves on from human "consciousness" to "ideology" and therefore to explaining how the German ideologists are placed in relation to the foundational human social activities that are indeed the substance of history. These passages that follow in Engels's hand again struggle somewhat through the argument. Note the interesting correction of "things" to "practice," that is, moving the language from a discourse of "material object" to one of "human activity":

The division of labour
only becomes an actual division at the moment
when a division of ~~mental & material~~ material
& mental labour takes place. From this
moment onwards consciousness <u>is able</u> to
conceive of itself as something other than the
consciousness of existing ~~things~~ practice,
~~something actual~~ actually representing
something without representing an actual thing
– from that moment onwards consciousness is
in a position to emancipate itself from the
world & to ascend to ~~pure~~ the formation of
"pure" theories, theology{,} philosophy{,}
morals
&c.
[07 Bogen, 15 Seite, L Column, p. 78]

Marx and Engels's "German ideology" Manuscripts

A telling correction by Marx occurs when—in a discussion of how humans are misrepresented in "ideological" discourse—he changes "single" (in Engels's hand) to "disaggregated," thus refusing a supposed biological bodily specificity but saddling the "ideologists" instead with an unrealistic and misleading abstraction away from *social* activity:

> the seeming representation of
> ~~single~~ **disaggregated** individuals
> [08 Bogen, 16 Seite, L Column, p. 84]

In the passages that follow there are also some anxieties over what is "natural" and what is not. The "natural" would generally stand for what cannot be altered, or should not be altered, and what therefore stands outside of history and historical development, which Marx and Engels are construing as a process of change in and through human productive activities that are necessarily social. These lines show a rejection of the idea that property had developed naturally, presumably in some process that was outside the trajectory that Marx and Engels are conceiving in terms of "forces" and "relations" of production. However, they seem to find a "natural" origin for property after all in "the family," given that "seed" is a naturalizing metaphor in this context (for a critical discussion of Marx on "the family," see Carver, 1998, Chapter 10). But then the two go on to articulate a trajectory of historical development for subsequent variations in property relations, which therefore makes them malleable:

> there also arises at the same time the
> dividing up ~~of the~~, & indeed the unequal
> division of labour & its products in both
> quantitative and qualitative terms, hence
> property {arises},
> which ~~had already developed naturally~~
> ~~within~~ already has its seed, its first form in
> the family, where the wife & the children
> are slaves of the husband.
> [08 Bogen, 16 Seite, L Column to 08 Bogen, 17 Seite, L Column, pp. 84, 86]

The previous discussion should not be taken to argue that these rough texts maintain a consistent view but rather that they struggle over this kind of conceptual distinction, and in a political way. The writers' aim is clearly to affirm a political battleground in the present within certain parameters, namely, those of social production—and, as we see in the passage above, nascent class struggle. Doing this requires not just a historical narrative but one that locates humanity both in a natural/material realm (e.g., bodily functions, socially catered for) and in a historical/natural realm of change (even if slow and un-self-conscious, often discontinuous). Perhaps rather typically the text in Engels's hand moves woman as "wife" into a natural/material realm of "family" relations and reproductive activity; as we have seen earlier, Marx had a sharper idea that critique should venture even here (though as also mentioned earlier he does not pursue this at any length). The point here is not to settle any of these substantive issues in terms of the text or indeed otherwise but rather to note the points of struggle and occasional correction (and inconsistency) as the discussion (in very rough draft) moves along.

Analytical Introduction

The text takes an interesting turn when "natural" comes to refer to social structures instituted unfreely and so constituting an "alien power" subjugating humans, whereas institutions arising "freely" would allow humans to control the structures to which their own activities give rise. Having thoroughly historicized the "natural," thus making it opposed to any notion of a timeless materiality, the text now takes the historicized "natural" and politicizes it negatively in relation to freedom:

> so long as men are living
> in societies that have arisen naturally, there
> exists a cleavage between particular &
> common interest, hence so long as ~~labour~~
> activity is not freely but rather naturally
> divided, man's own act becomes opposed to
> him as an alien power over and above him,
> which ~~controls~~ subjugates him instead of
> him controlling it.
> [08 Bogen, 17 Seite, L Column, p. 88]

The following passage in Engels's hand contains a correction of "social" to "historical," perhaps making sure that the "historical"—where the political excitement is located—is clearly separated from anything—such as a timeless concept of "society"—that might lazily be associated with the "natural":

> This fixation of social activity, this
> consolidation of ~~my~~ our own product into
> a ~~power~~ material sovereignty over ~~me~~ us,
> which escapes ~~my~~ our control, confounds
> ~~my~~ our expectations, brings our
> calculations to nothing, is one of the chief
> factors in the ~~existing soc{ial}~~ historical
> development up to now
> [08 Bogen, 18 Seite, L Column, p. 92]

In this passage that follows, "natural" refers to a process inside "history," namely, a development that occurs un-self-consciously, focusing in particular on property as a historical product, but not of self-conscious history-making:

> The social power, ~~which to~~
> ~~me{n}~~ i.e. the multiplied productive force,
> which develops through the cooperation,
> {*insertion*} conditional on the division of

17

> labour {*end insertion*}, of different
> individuals, appears to these individuals,
> because the cooperation itself is not
> voluntary but arises naturally, not as their
> own conjoined power, but rather as an
> alien sovereignty standing outside them,
> about which they know neither where it's
> come from nor where it's going ~~& with which they therefore no longer~~, which they
> therefore cannot control anymore, which
> on the contrary goes through a peculiar
> series of phases & stages of development
> independent of the will & action of men,
> even directing that very will & action.
> How else could e.g. property have a
> history at all
> [08 Bogen, 18 Seite, L Column, pp. 92, 94]

This passage below shows the consistency with which—in these rough texts—what is (in translation of course) described as "material" and "empirically verifiable" is to be explained in terms of human social activities and indeed quite mundane ones. Or, in other words, what is "material" is a practice and a process through which this view is "empirically verifiable" and is readily available to anyone, so who needs philosophers? And—see Marx's insertion "**world spirit's**"—especially Hegel and Hegelians:

> It follows from this that the ~~cha{nge}~~
> conversion from history to world history is by
> **world spirit's**
> no means a mere act of the "self-
> consciousness" or of any metaphysical spectre
> at all, but ~~is~~ rather a wholly material,
> empirically verifiable act, an act to which
> every individual affords the proof as he comes
> and goes, eats, drinks & clothes himself.[14]
> [08 Bogen, 21 Seite, L Column, p. 108]

Interestingly, this "ordinary experience" epistemology is said by Marx and Engels to extend quite dramatically to imminent and mass political conclusions, notwithstanding the "ideological" mystifications of "critical critics." "Ordinary experience" epistemology thus works to pit empirical verification against "philosophical," that is, nonordinary—and indeed inverted and purported—"truths."

Analytical Introduction

> In history up to now it is just as much an
> empirical fact that with the extension of their
> activities to ~~world history~~ the world-historical,
> disaggregated individuals have become more
> and more enslaved ~~to a power growing ever more massive to a power which has grown ever more massive~~ to a power alien to
> them (which burden they ~~then also~~
> then also conceive as trickery by the so-called
> world spirit &c)
> [09 Bogen, 21 Seite, L Column, p. 110]

In an insertion into the text that follows, Marx specifically includes "intellectual production" within "practical production." Doing this refuses any timeless distinction between the "intellectual" and the "practical," notwithstanding Marx and Engels's excoriating attack on the "intellectual production" of their contemporaries as the products of "ideologists." Their critique sees this as pointlessly impractical and indeed counterposed to any recognition of what their texts identify as a universal human interest, namely, a negation of the dominating and enslaving social forces that have developed "naturally," that is, un-self-consciously but yet within "history":

> put into practical
> **(including**
> connection with the production
> **intellectual production)**
> of the whole world &
> ~~are capable of enjoying the multifaceted production from the whole earth~~ **put themselves
> into position to acquire the capacity
> for enjoying this multifaceted production
> from the whole earth (**~~men's creations~~
> **creations of men).**
> [09 Bogen, 21 Seite, L Column, p. 112]

This process of refusing the traditional matter/consciousness dichotomy and with that the traditional ontological way of conceiving what there is to be known, and how and where it becomes known, was not without equivocation and ambiguity in these manuscript fragments. This passage in Engels's hand uses "praxis" to refer to human practical activities (as variously noted and described) but also "material praxis," as well as a (supposedly) persuasive "materialist" metaphor "bedrock" assuring truthful perception of historical fact. "This conception of history," so it says in Engels's hand,

> remains constantly standing
> on the actual <u>bedrock</u> of history, does not

explain praxis from the idea, ~~rather~~ explains
the formation of ideas from material praxis
[10 Bogen, 24 Seite, L Column, p. 130]

But if praxis is the epistemological guarantee of political truth (as opposed to "ideological" speculation), and given that knowledge of this then explains "the formation of ideas," how is praxis/material praxis also an ontological constituent of actuality, along with—but contrasted from—"ideas"? Evidently, the Marx/Engels view merges epistemology with ontology, what "is" with how we "know." In the passage that follows the insertion by Marx perhaps explains what "material" is otherwise ambiguously indicating:

at each
stage there is to hand a material result, a sum
of productive forces, {*insertion*} **a historically
created relation to nature and of individuals
to one another** {*end insertion*},
[10 Bogen, 24 Seite, L Column, p. 132]

Possibly, Marx's drafting is more consistent in avoiding ambiguous references to "material" and sticking with the "praxis" terminology:

**The
"conception", the "representation" of
these specific men concerning their
actual praxis is transformed into** ~~the
actual defining and active essence~~ **the
sole defining and active power** which
controls & defines the praxis of these men.
[10 Bogen, 25 Seite, L Colum, pp. 138, 140]

Notice in the previous passage the strike-through on "essence" (a classically philosophical term) and rephrasing in terms of power (much more this-worldly and experiential). The strike-through change in the next passage is possibly evidence of the hypothesis that Marx is refusing philosophy and the term "material" as regressive in terms of the new "outlook." Not even an "objective" (i.e., nonidealist, non-Hegelian) approach to history has got this right, not really grasping the praxis or "activity" perspective that the two are arguing for:

**So-called <u>objective</u> historiography consisted
precisely in conceiving of** ~~mater{ial}~~
**historical relations separated from activity.
Reactionary character.**
[10 Bogen, 26 Seite, R Column, p. 142]

Analytical Introduction

In Engels's hand, "facts & practical developments" are another locution for the "ground" from which a properly nonideological history can arise. In this passage, "they" are the "German ideologists" but "their" refers back to "histories of ideas":

> they give only a history of ideas torn
> away from the facts & practical developments
> which are their ground
> [11 Bogen, 27 Seite, L Column, p. 150]

Perhaps more prosaically we have this version of a "ground" in ordinary experience:

> While ~~one in ordinary life~~ in ordinary life
> every shopkeeper knows very well how to
> distinguish between what someone pretends
> to be, & what he actually is, yet our writing of
> history has still not arrived at this trivial
> insight. It takes every epoch at its word, what
> it says & imagines about itself.
> [21 Bogen, 35 Seite, L Column, p. 202]

Note the strike-through in the passage ahead where a reference to "consciousness," abstracted in a philosophical way, is replaced with one to activity as "self-conscious." This passage is thus the follow-on to the earlier identification of the (historical) "natural" as a realm in which social relations subjugate humans, whereas properly (i.e., nonideologically) informed self-conscious activity could empower "united individuals" instead:

> Communism distinguishes itself from all
> previous movements in that it overturns the
> basis of all previous production relations &
> relations of exchange, & for the first time
> ~~when with consciousness~~ self-consciously
> considers all naturally arising preconditions
> up to now
>   as human creations, strips away
>   power
> their naturalness & subjects them to the
> of
>   united p~~[ower]~~ individuals.
> [88 Bogen, 59 Seite, L Column, p. 320]

The discontinuous but lengthy run of *Bogen* numbered 84–92 record lengthy ruminations on the history of humanity from prehistory through to the present and on to the future. These discussions merge the latter two into a descriptive and predictive account of the economic, social, and political processes, which—so the two writers are arguing—can be discerned but only from their "ground" as previously developed. This "ground" is conceived in terms of ordinary experience and—crucially—ordinary experience is conceived historically, rather than as a timeless merger of human physical needs and capacities. Viewing humanity in this way gives the Marx/Engels account a social and indeed sociological edge, since human bodies/minds are conceived as socially interactive and reflexively self-creating and—importantly here—not just as producers of historical development as some "external" effect. Rather they are also conceived as further developing historically in terms of what their bodies/minds themselves actually are, changing in and of themselves through the activities that make history.

On the one hand, this narrative is now perhaps overly familiar to many readers, since it represents a very close draft of the material that emerged in the *Manifesto of the Communist Party*, which was produced within the next two years. On the other hand, in this very rough form the assertions and arguments are rather more straightforward in propositional terms, lacking the rhetorical questions and sarcastic jibes of the later work. The target for the *Manifesto* polemic of course is rather different; importantly, in that work, Marx and Engels are protesting the general views held by the bourgeois class, as promoted—so they argue—by bourgeois ideologists. Those views are self-serving, secondhand versions of political economy, historical mystifications and displacements (e.g., dynastic wars rather than a focus on economic development), and religious nonsense (deflecting attention from the realities of class struggle). The present *Bogen* are fragments of a more hermetic political exercise (aimed at the "critical critics" in their Hegelianizing "Germanness") than the later *Manifesto*, which was aimed at the wider European scene.

This short passage occurs within the development of "empirical" history, as Marx and Engels are working through their ideas, and it draws a clear contrast between their focus on the history of "estates & classes," as opposed to a notion that history consists in a conceptual development within which the "species" or "man" progresses as a mere effect of disembodied forces. These abstractions, so they say, are far removed from the sociohistorical activities through which individuals instantiate "the common conditions of existence":

> If one considers *philosophically* this development of individuals within ~~the give{n}, to them given to them in part considered philosophically in part through the further formation of the given conditions of existence~~ the common conditions of existence of the estates that follow one another & classes historically & within the general conceptions thereby imposed on these {individuals}, then one can indeed easily imagine ~~these individuals~~ that the species or man has developed in these individuals, or that they {species or man} have developed the men; a

conceit by which history is given some hard
knocks.

[87 Bogen, 55 Seite, L Column, pp. 296, 298]

The best supposition is that this extensive development of the Marx/Engels version of history was extracted from the immediate context as too much of an excursus and distraction from the polemical fray. Marx's next project turned out to be *The Poverty of Philosophy*, where again the political context is one of personal polemic against a philosopher/politician (Proudhon, in this case). Rather similarly, aspects of this view of human history-in-the-making appear by contrast with Proudhon's philosophizing and Hegelianizing of human activity (as Marx saw it).

Besides being a much more notable opponent, Proudhon was a philosopher-socialist writing in French for a very broad European public. The Frenchman was also a political economist in the sense that he had constructed a "system of economic contradictions" and "philosophy of poverty" (the title and subtitle of the work that Marx was attacking). In contradistinction to the polemics against Stirner and Bauer (and their Feuerbachianism) Marx organized his polemic around Proudhon's concepts of value and money (and a purported "communist" resolution of the "social" question, that is, the liberation of the impoverished classes). Marx also pillories Proudhon as a philosophizing dilettante (and a worse Hegelian than even Bauer and his ilk)—and indeed he attacks Proudhon's "dialectical" method with withering scorn.

In *The Poverty of Philosophy*, a work that is barely a year later in composition than these "German ideology" leftover fragments, Marx reviewed this "empirical" material very briefly in order to establish a clear contrast between himself and his rival (see especially CW 6, pp. 183–90). Somewhat the same method arises in Engels's two versions of founding declarations for the Communist League dating from 1847: his "Draft of a Communist Confession of Faith" (see CW 6, pp. 100–101) and especially his "Principles of Communism" from the same year (see especially ibid., pp. 341–48).

However, inasmuch as the material on *Bogen* 84–92—rough and thoughtful as it is—represents an authorial resource for later works, it also represents a more extended and detailed account of their thinking about historical development and class contradiction than is found elsewhere. Perhaps because it is more extended, and less polemically focused, the fragility of modern industry in historical terms and the tensions of class coalition-building in political terms come through rather more clearly than in subsequently published works. The passage closes with an argument that global relations of production and distribution will alter the situation, at least in terms of securing gains in what is produced and in industrial productivity:

> It depends solely on the extension of trade ~~the extent to which~~ whether or not the powers of production secured in a locality, particularly inventions, are lost for later development. As long as there is still no trade proceeding beyond the immediate vicinity, every invention has to be made in each locality ~~anew~~ in particular, & ~~only~~ mere accidents, like incursions of barbarian peoples, ~~wa{rs}~~ even the usual sort of wars, are sufficient to bring a

~~mass~~ country with ~~hard-won~~ developed productive forces & ~~inventions for a long time & again~~ requirements to such a state that it has to start over again from the beginning. In early history every invention had to be made afresh every day, & be made independently in every locality. How little even ~~a~~ developed productive forces are safe from complete destruction by their ~~quite~~ proportionate extension of trade is proved by ~~the history of~~ the Phoenicians, whose inventions were lost through the expulsion of their nation from trade, ~~& their conquest by Alexander~~ their conquest by Alexander & the subsequent long period of decline ~~of that natio{n}~~. {*insertion*} {It was} just the same in the middle ages – e.g. stained glass production.{*end insertion*} Only when trade has become worldwide & ~~a competitive struggle of all n{ations}~~ on the basis of large-scale industry & all nations are drawn into the competitive struggle is the permanence of hard-won productive forces secured.

[85 Bogen, 45 Seite, L Column, pp. 236, 238]

The comments that attempt to reconcile class struggle (bourgeoisie vs. proletarians) with human (i.e., communist) solidarity are particularly realistic here and poignant, even if similarly hopeful about the globalized future:

~~As~~ Competition isolates individuals from one another, not only middle class {*bourgeois*} but ~~also~~ even more the workers {*proletariat*}, in spite of the fact that it brings them together. Hence it is a long time till these individuals ~~are united once more~~ can unite themselves {*insertion*} besides the fact that for this union {*further insertion*} if it is not to be merely local {*end further insertion*} the necessary

means, the large-scale industrial cities & the
cheap & quick means of communication, must
first be produced by large-scale industry,{*end
insertion*} & hence every organised power
opposed to these isolated individuals, living in
relations which daily reproduce the isolation,
is only overcome after long struggles. To
demand the opposite would be just like
demanding that competition should not exist in
a specific historical period & or that
individuals, should expunge from their brains
the relations ~~over of which which they~~
~~as isolated individuals have no control~~ over
which they as isolated individuals have no
control.
[87 Bogen, 53 Seite, L Column, p. 284, 286]

The passage above clearly reprises the view that communist society must overcome the "alienation" that former social relations, and commodity-producing societies in particular, impose on individuals who are thus "isolated" from each other in the basic productive activities of social life. While these terms have been made familiar since the 1960s, when text and commentary relating to the "Economic and Philosophical Manuscripts of 1844" were central to scholarship on Marx, they hardly featured in his published works of the period, for example, they were but very briefly mentioned in *On the Jewish Question* of 1844 (CW 3: pp. 173–74) and were discussed with rather more critical edge in *The Holy Family* polemics of 1845. Famously the "German ideology" texts also record an anxiety about the actual term "alienation," even though at times the authors use it quite freely. Marx records his summary view very sharply in the passage here:

This "alienation", to keep things
intelligible to philosophers, can of
course only be transformed
{*aufgehoben*} under two practical
presuppositions.
[08 Bogen, 18 Seite, R Column, p. 94]

Possibly, "powers" in the following passage was Marx's preferred term, removing "alien" as a general qualifier and opting instead for other pejorative and less "philosophical" adjectives, such as "intolerable"; see this self-correction:

2)
the ~~alien~~ powers of commerce itself
could not have developed as universal,

hence intolerable powers,

[08 Bogen, 18 Seite, R Column, p. 98]

This later passage below records a discussion that reproduces quite accurately the "alienation" argument of the manuscript materials of 1844 undertaken by Marx in his notebook studies of political economy and now known after editorial construction as the "Economic and Philosophical Manuscripts of 1844" (CW 3: pp. 229–346; see Rojahn, 2002). However, the discussion here abjures the word "alienation" altogether. The authors have apparently "broken" with the term, for reasons recorded by Marx earlier (p. 94):

> With
> ~~the labouring class {Proletariat}~~ the labourers
> {*Proletariariern*}, on the other hand, their
> own conditions of life, work ~~for them~~
> ~~to{gether}~~ & hence all the conditions of
> existence of modern society have become
> something contingent for them, over which
> ~~they {have} no~~ the individual workers
> {*Proletarier*} have no control, {*insertion*} **and**
> **over which** ~~the~~ **no organisation** in
> commercial society **can~~not~~ give them control**
> {*end insertion*} & the ~~oppo{sition}~~
> contradiction between the individuality of the
> particular worker and labour, his conditions of
> life that are forced upon him, becomes
> ~~perspicu{ous}~~ obvious to him~~.~~
> [88 Bogen, 57 Seite, L Column, p. 308]

Note the interesting shift in the phrase below from a discourse of philosophical recuperation of something once lost (e.g., an alienation) to one of practical political activity (in presumably contingent circumstances):

> individuals ~~are united once more~~
> can unite themselves
> [87 Bogen, 53 Seite, L Column, p. 284]

Here is another example below of the "alienation" argument—a descriptive account that functions rhetorically as a call to arms in context. But from the contemporary perspective, it proceeds as Hamlet without the ghost, given the way that the views expressed have been understood since the early 1960s as "humanism" and the "theory of alienation." Ironically, that reading of the "early Marx" rephilosophized him, whereas the polemical works for publication from 1843 through these manuscript pages were resolutely tacking the opposite antiphilosophical tack:

> Thus on the one hand there is a totality of the forces of production which have taken on a material form, as it were, & are for the individuals themselves no longer the powers of individuals but rather of private property, & hence of individuals only in so far as they are owners of private property. In no earlier period have ~~these~~ the forces of production taken on this form, indifferent to the interaction of individuals *as* individuals, because their interaction itself was still such a limited one. On the other hand opposed to these forces of production are the majority of individuals ~~to whom~~ from whom these powers were stripped away & who have become abstract individuals, robbed of all the actual content of life, but who are only put by those means into a position to enter into relations with one another *as individuals.* The sole connection that is still between them and the forces of production & their own existence, labour, has lost all appearance of self-activity for them & only sustains their life [90 Bogen, 65 Seite, L Column, pp. 350, 352]

Marx and Engels, in referring to the "alienation" theorists of their day, limned in an uncanny fashion in the passage that follows below the way that their own outlook was rephilosophized in the 1960s:

> The whole process was understood as the process of self-alienation of "man" & this was essentially a matter of shifting the average individual of a later stage into the earlier one & later consciousness into earlier individuals. Through this inversion, which from the outset

abstracts from actual conditions, it was
possible to transform all of history into a
process of development of consciousness.
[91 Bogen, 68 Seite, L Column, p. 362]

While some of the "alienation" theorists of the 1960s and later may have argued that their views were neither idealist nor a history of consciousness, this was not always convincing, and indeed—as with "liberation theology"—not even denied (for a definitive discussion of this period and its modern reception; see Leopold, 2007).

By contrast Marx and Engels's new "outlook" linked their "ground" in historicized industry to the basic vocabulary of political economy, namely, economic relations through which forces of production were put to human social use. Note the way that social **activity or engagement** displaces individual "self-activity" as a correction. Interestingly, animals as the constitutive "outside" to human activities reappear in the passage that follows and are duly noted as also being historical products, rather than timelessly natural:

The relation of the
productive forces to the form of exchange is
the relation of the form of exchange to the
~~self-activity~~ **activity or engagement** of the
individuals. (The fundamental form of this
~~self-activity~~ **engagement** is naturally material,
on which all other {forms}, intellectual,
political, religious etc., depend. The varying
shape of material life is naturally dependent in
every case on the needs that have already been
developed, & the ~~development~~ production ~~or~~
as well as the satisfaction of these needs is
itself a historical process which does not take
place with sheep or dogs {*insertion*} (Stirner's
factitious
      main argument *against* humanity)
{*end insertion*}, although sheep and dogs in
their present form are certainly, albeit in spite
of themselves, the products of a historical
process.)[15]
[89 Bogen, 60 Seite, L Column, pp. 324, 326]

Note the strike-through in the passage that follows, where once again the philosophical and in this case economic term "material" is entered in the text but then refused in relation to the

"~~material~~ existence" of the state. Any economic connotation is replaced with more specific conceptualizations, for example, "commercial credit":

> To this
> modern private property corresponds the
> modern state, which is gradually purchased for
> themselves by the owners of private property
> through taxation, ~~is~~ completely delivered into
> their hands through state indebtedness &
> whose ~~material~~ existence has become wholly
> dependent on the commercial credit which the
> owners of private property, the commercial
> class {*Bourgeoisie*} extend to it, on state
> bonds which rise & fall on the exchange.
> [91 Bogen, 69 Seite, L Column, pp. 366, 368]

Marx's insertion in the passage below, which will be familiar to readers of his later 1859 "Preface" to *A Contribution to the Critique of Political Economy*, and thus to those who followed the "analytical Marxist" controversies of the late 1970s and 1980s over its internal ambiguities and confusions, is quite telling but also interesting in an independent methodological sense (for an overview, see Veneziani, 2012). Here, Marx asserts that "relations of production" are also "forces of production." While this is obviously at odds with much later Marxist views on technological determinism, in this context it demonstrates a consistency in refusing the matter/consciousness dichotomy, that is, "relations" would be aspects of shared consciousness, whereas "forces" would—so one might presume, following the traditional dichotomy—encompass material objects in contradistinction:

> a certain mode of production or stage
>   always
> of industry is   conjoined with a
> certain mode of social interaction or stage of
> society, {*insertion*}**and this mode of social
> interaction is itself a "force of production"**
> {*end insertion*}
> [07 Bogen, 13 Seite, L Column, p. 70]

Conclusions

Overall, these rough manuscript fragments give us a picture not of some decisive "break" or even "breakthrough" as a before/after moment of "self-clarification" but rather they show us some degree of discursive struggle over quite difficult issues. This is happening as a philosophizing "gaze" on humanity, organized around tropes of wholeness, loss, and recuperation (even redemption), gives way (albeit with some temporary and often corrected regressions) to a politicizing discourse of goal-directed history-making, which the two authors associate with communism as a movement.

Comparison with the earlier polemic *The Holy Family* of 1845—written just prior to the planned "German ideology" ripostes to much the same "critical critics"—shows Marx opening his attack by mounting a *defense* of Proudhon (to a degree) precisely on the subject of the historical development of economic technologies and relationships, as opposed to the philosophizing of these facts for which he excoriated the work of Edgar Bauer (CW 4, pp. 23–54). And indeed the "Economic and Philosophical Manuscripts of 1844" (extracted from Marx's "excerpt notebooks" of the period) are engaged in a preliminary way with the political economists and hence with their concerns—famously, production, consumption, distribution, and exchange, conceived in at least somewhat historical (and of course Eurocentric) terms (see Rojahn, 2002). As shown earlier, these are the terms through which "nature" is historicized and history made "natural" when viewed from a "ground" in human activity of mundane sorts.

Other than in the "German ideology" fragments, under discussion here, we have little or no testimony as to compositional processes through which tensions like this between Hegelianizing discourse (itself religious and quasi-Christian) and a more hardheaded empirical (indeed economic and everyday) discourse come to the fore. Part of the picture could well be a need to communicate—even with implacably hopeless opponents—in terms that they could conceivably understand and which could possibly move them to another position; note that in his own hand Marx offered "alienation" (in heavy scare quotes) as a concession to keep things "intelligible to philosophers." The tension in these polemical strategies is between backsliding and making concessions, as opposed to stating a clear position and backing it up with irrefutable arguments (not excluding sarcasm, send-up, mockery, and the like, of course). Genre and associated discourses—including tropes, tone, and rhetorical devices—are in Marx's works just as much determinants of what we see (and therefore think we understand) as any supposed "breaks" or even developments in his thinking. Or rather it is far from obvious that—intellectual biographers notwithstanding—Marx was intent on system or doctrine as such (see especially Berlin, 2013 [1939], Introduction) rather than on the use of ideas to "do" politics.

As we have seen demonstrated in Carver and Blank (2014), the temptation to exploit a mysticism of the manuscript and fetishism of the archive has been overwhelming, given the way that scholars have had to capitalize on these "hooks" to get their projects under way. This has had the result that works actually published by Marx and Engels (variously) have been somewhat undervalued, or at least overshadowed, given the popularity of, say, the "Economic and Philosophical Manuscripts of 1844" (which were at least advertised as manuscripts) and the—if possible—even more influential and mandatory worship of the "German ideology" as a supposed "book" that—even if a bit rough in places—could still be editorially pieced together and presented as a "last hand" text. Ironically the roughest manuscripts—as surveyed here—are the ones of most interest, not because they prove something we already know, or indeed mark a point of origin for a "break" but because they lead us—if perspicuously presented—to enquire in a more open-minded way into just what questions were being asked by the collaborative authors and just how much they struggled over the answers.

Rather than doctrinaires who cogitated something quite distinctly original and then somehow stumbled here and there in getting *it* down on paper, the present study has made the *it* rather more problematic in terms of substantive content and the struggles rather more visible and significant. While there is every authorial certainty in these fragments that the "German ideologists" are wrong and wrongheaded, there is rather less certainty—even reading through the "smooth" text and setting aside the variants—that Marx and Engels are quite so certain as they go along with respect to what exactly they need to say to put the "critical critics" to rights (and indeed to neutralize them politically). By focusing on the "variants" in these fragments we hope to have created a certain sense of contingency and experimentation in the joint process of composition that these pages record, even in places marking debates between the two (indeed, unsurprisingly, given what we know of Marx) to the point of actual sarcasm.

The authors of the present volume entrust this work to readers, hoping that they will enjoy this excursion into the intellectual "laboratory" (and political "retort") that the present translation and re-presentation provides and will resist the reductionist temptation to "boil it all down" to a dusty precipitate that will fit conventional expectations. Marx and Engels deserve considerable credit, not just for developing an "outlook" (*Ansicht/Auffassung/Theorie*)—on humanity, civilization, industry, politics, society, change, and the future—but for exposing the kinds of questions that need to be asked in order to get that discussion going. They—and we—are up against the weight of supposed common sense and received—even academically or politically authorized—opinion. This pattern of reception and inertia applies to Marxism, and to Marxology, as much as anything else. The present study is thus offered up in a spirit of comradely struggle with the world that humanity has made since prehistory and with a will to fight for the right to ask questions that challenge long-settled views.

Notes

1. The historical background to the editorial fabrication of *The German Ideology* as a "book" solely authored by Marx and Engels, with an opening "chapter" "I. Feuerbach," is covered in Terrell Carver and Daniel Blank, *A Political History of the Editions of Marx and Engels's "German ideology Manuscripts"* (Palgrave Macmillan, 2014); hereafter Carver and Blank (2014). The present volume includes manuscript materials not previously published as part of the "Feuerbach chapter"; see Carver and Blank (2014: pp. 124–25).
2. Engels's phrase from 1859, never used by Marx; see Carver (2003), Chapter 5.
3. Marx [Declaration against Karl Grün], in *Collected Works*, vol. 6 (London: Lawrence & Wishart, 1976), pp. 72 note b, 73; the newspaper note had no title so the editors have assigned the one in square brackets; see also Taubert, Pelger, and Grandjonc (1998).
4. See Carver and Blank (2014), Chapter 7.
5. See ibid., Chapter 6.
6. As in the Hiromatsu edition; see ibid., Chapter 7.
7. These are promised in future for the Marx-Engels-Gesamtausgabe website: www.bbaw.de/en/research/mega.
8. See Carver and Blank (2014), Chapter 6.
9. See ibid.
10. See CW 26: p. 520; and Carver and Blank (2014), Chapter 2.
11. Marx's emphasis at these two points; *Jahrbuch 2003*, vol. 2, p. 213, ref. 7.17–18 l.
12. Bruno Bauer, "Charakteristik Ludwig Feuerbachs," *Wigand's Vierteljahrsschrift*, vol. 3 (1845).
13. The editors of *Jahrbuch 2003* state that this insertion was written down later than the previous one; vol. 2, p. 216, ref. 11.3–6 l.
14. The editors of *Jahrbuch 2003* give the original word order in this phrase as: eats & drinks, {clothes} himself; vol. 2, p. 230, ref. 25.20 l.
15. Marx's parentheses around this passage.

Analytical Introduction

Brief Apparatus Criticus

deletion = ~~excised word or phrase~~

inserted word or phrase by Marx or Engels = ^{appears here}   ^{later insertion appears here}

{*insertion*}/{*end insertion*} = insertions by Marx or Engels too long to go easily above the line

[square brackets] = insertions by the editors of *Jahrbuch 2003*

{braces} = insertions by present editors

roman typeface = Engels's handwriting

bold typeface = Marx's handwriting

<u>underline</u> = emphasis in the manuscript

pp = German abbreviation for "and so forth"

Punctuation and capitalization are in conformity with English usage, but I have taken the transcription of the German manuscript into account as much as possible.

Fragment page numbered '1' by Marx, possibly from printer's sheet '1' (in Engels's sequence)

~~according to~~ {*The Holy Fa*}*mily* refutes {the idea} over & over again that the holy philosophers & theologians have "produced" the "non-autonomy of the individual", "by" – serving up a few chewed over phrases about absolute spirit. As if the "individual", i.e. each man, would become "non-autonomous" by that means, would actually be "transformed {*aufgehoben*} "into absolute spirit" by that means, {as} if a few ~~speculati{ve}~~ speculating word-merchants – ~~because~~ not because of the "~~dependence~~ non-autonomy of the individual" but rather because of a miserable condition of society {–}, could start up their philosophical fancies all by themselves, {could} prate this to the "individual", command him that he should suddenly & without thinking about it "be absorbed into absolute spirit"! Naturally of course we will not take the trouble to enlighten ~~to~~ our wise philosophers with the fact that the "liberation" of "man" does not get a single step further when they have dissolved philosophy, theology, substance & all that foolery into "self-consciousness", when they have liberated "man" from domination by these phrases to which he had never been in

Philosophical hairsplitting{.}
Just like his rivals Feuerbach believes {himself} to have transcended philosophy! ~~The act{ual}~~ The struggle against general conceptions, which have previously oppressed the individual, summarises the standpoint of German philosophical criticism. We maintain that this struggle, pursued in this manner, is itself founded on philosophical illusions of the sovereignty of general conceptions.

<u>Feuerbach.</u>
<u>Philosophical and actual liberation.</u>
<u>Man</u>. <u>Individuality</u>. The <u>Individual</u>.
Geological, hydrographical etc. conditions. The human body. Needs and labour.

Fragment page numbered '1' by Marx, possibly from printer's sheet '1' (in Engels's sequence)

{*The Holy F*}*amily* refutes {the idea} over & over again that the holy philosophers & theologians have "produced" the "non-autonomy of the individual", "by" – serving up a few chewed over phrases about absolute spirit. As if the "individual", i.e. each man, would become "non-autonomous" by that means, would actually be "transformed {*aufgehoben*} into absolute spirit" by that means, {as} if a few speculating word-merchants – not because of the "non-autonomy of the individual" but rather because of a miserable condition of society {–}, could start up their philosophical fancies all by themselves, {could} prate this to the "individual", command him that he should suddenly & without thinking about it "be absorbed into absolute spirit"! Naturally of course we will not take the trouble to enlighten our wise philosophers with the fact that the "liberation" of "man" does not get a single step further when they have dissolved philosophy, theology, substance & all that foolery into "self-consciousness", when they have liberated "man" from domination by these phrases to which he had never been in

Philosophical hair-splitting{.}
Just like his rivals Feuerbach believes {himself} to have transcended philosophy! The struggle against general conceptions, which have previously oppressed the individual, summarises the standpoint of German philosophical criticism. We maintain that this struggle, pursued in this manner, is itself founded on philosophical illusions of the sovereignty of general conceptions.
Feuerbach.
Philosophical and actual liberation.
Man. The Ego. The Individual.
Geological, hydrographical etc. conditions. The human body. Needs and labour.

Fragment page numbered '1' by Marx, possibly from printer's sheet '1' (in Engels's sequence)

thrall; that it is not possible to achieve actual liberation other than in the actual world & with actual means, that slavery cannot be transformed {*aufheben*} without the steam-engine & spinning machines, serfdom without improved agriculture, that in any case men cannot be liberated so long as they are not in a position to obtain food & drink, shelter & clothing ~~adequate~~ sufficient in quality & quantity. "Liberation" is a historical action, not a conceptual action, & it is accomplished through historical relations, through the state of industry, of trade, of agriculture, of social interaction {relation}s{,}

Fragment page numbered '1' by Marx, possibly from printer's sheet '1' (in Engels's sequence)

thrall; that it is not possible to achieve actual liberation other than in the actual world & with actual means, that slavery cannot be transformed {*aufheben*} without the steam-engine & spinning machines, serfdom without improved agriculture, that in any case men cannot be liberated so long as they are not in a position to obtain food & drink, shelter & clothing sufficient in quality & quantity. "Liberation" is a historical action, not a conceptual action, & it is accomplished through historical relations, through the state of industry, of trade, of agriculture, of social interaction {relation}s{,}

Fragment page numbered '2' by Marx, possibly from printer's sheet '1' (in Engels's sequence)

then subsequently, in accord with ~~their given~~ their different stages of development, {they conceive} the nonsense of substance, subject, self-consciousness & pure critique ~~& dispel it again~~ just like religious & theological nonsense, & after that dispel it {nonsense} again when they {stages of development} are developed far enough. Naturally ~~in this a land like Germany, where no historical development is taking place, these developments-in-thought take the place of historical {development} & {they} get a grip~~ & in a land like Germany, where ~~no~~ only a miserable level of historical development is taking place, these developments-in-thought, {*insertion*} these misperceived & ineffectual miseries {*end insertion*} replace the deficit in historical {development}, {they} get a grip & must be resisted. However, that is a battle ~~of merely local signi{ficance}, not historical, general significance, a battle which brings men to the mass of men new fa{cts} results, like the battle of civilisation against the barbarians, the battle of the w{orker}~~ **of local significance.** ~~has, a struggle~~ The holy Bruno has ~~therefore~~ rendered a "Profile of Ludwig Feuerbach" i.e. an improved edition of ~~the~~ a

Phrases and actual movement.

Significance of phrases for Germany.

~~The language is the language of ac{tual life}~~ <u>Feuerbach. Bauer.</u>

<u>St. Bruno over Feuerbach as the champion of substance.</u>

Fragment page numbered '2' by Marx, possibly from printer's sheet '1' (in Engels's sequence)

then subsequently, in accord with their different stages of development, {they conceive} the nonsense of substance, subject, self-consciousness & pure critique just like religious & theological nonsense, & after that dispel it {nonsense} again when they {stages of development} are developed far enough. Naturally in a land like Germany, where only a miserable level of historical development is taking place, these developments-in-thought, these misperceived & ineffectual miseries replace the deficit in historical {development}, {they} get a grip & must be resisted. However, that is a battle **of local significance**. The holy Bruno has rendered a "Profile of Ludwig Feuerbach" i.e. an improved edition of a **piece** already published

Phrases and actual movement.
Significance of phrases for Germany.

Feuerbach. Bauer.

St. Bruno over Feuerbach as the champion of substance.

Fragment page numbered '2' by Marx, possibly from printer's sheet '1' (in Engels's sequence)

piece already published in the "~~n~~North German Newsletter". ~~With this holy character wherein becomes in both Feuerbach is represented as the defen{der} champion of "Substance", is what serves the purpose of making the Bauer-ish "self-consciousness" somewhat brighter.~~ **Feuerbach is portrayed as the champion of "Substance"** ~~so that~~ **in order** ~~to give~~ **to throw Bauer-ish "self-consciousness"** ~~shines more brightly~~ **into greater relief. In general** ~~his~~ **pure critique limits itself lately to talking about any and everything that would be "Substance".** With this transubstantiation of Feuerbach the holy man **by** jumps from F{euerbach}'s writings on ~~Bayle & Leibnitz~~ **Leibnitz & Bayle** immediately to the Essence of Christianity ~~without mentioning Feuerbach's piece against the "positive" philosophy at in the Deutsche Jahrbücher for the simple reason because here Feuerbach , as opposed to the positive representatives of "Substance" expressed the entire wisdom of "absolute self-consciousness" at a point~~ **and skips over** ~~Feuerbach's~~ **the piece against "positive" philosophy in the Hallische Jahrbücher.**

Fragment page numbered '2' by Marx, possibly from printer's sheet '1' (in Engels's sequence)

in the "North German Newsletter". **Feuerbach is portrayed as the champion of "Substance" in order to throw Bauer-ish "self consciousness" into greater relief. In general pure critique limits itself lately to talking about any and everything that would be "Substance".** With this transubstantiation of Feuerbach the holy man jumps from F{euerbach}'s writings on **Leibnitz & Bayle** immediately to the Essence of Christianity, **and skips over the piece against "positive" philosophy in the Hallische Jahrbücher. This was "a mistake"**

Fragment page numbered '2' by Marx, possibly from printer's sheet '1' (in Engels's sequence)

~~This was necessary because~~ This was ~~carelessness~~ "a mistake" "at this point" ~~because~~. Here, as opposed to the positive representatives of "Substance", Feuerbach revealed precisely the whole wisdom of "self-consciousness" at a time when the holy Bruno still [specula]ted on the immaculate conception ~~& and much more clearly, mu[ch more pertinent]ly expressed, than the holy Bruno has ever done~~.

In just that piece Feuerbach seeks the secret, with which St. Bruno constantly busies himself, of the r{epresentatives of Substance}...

Fragment page numbered '2' by Marx, possibly from printer's sheet '1' (in Engels's sequence)

"at this point". Here, as opposed to the positive representatives of "Substance", Feuerbach revealed precisely the whole wisdom of "self-consciousness" at a time when the holy Bruno still [specula]ted on the immaculate conception.

In just that piece Feuerbach seeks the secret, with which St. Bruno constantly busies himself, of the r{epresentatives of Substance}...

First page on printer's sheet '6' (in Engels's sequence), numbered '8' by Marx

[. . .] in reality {it} ~~is a matter of~~ & for the **practical** materialists, i.e. the **communists**,[1] it   **Feuerbach**
is a matter of revolutionising the existing
world, of getting to grips with things to hand
& changing them. If we occasionally find such
views in Feuerbach, they never reach
beyond isolated instances & have much too
little influence on his way of viewing things
to be regarded here as anything other than
hints that could be developed. Feuerbach's
~~theoretical conception~~ "**conception**" of
~~perceptibility~~ the perceptible world
is limited on the one hand to
merely viewing it, & on the
                to merely
other   feeling {it}, {insertion}
{**he**} considers "**man**" instead of "**actual historical man**". "**Man**" is in reality "**German man**". {end insertion} In the first
case, in viewing ~~nature~~ the perceptible world,
he necessarily engages with things
which contradict his consciousness &
                                ~~of his~~
his emotions, which disturb the harmony
                        of all ~~members~~ parts of
that he presupposes
the perceptible world, & in particular
                                of man

---

1. Marx's emphasis at these two points; *Jahrbuch 2003*, vol. 2, p. 213, ref. 7.17–18 l.

[. . .] in reality & for the **practical** materialists, i.e. the **communits**,[1] it is a matter of revolutionising the existing world, of getting to grips with things to hand & changing them. If we occasionally find such views in Feuerbach, they never reach beyond isolated instances & have much too little influence on his way of viewing things to be regarded here as anything other than hints that could be developed. Feuerbach's **"conception"** of the perceptible world is limited on the one hand to merely viewing it, & on the other to merely feeling {it}, {**he**} **posits "<u>man</u>" instead of "actual historical man". "<u>Man</u>" is in reality "German man".** In the first case, in <u>viewing</u> the perceptible world, he necessarily engages with things which contradict his consciousness & his emotions, which disturb the harmony of all parts of the perceptible world that he presupposes, & in particular of man with

Feuerbach

---

1. Marx's emphasis at these two points.

First page on printer's sheet '6' (in Engels's sequence), numbered '8' by Marx

with nature. In order to resolve this, he has then ~~to a dual conception~~ to find refuge in a dual conception, between a profane one which describes only "the immediately apparent" & a higher, philosophical one, which describes the "true essence" of things. He does not see how the perceptible world surrounding him is not[1] **a thing** handed down directly from eternity, staying always the same, **but rather the product of industry & of social conditions & to be sure in the sense that it is a historical product, the result of the activity of a whole series of generations**, each of which stood on the shoulders of its predecessors, {was} further ~~advanced, its social institu{tions} social order in accordance with different conditions~~ advanced its industry

NB. F[euerbach's] mistake is not that he subordinates the immediately apparent, perception, to the perceptible actuality attested by precise investigation of perceptible circumstances, but that he cannot in the end cope with perceptibility except by considering it with the "eyes", i.e. through the "spectacles", of the philosophers.

---

1. The *Jahrbuch 2003* editors read two thoughts in Engels's hand that precede Marx's final version; vol. 2, p. 214, ref. 8.14–19 l.
{1} ~~product, rather the result of activity, the product of a whole series of generations~~
{2} ~~thing, rather the product of industry & of social conditions & to be sure in the sense that it~~
  ~~in every historical epoch, which~~
~~is~~   ~~result~~
  ~~the product~~   ~~of the activity of a whole series of generations~~

First page on printer's sheet '6' (in Engels's sequence), numbered '8' by Marx

nature. In order to resolve this, he has then to find refuge in a dual conception, between a profane one which describes only "the immediately apparent" & a higher, philosophical one, which describes the "true essence" of things. He does not see how the perceptible world surrounding him is not **a thing** handed down directly from eternity, staying always the same, **but rather the product of industry & of social conditions & to be sure in the sense that it is a historical product, the result of the activity of a whole series of generations**, each of which stood on the shoulders of its predecessors, further advanced its industry and its social

NB. F[euerbach's] mistake is not that he subordinates the immediately apparent, perception, to the perceptible actuality attested by precise investigation of perceptible circumstances, but that he cannot in the end cope with perceptibility except by considering it with the "eyes", i.e. through the "spectacles", of the philosophers.

First page on printer's sheet '6' (in Engels's sequence), numbered '8' by Marx

and its social interactions, modified its social order according to the changed conditions. Even the objects of the simplest "sense-certainty", ~~e.g. a cherry tree~~, are provided for him only through social development, industry & commercial interaction. As is well known, the cherry tree ~~like almost all fruit trees~~, like almost all fruit trees, was only transplanted by <u>trade</u> into our geographical zone a few centuries ago, & ~~could~~ was therefore only

First page on printer's sheet '6' (in Engels's sequence), numbered '8' by Marx

interactions, modified its social order according to the changed conditions. Even the objects of the simplest "sense-certainty" are provided for him only through social development, industry & commercial interaction. As is well known, the cherry tree, like almost all fruit trees, was only transplanted by <u>trade</u> into our geographical zone a few centuries ago, & was therefore only

Second page on printer's sheet '6' (in Engels's sequence), numbered '9' by Marx

provided for Feuerbach's "sense-certainty" through this action by a certain kind of society at a certain point. Moreover in this conception ~~also the~~ of things as they actually are & have happened, every profound philosophical problem resolves itself quite simply into an empirical fact, as is shown even more clearly below. E.g. the important question of the relation of man to nature ~~on which~~, {*insertion*} **(or especially ~~the "relation between~~ as Bruno says (p. 110)**[1] **the "antitheses in nature and history", as if** {*further insertion*} **the two were quite separate "things",** {*end further insertion*} **{as if} man is not always confronted with a historical nature and a natural history,)** {*end insertion*} from which arose all the ~~unfathomable lofty works~~ "unfathomable lofty works" on "substance" & "self-consciousness", collapses with the insight that the much ~~famed~~ vaunted "unity of man with nature" has always existed in industry & has existed variously in every epoch depending on the lesser or greater development of industry, {*insertion*} **just the same as the "struggle" of**

Feuerbach

---

1. Bruno Bauer, "Charakteristik Ludwig Feuerbachs," *Wigand's Vierteljahrsschrift*, vol. 3 (1845).

provided for Feuerbach's "sense-certainty" <u>through</u> this action by a certain kind of society at a certain point. Moreover in this conception of things as they actually are & have happened, every profound philosophical problem resolves itself quite simply into an empirical fact, as is shown even more clearly below. E.g the important question of the relation of man to nature **(or especially as Bruno says (p. 110)**[1] **the "antitheses in nature and history", as if the two were quite separate "things", {as if} man is not always confronted with a historical nature and a natural history,)** from which arose all the "unfathomable lofty works" on "substance" & "self-consciousness", collapses with the insight that the much vaunted "unity of man with nature" has always existed in industry & has existed variously in every epoch depending on the lesser or greater development of industry, **just the same as the "struggle" of man with nature right up to**

Feuerbach

---

1. Bruno Bauer, "Charakteristik Ludwig Feuerbachs," *Wigand's Vierteljahrsschrift*, vol. 3 (1845).

man with nature right up to the ~~complete~~ **development of his productive forces on a corresponding basis.** {*end insertion*} ~~These~~ Industry & trade, production and exchange of life's necessities, for their part, condition, and again in their mode of operation {they} are conditioned by, the distribution {of goods}, the structure of the different social classes – & so it happens that Feuerbach sees in Manchester, e.g., only fabrics & machines, where ~~he saw~~ a hundred years earlier there were only spinning wheels and weaving looms to be seen, or in the Roman Campagna he discovers only pastures & swamps whereas ~~before~~ in the time of Augustus ~~he~~ he would have found only vineyards & villas of Roman capitalists. Feuerbach speaks ~~in his~~ particularly of the natural scientific view, he alludes to mysteries which become clear only to the eyes of physicists & chemists; but where would natural science be without industry & trade? Even this "pure" natural science acquires its purpose as well as its materials only
    through trade & industry, through the perceptible activity of men. {*insertion*} So much is this activity {one} of unceasing

Feuerbach

the development of his productive forces on a corresponding basis. Industry & trade, production and exchange of life's necessities, for their part, condition, and again in their mode of operation {they} are conditioned by, the distribution {of goods}, the structure of the different social classes – & so it happens that Feuerbach sees in Manchester, e.g., only fabrics & machines, where a hundred years earlier there were only spinning wheels and weaving looms to be seen, or in the Roman Campagna he discovers only pastures & swamps whereas in the time of Augustus he would have found only vineyards & villas of Roman capitalists. Feuerbach speaks particularly of the natural scientific view, he alludes to mysteries which become clear only to the eyes of physicists & chemists; but where would natural science be without industry & trade? Even this "pure" natural science acquires its purpose as well as its materials only through trade & industry, through the sensuous activity of men. So much is this activity {one} of unceasing perceptible

Feuerbach

Second page on printer's sheet '6' (in Engels's sequence), numbered '9' by Marx

perceptible labour and creation, {so much is} this production the foundation ~~of all~~ of the whole perceptible world as it now exists, that if it were interrupted for even a year, Feuerbach ~~not only innumerable fa{cts}~~ would find not only a tremendous change in the natural world but also that the whole human world and his own capacity to form a view, even his own existence, had very swiftly gone missing. ~~For~~ In any case the {temporal} priority of   external   nature remains intact here, ~~& it is no accident for us &~~ & in any case ~~this nature no distinction~~ all this has no {*insertion continues onto the following page*}

Second page on printer's sheet '6' (in Engels's sequence), numbered '9' by Marx

labour and creation, {so much is} this production the foundation of the whole perceptible world as it now exists, that if it were interrupted for even a year, Feuerbach would find not only a tremendous change in the natural world but also that the whole human world and his own capacity to form a view, even his own existence, had very swiftly gone missing. In any case the {temporal} priority of external nature remains intact here, & in any case all this has no
{*insertion continues onto the following page*}

Third page on printer's sheet '6' (in Engels's sequence), numbered '10' by Marx

application to the first men produced through spontaneous generation; this distinction, however, only has meaning in so far as one considers man to be distinguished from nature. Moreover this nature, which precedes human history, is really not ~~Feuerbach's, in which~~ the nature in which Feuerbach lives, not the nature which no longer exists anywhere today except perhaps ~~in the interior of newly f{ormed}~~ on isolated Australian coral islands of recent origin, hence does not exist for Feuerbach either. {*end insertion from previous page*} – Feuerbach has in any case a big advantage over the "pure" materialists because he ~~also realises how~~ realises how man too is "a perceptible object"; however, {*insertion*}[1] **apart from the fact that he only conceives of him as ~~"perceptible~~ a "perceptible object" not as "perceptible activity"**,{*end insertion*} because he thereby ~~at the~~ remains only in the realm of theory, ~~so he does not arrive at men~~ {he} conceives of ~~the actual "individual, embodied man"~~ men not in ~~his~~ their given social ~~historical~~ connection, not under ~~his~~ their current conditions of life which have made

---

1. The editors of *Jahrbuch 2003* state that this insertion was written down later than the previous one; vol. 2, pp. 216, ref. 11.3–6 l.

Third page on printer's sheet '6' (in Engels's sequence), numbered '10' by Marx

application to the first men produced through spontaneous generation; this distinction, however, only has meaning in so far as one considers man to be distinguished from nature. Moreover this nature, which precedes human history, is really not the nature in which Feuerbach lives, not the nature which no longer exists anywhere today except perhaps on isolated Australian coral islands of recent origin, hence does not exist for Feuerbach either. – Feuerbach has in any case a big advantage over the "pure" materialists because he realises how man too is "a perceptible object"; however, **apart from the fact that he only conceives of him as a "perceptible object" not as "perceptible activity",** because he thereby remains only in the realm of theory, {he} conceives of men not in their given social connection, not under their current conditions of life which have made

Third page on printer's sheet '6' (in Engels's sequence), numbered '10' by Marx

~~him~~ them into what they are, hence he never arrives at actually existing active men, but rather stops ~~with all~~ with the abstraction "man", & only gets as far as recognising the "actual, individual, embodied men" in terms of emotion, i.e. he ~~arrives at~~ knows no other "human relations" "of man to man" other than love & friendship, {*insertion*} **and idealised at that. There is no critique of present-day loving relations.** {*end insertion*} Hence he never arrives at a conception of the perceptible world as the ~~unified perceptible unified perceptible~~ **whole perceptible** whole living perceptible <u>activity</u> of the individuals who compose it ~~& where the practical~~, hence if he sees e.g. a heap of scrofulous, overworked & consumptive starvelings instead of healthy men, then he is forced to take his refuge in the "higher view" & the "ideal "reconciliation in the species", thus relapsing into idealism precisely at the point where the communist materialist sees the necessity & at the same time the condition for a transformation of industry as well as ~~societal~~ the social structure. ~~With Feuerbach~~

 In so far as Feuerbach is a materialist,

F.

Feuerbach.

them into what they are, hence he never arrives at actually existing active men, but rather stops with the abstraction "man", & **F.** only gets as far as recognising the "actual, individual, embodied men" in terms of emotion, i.e. he knows no other "human relations" "of man to man" other than love & friendship, **and idealised at that. There is no critique of present-day loving relations.** Hence he never arrives at a conception of the perceptible world as the **whole living perceptible** <u>activity</u> of the individuals who **Feuerbach.** compose it, hence if he sees e.g. a heap of scrofulous, overworked & consumptive starvelings instead of healthy men, then he is forced to take his refuge in the "higher view" & the ideal "reconciliation in the species", thus relapsing into idealism precisely at the point where the communist materialist sees the necessity & at the same time the condition for a transformation of industry as well as the social structure.

In so far as Feuerbach is a materialist,

Third page on printer's sheet '6' (in Engels's sequence), numbered '10' by Marx

history does not register with him, & in so far as he brings history into consideration, he is no materialist. With him materialism & history diverge completely, which, by the way, is already evident from what has been said. ~~The reason we nevertheless examine so-called history so closely here is because the Germans are used~~

Third page on printer's sheet '6' (in Engels's sequence), numbered '10' by Marx

history does not register with him, & in so far as he brings history into consideration, he is no materialist. With him materialism & history diverge completely, which, by the way, is already evident from what has been said.

Fourth page on printer's sheet '6' (in Engels's sequence), numbered '11' by Marx

~~to the words history & historical representing all things possible except all reality to which, of which Saint Bruno in particular with his "pulpit eloquence" offers a shining example.~~ — We have ~~therefore~~[1] to make a start with the ~~Germans presupposition{less}~~ Germans, who are devoid of premises, by setting forth the first premise of all human existence, ~~namely~~ and therefore of all history, namely the premise that men have to be in a position to live in order to be able to "make history". But living requires above all else eating & drinking,[2] shelter, clothing & yet other things. The first historical act is therefore the production of the means to satisfy these needs, the production of material life itself, & indeed this is a historical act, a founding condition of all history, which must be fulfilled today, on a daily & hourly basis, just as it was thousands of years ago, simply for men to stay alive. ~~Hence the first thing~~ {*insertion*} Even if perceptibility is reduced to a stick, to a minimum, as it is with the holy Bruno, it presupposes the activity of producing

History.

Hegel.
Geological, hydrographical etc. relations.
Human bodies. Needs, labour.

---

1. The editors of *Jahrbuch 2003* indicate that Marx struck out this word; vol. 2, p. 217, ref. 12.8 l.

2. The editors of *Jahrbuch 2003* indicate that the first formulation of this phrase was: "eating & drinking, above all else"; vol. 2, p. 218. ref. 12.17–18 l.

Fourth page on printer's sheet '6' (in Engels's sequence), numbered '11' by Marx

— We have to make a start with the Germans, who are devoid of premises, by setting forth the first premise of all human existence, and therefore of all history, namely the premise that men have to be in a position to live in order to be able to "make history". But living requires above all else eating & drinking, shelter, clothing & yet other things. The first historical act is therefore the production of the means to satisfy these needs, the production of material life itself, & indeed this is a historical act, a founding condition of all history, which must be fulfilled today, on a daily & hourly basis, just as it was thousands of years ago, simply for men to stay alive. Even if perceptibility is reduced to a stick, to a minimum, as it is with the holy Bruno, it presupposes the activity of producing that

History.

Hegel.
Geological, hydrographical etc. relations.
Human bodies. Needs, labour.

Fourth page on printer's sheet '6' (in Engels's sequence), numbered '11' by Marx

that stick. {*end insertion*} Hence with any conception of history the first thing is to observe this fa{ct} fundamental fact in its full significance & its full implications & do it justice. As is well known the Germans have never done this, hence have never had an earthly basis for history & consequently never had an historian. The French & the English at least, even when they have conceived conceived of the connection of this fact with so-called history in a highly tendentious way, particularly as long as they were biased by political ideology, have always all the same made the first attempts to give a materialistic basis to the writing of history by being the first to write histories of civil society, of trade & of industry. – The second thing {with any acquired conception of history} is, that the ease of — men produces liberation from primary needs as well as {providing} new needs

Fourth page on printer's sheet '6' (in Engels's sequence), numbered '11' by Marx

stick. Hence with any conception of history the first thing is to observe this fundamental fact in its full significance & its full implications & do it justice. As is well known the Germans have never done this, hence have never had an <u>earthly</u> basis for history & consequently never had an historian. The French & the English, even when they conceived of the connection of this fact with so-called history in a highly tendentious way, particularly as long as they were biased by political ideology, have all the same made the first attempts to give a materialistic basis to the writing of history by being the first to write histories of civil society, of trade & of industry. – The second thing {with any conception of history} is

First page on printer's sheet '7' (in Engels's sequence), numbered '12' by Marx

that ~~the satisfaction of the {need} of needs~~ the first ~~already~~ satisfied need itself, the action of satisfying it & the instrument acquired for this satisfaction, leads to new needs – & this production of new needs is the ~~history~~ first historical act. With this we see at the same time whose spiritual child the great ~~wis{dom}~~ historical wisdom of the Germans is, hence where their positive material runs out, & where neither theological, nor political, nor literary nonsense is under consideration, it brings up the "prehistoric era", not history at all, without making clear to us how one gets from this nonsense about "prehistory" to proper history – although on the other hand their historical speculation casts itself in particular on "prehistory" because it is believed to be safe there ~~&~~ from the intrusion of "crude facts" & at the same time because they give full rein to their speculative impulse & {it} can set up & knock down ~~non{sense}~~ ~~irre{futable}~~ hypotheses by the thousand. – The third relation {in any conception of history}, which enters here into historical development on equal terms right from the start, is that men, who make their bodies anew

First page on printer's sheet '7' (in Engels's sequence), numbered '12' by Marx

that the first satisfied need itself, the action of satisfying it & the instrument acquired for this satisfaction, leads to new needs – & this production of new needs is the first historical act. With this we see at the same time whose spiritual child the great historical wisdom of the Germans is, hence where their positive material runs out, & where neither theological, nor political, nor literary nonsense is under consideration, it brings up the "prehistoric era", not history at all, without making clear to us how one gets from this nonsense about "prehistory" to proper history – although on the other hand their historical speculation casts itself in particular on "prehistory" because it is believed to be safe there from the intrusion of "crude facts" & at the same time because they give full rein to their speculative impulse & {it} can set up & knock down hypotheses by the thousand. – The third relation {in any conception of history}, which enters here into historical development on equal terms right from the start, is that men, who make their bodies anew every day, set about making other

First page on printer's sheet '7' (in Engels's sequence), numbered '12' by Marx

every day, set about making other men, propagating themselves – the relation between man & wife, elders & children, the <u>family</u>. This family, which at the beginning is the sole social relation, later turns into a subordinate one (except in Germany), when increased   , & the needs produce new social relations increased numbers of men new needs,   & must therefore be treated & developed according to existing empirical data, not according to the "concept of the family", as one is obliged to do in Germany. {*insertion*} [1]In any case these three aspects of social activity are not to be understood as three different stages, but rather only as three aspects, or in order to write transparently for the Germans, three   simultaneously "moments" that have existed ~~at the onset of history~~ from the beginning of history & since the first men & are still at work in history today.{*end insertion*} – The production of life, of one's own in labouring as well as of other life in procreating, appears here at the same time as a double

---

1. The editors of *Jahrbuch 2003* state that this insertion was written down later than the previous one; vol. 2, p. 219, ref. 14.22–32 l.

men, propagating themselves – the relation between man & wife, elders & children, the <u>family</u>. This family, which at the beginning is the sole social relation, later turns into a subordinate one (except in Germany), when increased needs produce new social relations , & the increased numbers of men new needs,

&

must therefore be treated & developed according to existing empirical data, not according to the "concept of the family", as one is obliged to do in Germany. In any case these three aspects of social activity are not to be understood as three different stages, but rather only as three aspects, or in order to write transparently for the Germans, three "moments" that have existed simultaneously from the beginning of history & since the first men & are still at work in history today. – The production of life, of one's own in labouring as well as of other life in procreating, appears here at the same time as a double

Second page on printer's sheet '7' (in Engels's sequence), numbered '13' by Marx

relation – on the one hand as a natural relation, on the other hand as a social relation – social in the sense that the interaction of several individuals, no matter under whatever conditions, in whatever way and for whatever purpose, is hereby understood. It follows from this that a certain mode of production or stage of industry is always conjoined with a certain mode of social interaction or stage of society, {*insertion*}**and this mode of social interaction is itself a "force of production"** {*end insertion*}, so that the ~~state~~ aggregate of productive forces accessible to men affects the condition of society & therefore the "history of mankind" must always be studied and treated in connection with the history of industry & of exchange. However it is also clear how it is impossible in Germany to write such ~~jour{nals}~~ history since the Germans in this matter lack not only the capacity to understand & the material but also the "perceptible certainty", & one can get no experience of these things on that side of the

Second page on printer's sheet '7' (in Engels's sequence), numbered '13' by Marx

relation – on the one hand as a natural relation, on the other hand as a social relation – social in the sense that the interaction of several individuals, no matter under whatever conditions, in whatever way and for whatever purpose, is hereby understood. It follows from this that a certain mode of production or stage of industry is always conjoined with a certain mode of social interaction or stage of society, **and this mode of social interaction is itself a "force of production"**, so that the aggregate of productive forces accessible to men affects the condition of society & therefore the "history of mankind" must always be studied and treated in connection with the history of industry & of exchange. However it is also clear how it is impossible in Germany to write such history since the Germans in this matter lack not only the capacity to understand & the material but also the "perceptible certainty", & one can get no experience of these things on that side of the Rhine because there is no

Second page on printer's sheet '7' (in Engels's sequence), numbered '13' by Marx

Rhine ~~since~~ because there is no history going on over there any more. Thus it is obvious from the outset that there is a materialistic connection of men with one another which {is} conditioned by the needs {of men} & the mode of production & is thus as old as humanity itself – ~~that hence for "history"~~ a connection which is always ~~taking on~~ taking on new forms ~~&~~ & thus offering a "history" without the existence of any kind of superfluous political or religious nonsense which would additionally hold men together. – Only now, after we have considered four moments, four aspects of original, historical relations do we find that man ~~among other things also has "mind", & that this "mind" "manifests" itself~~ also has "consciousness". ~~as "consciousness"~~ But even this {is} not from the outset "pure" consciousness. The "mind" has from the start

Men have history, because they must produce their life, and indeed must do so in a specific way; ~~they ha{ve}~~ this is given by their physical organisation; just the same as their consciousness.

Second page on printer's sheet '7' (in Engels's sequence), numbered '13' by Marx

history going on over there any more. Thus it is obvious from the outset that there is a materialistic connection of men with one another which {is} conditioned by the needs {of men} & the mode of production & is thus as old as humanity itself – a connection which is always taking on new forms & thus offering a "history" without the existence of any kind of superfluous political or religious nonsense which would additionally hold men together. – Only now, after we have considered four moments, four aspects of original, historical relations do we find that man **also has "consciousness"**. But even this {is} not from the outset "pure" consciousness. The "mind" has from the start

Men have history, because they must produce their life, and indeed must do so in a specific way; this is given by their physical organisation; just the same as their consciousness.

the curse of being "burdened" with matter, which ~~here in the form of vibrating layers of air, sounds, in short, language~~ occurs here in the form of vibrating layers of air, sounds, in short, language. Language is as old as consciousness – language is practical, actual consciousness existing for other men as well {*insertion*}, only therefore does it also exist for me myself {*end insertion*}, & like consciousness, language only arises from the ~~social interaction~~ need, the necessity of social interaction with other men. Consciousness is therefore from the outset a social product & remains so as long as men exist at all. Naturally at first[1] consciousness is simple **immediate** ~~percep{tible}~~ consciousness of the perceptible environment & consciousness of the **limited** interconnection with other persons & things outside the increasingly self-conscious individual; at the same time it is consciousness ~~about the~~ of nature which confronts men in the beginning as a thoroughly alien, all-powerful & incomprehensible force, to which men relate

~~My relationship to my environment is my consciousness~~ Where there exists a relationship it exists for me, the animal **not for itself to an{other}** "relates"[2] itself to nothing & {does} not {relate itself} at all. {insertion}[3] **For the animal its relationship to others does not exist as a relationship.** {end insertion}

---

1. The editors of *Jahrbuch 2003* state that the word order in this phrase was originally: "At first naturally"; vol. 2, p. 220, ref. 16–22 l.

2. Marx's quotation marks.
3. The editors of *Jahrbuch 2003* state that this insertion was written down later than the two nearby insertions in the left-hand column; vol 2, p. 220, ref. 16.20–21 r.

Third page on printer's sheet '7' (in Engels's sequence), numbered '14' by Marx

the curse of being "burdened" with matter, which occurs here in the form of vibrating layers of air, sounds, in short, language. Language is as old as consciousness – language is practical, actual consciousness existing for other men as well, only therefore does it also exist for me myself, & like consciousness, language only arises from the need, the necessity of social interaction with other men. Consciousness is therefore from the outset a social product & remains so as long as men exist at all. Naturally at first consciousness is simple consciousness of the **immediate** perceptible environment & consciousness of the **limited** interconnection with other persons & things outside the increasingly self-conscious individual; at the same time it is consciousness of nature which confronts men in the beginning as a thoroughly alien, all-powerful & incomprehensible force, to which men relate

Where there exists a relationship it exists for me, the animal "relates"[1] itself to nothing & {does} not {relate itself} at all. **For the animal its relationship to others does not exist as a relationship.**

---

1. Marx's quotation marks.

Third page on printer's sheet '7' (in Engels's sequence), numbered '14' by Marx

in a purely animal way, ~~which to them~~ by which they are overawed like beasts, & hence a purely animal consciousness of nature (natural religion) – & on the other hand consciousness of the ~~necessary~~ necessity of entering into relations with nearby individuals, the beginning of ~~social~~ consciousness of the fact that he is living in society at all. This beginning is as ~~beast-like~~ animalistic as social life is at this stage, it is mere herd-consciousness, & ~~is distinguished~~ man distinguishes himself here from a sheep only in that with him his consciousness takes the place of instinct, or that his instinct is a conscious one ~~sheep or tribal consciousness~~. This sheep- or tribal-consciousness obtains its further development & improvement through increased productivity, the expansion of needs &, fundamental to both of these, the

precisely because nature is still ~~no{t}~~ ~~little~~ scarcely modified historically.

One sees {this} here at once. This natural religion ~~is conditioned by the social inter{action} form of society and~~ or this specific way of relating to nature is conditioned ~~with~~ by the form of society and the other way round. Here as everywhere the identity of nature and man also comes up because men's limited way of relating to

in a purely animal way by which they are overawed like beasts, & hence a purely animal consciousness of nature (natural religion) – & on the other hand consciousness of the necessity of entering into relations with nearby individuals, the beginning of consciousness of the fact that he is living in society at all. This beginning is as animalistic as social life is at this stage, it is mere herd-consciousness, & man distinguishes himself here from a sheep only in that with him his consciousness takes the place of instinct, or that his instinct is a conscious one. This sheep- or tribal-consciousness obtains its further development & improvement through increased productivity, the expansion of needs &, fundamental to both of these, the

precisely because nature is still scarcely modified historically.

One sees {this} here at once. This natural religion or this specific way of relating to nature is conditioned by the form of society and the other way round. Here as everywhere the identity of nature and man also comes up because men's limited way of relating to

increase in population.[1] Along with these there develops a division of labour, the ~~pre{vious}~~ original of which was nothing but the division of labour in the reproductive act, then ~~the~~ division of labour which makes use of natural aptitude in and of itself (e.g. physical strength, needs, variations &c &c) ~~therefore~~ or "developing naturally". The division of labour only becomes an actual division at the moment when a division of ~~mental & material~~ material & mental labour takes place. From this moment onwards consciousness is able to conceive of itself as something other than the consciousness of existing ~~things~~ practice, ~~something actual~~ actually representing something without representing an actual thing – from that moment onwards consciousness is in a position to emancipate itself from the world & to ascend to ~~pure~~ the formation of "pure" theories, theology{,} philosophy{,} morals
&c. But even if this theory, theology, philosophy, morals &c enters into contradiction with existing relations, then this can only happen when the existing social relations ~~enter~~ have thereby entered into

nature conditions their restricted relation to one another, and their restricted way of relating to one another conditions their restricted relationship with nature.

~~Men develop their to~~
~~Consciousness develops~~
~~within the actual historical development.~~
~~Through the division of labour~~
Coincides with the first form of ideology. Priests.

---

1. According to the editors of *Jahrbuch 2003* Engels wrote Pop{ulation} and then deleted it in favor of *Bevölkerung*; vol. 2, p. 221, ref. 17.14 l.

Fourth page on printer's sheet '7' (in Engels's sequence), numbered '15' by Marx

increase in population. Along with these there develops a division of labour, the original of which was nothing but the division of labour in the reproductive act, then division of labour which makes use of natural aptitude in and of itself (e.g. physical strength, needs, variations &c &c) or "developing naturally". The division of labour only becomes an actual division at the moment when a division of material & mental labour takes place. From this moment onwards consciousness <u>is able</u> to conceive of itself as something other than the consciousness of existing practice, actually representing something without representing an actual thing – from that moment onwards consciousness is in a position to emancipate itself from the world & to ascend to the formation of "pure" theories, theology{,} philosophy{,} morals &c. But even if this theory, theology, philosophy, morals &c enters into contradiction with existing relations, then this can only happen when the existing social relations have thereby entered into

nature conditions their restricted relation to one another, and their restricted way of relating to one another conditions their restricted relationship with nature.

Coincides with the first form of ideology. Priests.

Fourth page on printer's sheet '7' (in Engels's sequence), numbered '15' by Marx

contradiction with the existing forces of production – which can also happen in any case in a specific national sphere of relations in such a way that the contradiction does not itself occur within this national space but rather ~~very simply occ{urs} arises in the sphere of the consciousness belonging to it~~ between this national consciousness & the practice of other nations, i.e. between the national & general consciousness of a nation (like Germany at present) – where to that nation then, because this contradiction ~~itself~~ seems to appear ~~to occur~~ only inside national as a contradiction of the consciousness, the struggle also appears to be limited to this

Religions. The German with the <u>ideology</u> as such.

contradiction with the existing
forces of production – which can also happen
in any case in a specific national sphere
of relations in such a way that the
contradiction does not itself occur within this
national space but rather between this national
consciousness & the practice of other
nations, i.e. between the national & general
consciousness of a nation (like Germany at
present) – where to that nation then, because
this contradiction seems to appear only
as a contradiction inside of the national
consciousness, the struggle also appears to
be limited to this

Religions. The German with the <u>ideology</u> as such.

First page on printer's sheet '8' (in Engels's sequence), numbered '16' by Marx

national shit precisely because this nation is shit through and through. Moreover {it is} completely irrelevant what this consciousness starts to do on its own, we get ~~only from this whole mess~~ from this whole mess the sole result that these three moments, the force of production, the condition of society & consciousness can & must come into contradiction with one another, because with the <u>division of labour</u> there arises the possibility, indeed the actuality, that mental & material ~~labour~~ activity, {*insertion*}[1] — ~~activity and thought, i.e. unselfconscious activity and unself{conscious} pointless thought~~ {*end insertion*} that use & labour, production & consumption fall to different individuals, & the possibility that they do not come into contradiction lies only in transforming {*aufgehoben*} the division of labour in turn. In any case it is self-evident that "spectres", "ties", "higher being", "concept", "thoughtfulness" ~~are, inne{r}~~ are merely the speculative idealist mental

11, 12, 13, 14, 15, 16[2]

---

1. The editors of *Jahrbuch 2003* state that this insertion was written down later than the previous change, where "work" was deleted; vol. 2, p. 222, ref. 18.33 l.

2. The editors of *Jahrbuch 2003* state that this insertion by Marx was written down later than the nearby "portrait sketch" by Engels but do not comment on the meaning of the sequence; vol. 2, p. 222, ref. 18.26 r.

First page on printer's sheet '8' (in Engels's sequence), numbered '16' by Marx

national shit precisely because this nation is shit through and through. Moreover {it is} completely irrelevant what this consciousness starts to do on its own, we get from this whole mess the sole result that these three moments, the force of production, the condition of society & consciousness can & must come into contradiction with one another, because with the <u>division of labour</u> there arises the possibility, indeed the actuality, that mental & material activity, that use & labour, production & consumption fall to different individuals, & the possibility that they do not come into contradiction lies only in transforming {*aufgehoben*} the division of labour in turn. In any case it is self-evident that "spectres", "ties", "higher being", "concept", "thoughtfulness" are merely the speculative idealist mental expression,

11, 12, 13, 14, 15, 16[1]

---

1. The editors of *Jahrbuch 2003* state that this insertion by Marx was written down later than the nearby "portrait sketch" by Engels but do not comment on the meaning of the sequence; Apparat p. 222, ref. 18.26 r.

First page on printer's sheet '8' (in Engels's sequence), numbered '16' by Marx

expression, the seeming representation of ~~single~~ **disaggregated** individuals, the representation of very empirical fetters & limitations within which are operating the mode of production of life & the form of social interaction corresponding to it. ~~These idealistic This idealistic expression of existing economic limitations is not only present purely theoretically but also in practical consciousness, i.e. it ma{kes} the consciousness which is emancipating itself~~ {*insertion*} ~~& entering into com{pulsion} contradiction with the existing mode of production~~ {*end insertion*} ~~does not only form religion and philosophy but also the state.~~

With the division of labour in which all these contradictions take place, & which for their part are resting in turn on the division of labour that arises naturally in the family & in the division of ~~societies~~ society into individual families confronting one another — there also arises at the same time the dividing up ~~of the~~, & indeed the unequal division of labour & its products in both quantitative and qualitative terms, hence property {arises},

First page on printer's sheet '8' (in Engels's sequence), numbered '16' by Marx

the seeming representation of **disaggregated** individuals, the representation of very empirical fetters & limitations within which are operating the mode of production of life & the form of social interaction corresponding to it.

With the division of labour in which all these contradictions take place, & which for their part are resting in turn on the division of labour that arises naturally in the family & in the division of society into individual families confronting one another – there also arises at the same time the dividing <u>up</u>, & indeed the <u>unequal</u> division of labour & its products in both quantitative and qualitative terms, hence property {arises},

Second page on printer's sheet '8' (in Engels's sequence), numbered '17' by Marx

which ~~had already developed naturally within~~ already has its seed, its first form in the family, where the wife & the children are slaves of the husband. The obvious, still very crude ~~&~~, latent slavery in the family is the first property, which ~~by the way already here itself~~, by the way, already fulfils the modern economist's definition, according to which it   is   the command over alien labour-power. {*insertion*[1]} After all, division of labour & private property are identical expressions – in the one the same thing is attested in relation to the activity as is attested in the other in relation to the product of the activity. – {*end insertion*}

Furthermore with the division of labour we have at the same time the contradiction between the interest of the single & individual or the single family & the common interest of all individuals who are {engaging} in social interchange with one another, and to be sure this common [2]out of this very contradiction between particular interest & common interest, ~~there is formed the common interest itself as state~~ the common interest takes on an independent form as the <u>state</u>, separated from the actual individual & collective

---

1. In the right-hand column but adjacent to this passage.

2. This insertion is said by the editors of *Jahrbuch 2003* to be later than the "ground level" text; Apparat p. 223, ref. 19.39–20.41 r.

Second page on printer's sheet '8' (in Engels's sequence), numbered '17' by Marx

which already has its seed, its first form in the family, where the wife & the children are slaves of the husband. The obvious, still very crude, latent slavery in the family is the first property, which, by the way, already fulfils the modern economist's definition, according to which it is the command over alien labour-power. After all, division of labour & private property are identical expressions – in the one the same thing is attested in relation to the activity as is attested in the other in relation to the product of the activity. – Furthermore with the division of labour we have at the same time the contradiction between the interest of the single individual or the single family & the common interest of all individuals who are {engaging} in social interchange with one another, and to be sure this common out of this very contradiction between particular interest & common interest, the common interest takes on an independent form as the <u>state</u>, separated from the actual individual & collective

interest does not exist merely as an idea, like for instance, "what is general", but immediately in reality as the mutual dependence of the individuals amongst whom the labour is divided. And finally the division of labour offers us in a similar way the first example of the fact that ~~man's own act so long as this act {is} not a free~~ ~~actual social~~ so long as men are living in societies that have arisen naturally, there exists a cleavage between particular & common interest, hence so long as ~~labour~~ activity is not freely but rather naturally divided, man's own act becomes opposed to him as an alien power over and above him, which ~~controls~~ subjugates him instead of him controlling it. Therefore as soon as the division of labour ~~is~~ starts to develop, each man has a particular, exclusive area of activity that constrains him, that he cannot get out of; he is a hunter, fisherman or **or critical critic** herdsman & must remain

& at the same time as an illusory interests, communality, however always on the real basis of ~~assoc{iations}~~ the existing ties in every family & tribal-conglomerate, such as flesh & blood, language,[1] ~~inte{rests}~~ division of labour on the larger scale & various interests ~~& like~~ – & in particular, as we will be developing later, the {contradiction} of the classes, already conditioned by the division of labour, which are separating themselves out in any kind of human mass & of which one dominates all the others. It follows from this that all struggles within the state, ~~between~~ the struggle between democracy, aristocracy & monarchy, the struggle for the franchise &c &c ~~everything out~~ are nothing but the illusory forms {*insertion*} – on the whole what is general {is} the illusory form of the common {interest} – {*end insertion*} in which the actual struggles of the different classes are

---

1. The editors of *Jahrbuch 2003* give the original order in this phrase as: language, flesh & blood; vol. 2, p. 224, ref. 20.8 r.

interest does not exist merely as an idea, like for instance, "what is general", but immediately in reality as the mutual dependence of the individuals amongst whom the labour is divided. And finally the division of labour offers us in a similar way the first example of the fact that so long as men are living in societies that have arisen naturally, there exists a cleavage between particular & common interest, hence so long as activity is not freely but rather naturally divided, man's own act becomes opposed to him as an alien power over and above him, which subjugates him instead of him controlling it. Therefore as soon as the division of labour starts to develop, each man has a particular, exclusive area of activity that constrains him, that he cannot get out of; he is a hunter, fisherman or herdsman **or critical critic** & must remain as such & at the same time as an illusory communality, however always on the real basis of the existing ties in every family & tribal-conglomerate, such as flesh & blood, language, division of labour on the larger scale & various interests – & in particular, as we will be developing later, the {contradiction} of the classes, already conditioned by the division of labour, which are separating themselves out in any kind of human mass & of which one dominates all the others. It follows from this that all struggles within the state, the struggle between democracy, aristocracy & monarchy, the struggle for the franchise &c &c are nothing but the illusory forms – on the whole what is general {is} the illusory form of the common {interest} – in which the actual struggles of the different classes are

Second page on printer's sheet '8' (in Engels's sequence), numbered '17' by Marx

as such unless he wants to lose ~~his~~ the means to live – whereas in communist society, where each man does not have an exclusive area of activity~~, rather~~ but can rather develop himself in any branch~~es~~ he likes, society ~~merely~~ regulates the general production & thus makes it possible for me to do one thing today and another to hunt, tomorrow, in the morning ~~to be a shoemaker & at midday~~ in the afternoon ~~a~~ to fish, to herd livestock, ~~gardner~~, in the evening ~~to be a playwright,~~ **and to criticise after dinner**, just as I have without ever becoming hunter{,} a mind. **or critic**. fisherman ~~or~~ herdsman.

conducted among themselves, (of which the German theoreticians have not the faintest inkling, in spite of the fact that they were given sufficient ~~mat{erial}~~ instruction on the subject in the Deutsch-Französische Jahrbücher & The Holy Family) & furthermore that each class striving ~~toward~~ for dominance, even if its dominance, as is the case with the proletariat, is the general condition of the transformation {*Aufhebung*} of the old form of society in its entirety **and of dominance generally**, {each class} must itself first ~~to the political power~~ seize political power in order to represent its interest in turn as the general interest, which it is forced to do at the outset. [1]**Just because individuals** <u>only</u> **seek their particular interest – for them not coinciding with their common interest – is the latter made to serve as an interest "alien" to them and** ~~over~~

---

1. Written on both pages *17* and *18* (as numbered by Marx) and, according to the editors of *Jahrbuch 2003*, at a later stage; vol. 2, p. 225, ref. 20.41–21.19 r.

unless he wants to lose the means to live – whereas in communist society, where each man does not have an exclusive area of activity, but can rather develop himself in any branch he likes, society regulates the general production & thus makes it possible for me to do one thing today and another tomorrow, in the morning to hunt, in the afternoon to fish, in the evening to herd livestock **and to criticise after dinner**, just as I have a mind, without ever becoming hunter{,} fisherman, herdsman **or critic**.

conducted among themselves, (of which the German theoreticians have not the faintest inkling, in spite of the fact that they were given sufficient instruction on the subject in the Deutsch-Französische Jahrbücher & The Holy Family) & furthermore that each class striving for dominance, even if its dominance, as is the case with the proletariat, is the general condition of the transformation {*Aufhebung*} of the old form of society in its entirety **and of dominance generally**, {each class} must itself first seize political power in order to represent its interest in turn as the general interest, which it is forced to do at the outset. **Just because individuals seek <u>only</u> their particular interest – for them not coinciding with their common interest – is the latter made to serve as an interest "alien" to them and**

Third page on printer's sheet '8' (in Engels's sequence), numbered '18' by Marx

This fixation of social activity, this consolidation of ~~my~~ our own product into a ~~power~~ material sovereignty over ~~me~~ us, which escapes ~~my~~ our control, confounds ~~my~~ our expectations, brings our calculations to nothing, is one of the chief factors in the ~~existing soc{ial}~~ historical development up to now ~~, & in property, which, at first through a particular institution set up by men themselves, soon gives to society a particular change of direction in no way intended by its originators, self evident to anyone who is not stuck fast in "self-consciousness" or "the ego"~~. The social power, ~~which to me{n}~~ i.e. the multiplied productive force, which develops through the cooperation, {insertion} conditional on the division of labour {end insertion}, of different individuals, appears to these individuals, because the cooperation itself is not voluntary but arises naturally, not as their own conjoined power, but rather as an "independent" of them, as yet again a particular and characteristic "general"-interest, or they themselves must be occupied within this dualism, as in democracy. On the other hand then the **practical** struggle of these particular interests, **in reality** always confronting common and illusory common interests, also makes **practical** intervention and regulation necessary through the illusory

"general"-interest as the state.
{marginal note¹}
Communism is not for us a state of affairs, which is to be established, an **ideal**, ~~which Feuerbach~~ according to which actuality has to be set aright. We call communism the ~~pra{ctical}~~ actual movement, ~~which the practical~~ which transforms {*aufhebt*} the current state of affairs. ~~We have merely to write. The conditions for this movement are to be jud{ged} according to the actual~~

---

1. According to the editors of *Jahrbuch 2003*, this was written later than the next insertion; vol. 2, p. 226, ref. 21.21–30 r.

Third page on printer's sheet '8' (in Engels's sequence), numbered '18' by Marx

This fixation of social activity, this consolidation of our own product into a material sovereignty over us, which escapes my control, confounds our expectations, brings our calculations to nothing, is one of the chief factors in the historical development up to now. The social power, i.e. the multiplied productive force, which develops through the cooperation, conditional on the division of labour, of different individuals, appears to these individuals, because the cooperation itself is not voluntary but arises naturally, not as their own conjoined power, but rather as an alien sovereignty standing

"independent" of them, as yet again a particular and characteristic "general"-interest, or they themselves must be occupied within this dualism, as in democracy. On the other hand then the practical struggle of these particular interests, in reality always confronting common and illusory common interests, also makes practical intervention and regulation necessary through the illusory "general"-interest as the state. Communism is not for us a state of affairs, which is to be established, an ideal, according to which actuality has to be set aright. We call communism the actual movement, which transforms {*aufhebt*} the current state of affairs. The conditions for this movement result

Third page on printer's sheet '8' (in Engels's sequence), numbered '18' by Marx

alien sovereignty standing outside them, about which they know neither where it's come from nor where it's going ~~& with which they therefore no longer~~, which they therefore cannot control anymore, which on the contrary goes through a peculiar series of phases & stages of development independent of the will & action of men, even directing that very will & action. How else could e.g. property have a history at all, taken on different forms, & say landed property ~~e.g.~~ in France, all the more in terms of the different situation there, have been able to move on from ~~great estates~~ enclosures to centralisation in a few hands, in England from centralisation in a few hands to enclosures, as is actually the case today? Or how does it happen that trade, which is after all nothing more than ~~the relation~~ the exchange of the ~~particular~~ products of different individuals & countries, controls

~~present reality itself~~ **result from the situation that now exists.**
{marginal note[1]}
This "alienation", to keep things intelligible to philosophers, can of course only be transformed {*aufgehoben*} **under two practical presuppositions. For it to become an "intolerable" power, i.e. a power, against which men rebel, it must necessarily have rendered ~~a~~ the mass of mankind thoroughly "propertyless" ~~,which~~ and at the same time in contradiction with an existing world of wealth and culture, both of which presuppose a huge rise in the force of production – a high level of its development – , and on the other hand this development of the forces of production (with which at the same time we already have ~~the world historical instead of the local~~ the present empirical existence of men in world historical**

---

1. The editors of *Jahrbuch 2003* note that Marx wrote this passage in the right-hand column but directed it into the left. But because they can find no continuity of thought, they have left it in the right-hand column; vol. 2, p. 227 ref. 21.32–23.5 r.

outside them, about which they know neither where it's come from nor where it's going, which they therefore cannot control anymore, which on the contrary goes through a peculiar series of phases & stages of development independent of the will & action of men, even directing that very will & action. How else could e.g. property have a history at all, taken on different forms, & say landed property in France, all the more in terms of the different situation there, have been able to move on from enclosures to centralisation in a few hands, in England from centralisation in a few hands to enclosures, as is actually the case today? Or how does it happen that trade, which is after all nothing more than the exchange of the products of different individuals & countries, controls the whole world

from the situation that now exists. This <u>"alienation"</u>, to keep things intelligible to philosophers, can of course only be transformed {*aufgehoben*} under two <u>practical</u> presuppositions. For it to become an "intolerable" power, i.e. a power, against which men rebel, it must necessarily have rendered the mass of mankind thoroughly "propertyless" and at the same time in contradiction with an existing world of wealth and culture, both of which presuppose a huge rise in the force of production – a high level of its development – , and on the other hand this development of the forces of production (with which at the same time we already have the present empirical existence of men in <u>world historical</u>

Third page on printer's sheet '8' (in Engels's sequence), numbered '18' by Marx

the whole world through the relation of supply & demand – a relation which, as an English economist says, hovers over the earth like the fate of the ancients & with an invisible hand allots fortune and misfortune to men, erects empires

rather than local mode) ~~already~~ on that account an absolutely necessary practical presupposition, because without it poverty \ destitution is merely generalised, hence with destitution the struggle for necessities also begins again, and all the old shit would have to be re-established, because only ~~in future~~ with this *universal* development of the forces of production *does* a universal social interaction among men take place, hence on the one hand the phenomenon of the "propertyless" "mass" ~~appears~~ arises in all peoples at the same time, (the general competition) – makes each of them dependent on the changes in the others ~~. Without this~~ , and finally empirically has set up world historical, universal individuals in place of local ones. Without this 1) communism could only exist as a local phenomenon, ~~and~~

through the relation of supply & demand – a relation which, as an English economist says, hovers over the earth like the fate of the ancients & with an invisible hand allots fortune and misfortune to men, erects empires

rather than local mode) is on that account an absolutely necessary practical presupposition, because without it poverty \ destitution is merely generalised, hence with destitution the struggle for necessities also begins again, and all the old shit would have to be re-established, because only in future with this universal development of the forces of production does a universal commerce among men take place, hence on the one hand the phenomenon of the "propertyless" "mass" arises in all peoples at the same time, (the general competition) – makes each of them dependent on the changes in the others, and finally has set up world historical, empirically universal individuals in place of local ones. Without this 1) communism could only exist as a local phenomenon,

Third page on printer's sheet '8' (in Engels's sequence), numbered '18' by Marx

2)
the ~~alien~~ <u>powers</u> of commerce itself could not have developed as <u>universal</u>, hence intolerable powers, they would remain homegrown-superstition-ridden
and 3)
"circumstances"   each advance in commerce would transform {*aufheben*} local
communism. Communism is empirically possible only as the act of the dominant peoples "all at once" and at the same time, which presupposes the universal development of the forces of production and the worldwide commerce that goes together with them.

Third page on printer's sheet '8' (in Engels's sequence), numbered '18' by Marx

2) the <u>powers</u> of commerce itself could not have developed as <u>universal</u>, hence intolerable powers, they would remain homegrown superstition-ridden "circumstances" and 3) each advance in social interaction would transform {*aufheben*} local communism. Communism is empirically possible only as the act of the dominant peoples "all at once" and at the same time, which presupposes the universal development of the forces of production and the worldwide commerce that goes together with them.

Fourth page on printer's sheet '8' (in Engels's sequence), numbered '19' by Marx

& overthrows empires, gives rise to nations and makes them disappear – while with the transformation of the basis, private property, with the communistic regulation of production & ~~the abolition~~ the consequent abolition ~~of the appearance, as if~~ of the alienation which men are undergoing in relation to their own product, the power ~~of the demand~~ of the relation between supply &
&
demand is dissolved into nothing, men once more get control over exchange, production, ~~its~~ the way they conduct their mutual relations?

The form of social interaction conditioned by the forces of productions at all previous historical stages & in turn conditioning them, is civil society {*bürgerliche Gesellschaft*}, which, as ~~we already from the above~~ obviously follows from the above discussion, ~~to the~~ has for its presupposition and foundation the simple family & and extended family, the so-called tribe, & whose more precise

Communism.[1]

Incidentally the mass of mere labourers – massed labour-power ~~of capital, or~~ cut off from capital or ~~working-class~~ labour-power cut off from any even limited restricted satisfaction, – and
no longer temporary,
also the loss, of
that labour as itself a secure source of life, the purely precarious position,
presupposes
through competition the world market. The proletariat ~~therefore presupposes world empirical history as practical~~ existence can therefore only exist world-historically, as
, its action
communism can only come into being as "world-historical" existence altogether; world historical existence of individuals, i.e. existence of individuals who are ~~materially~~ directly connected with ~~history of all~~ world history.

---

1. The editors of *Jahrbuch 2003* suggest that "Communism" was written down by Marx later than the passage that follows; vol. 2, p. 228, ref. 23.6–24 r.

& overthrows empires, gives rise to nations and makes them disappear – while with the transformation of the basis, private property, with the communistic regulation of production & the consequent abolition of the alienation which men are undergoing in relation to their own product, the power of the relation between supply & demand is dissolved into nothing, & men once more get control over exchange, production, the way they conduct their mutual relations?

The form of social interaction conditioned by the forces of productions at all previous historical stages & in turn conditioning them, is civil society {*bürgerliche Gesellschaft*}, which, as obviously follows from the above discussion, has for its presupposition and foundation the simple family & and extended family, the so-called tribe, & whose more precise

Communism.

Moreover the mass of mere labourers – massed labour-power cut off from capital or from any even restricted satisfaction, – and also the loss, no longer temporary, of that labour as itself a secure source of life, the purely precarious position, presupposes through competition the world market. The proletariat can therefore only exist world-historically, as communism, its action can only come into being as "world-historical" existence altogether; world historical existence of individuals, i.e. existence of individuals who are directly connected with world history.

Fourth page on printer's sheet '8' (in Engels's sequence), numbered '19' by Marx

specifications are laid out in the above discussion. It is already clear at this point that this civil society is the true foundry & showground of all history, & how ~~false~~ absurd the former conception of history is, neglecting the actual relations, confining itself to high-sounding top-level & state actions.

~~Only now after we ourselves over all of that real, of the~~

                             mainly
Up to now we have considered only one aspect of human activity, the <u>remaking of nature</u> by men. The other aspect, the <u>remaking of men</u> by <u>men</u> – – {*insertion by Marx of emphasis at three points above*}

Origin of the state & relation of the state to civil society {*bürgerlichen Gesellschaft*}.

Social interaction and productive power.

Fourth page on printer's sheet '8' (in Engels's sequence), numbered '19' by Marx

specifications are laid out in the above discussion. It is already clear at this point that this civil society is the true foundry & showground of all history, & how absurd the former conception of history is, neglecting the actual relations, confining itself to high-sounding top-level & state actions.

Up to now we have mainly considered only one aspect of human activity, the remaking of nature by men. The other aspect, the remaking of men by men – – {*insertion by Marx of emphasis at three points above*}

Origin of the state & relation of the state to civil society {*bürgerlichen Gesellschaft*}.

Social interaction and productive power.

First page on printer's sheet '9' (in Engels's sequence), numbered '20' by Marx

History is nothing but the succession of individual generations, each of which exploits the improved materials, capital resources,[1] powers of production from all the ones prior ~~bequeath{ed}~~ to it, and thus on the one hand pursues the ~~old~~ inherited activity under wholly altered circumstances & on the other hand modifies the old circumstances with a wholly altered activity, which lends itself to speculative distortion such that the later history is made into the purpose of the earlier, e.g. that ~~Ame{rica}~~ the basic purpose ~~of~~ ascribed to the discovery of America is to promote the outbreak of the French Revolution, through which then history receives its ~~pur{poses}~~ peculiar purposes and becomes a "person just like other persons" (just as are "self-consciousness,

&c

critique, the ego"   ), while that which is designated with the words "aim", "purpose", "seed", idea" of earlier history is

from

nothing else but an abstraction ~~out of~~

is precisely

the later history,   an abstraction

---

[1]. The editors of *Jahrbuch 2003* indicate that the original word order in this phrase was: capital resources, materials; vol. 2, p. 229, ref. 23.39 l.

First page on printer's sheet '9' (in Engels's sequence), numbered '20' by Marx

History is nothing but the succession of individual generations, each of which exploits the improved materials, capital resources, powers of production from all the ones prior to it, and thus on the one hand pursues the inherited activity under wholly altered circumstances & on the other hand modifies the old circumstances with a wholly altered activity, which lends itself to speculative distortion such that the later history is made into the purpose of the earlier, e.g. that the basic purpose ascribed to the discovery of America is to promote the outbreak of the French Revolution, through which then history receives its peculiar purposes and becomes a "person just like other persons" (just as are "self-consciousness, critique, the ego" &c), while that which is designated with the words "aim", "purpose", "seed", idea" of earlier history is nothing else but an abstraction from the later history, is precisely an abstraction from the active influence which the earlier history

First page on printer's sheet '9' (in Engels's sequence), numbered '20' by Marx

~~out of~~ from the ~~result and production of that~~

active

~~in which one seeks these secrets~~ influence which the earlier history exercises upon the later. – The further the separate mutually interacting spheres extend themselves in the course of this development, the ~~les{s}~~ more the original isolation of the individual nationalities is extinguished by the more developed ~~rel{ations}~~ mode of production, ~~form of~~ social interaction and the ~~transformed {aufgehoben}~~ division of labour ~~massively arising in that~~ between ~~way~~ arising naturally in that way different nations , the more does history become world history, so that e.g. if in England a machine is invented which deprives countless labourers in India & China of bread & revolutionises the entire form of existence of these empires, this invention becomes a world-historical fact; or that sugar and coffee have demonstrated their world-historical importance in the nineteenth century because the ~~necessarily soc{ial}~~ lack of these products caused by the Napoleonic continental system brought ~~for{th}~~ the Germans

First page on printer's sheet '9' (in Engels's sequence), numbered '20' by Marx

exercises upon the later. – The further the separate mutually interacting spheres extend themselves in the course of this development, the more the original isolation of the individual nationalities is extinguished by the more developed mode of production, social interaction and the division of labour arising naturally in that way between different nations, the more does history become world history, so that e.g. if in England a machine is invented which deprives countless labourers in India & China of bread & revolutionises the entire form of existence of these empires, this invention becomes a world-historical fact; or that sugar and coffee have demonstrated their world-historical importance in the nineteenth century because the lack of these products caused by the Napoleonic continental system brought the Germans

Second page on printer's sheet '9' (in Engels's sequence), numbered '21' by Marx

to rise up against Napoleon & thus become the real basis of the glorious wars of liberation of 1813 . It follows from this that the ~~cha{nge}~~ conversion from history to world history is by no means a mere act of the **world spirit's** "self-consciousness" or of any metaphysical spectre at all, but ~~is~~ rather a wholly material, empirically verifiable act, an act to which every individual affords the proof as he comes and goes, eats, drinks & clothes himself.[1]

– {insertion} ~~the holy Max Stirner himself carries world history around on his back & eats & drinks it every day, like in times past the body & blood of our Lord Jesus Christ.~~ [2] ~~Hence it follows that in "world history" the individuals are just as much & just as little "their own" in it as in every Stirneresque "association" of students and free seamstresses. Consequently~~ {end insertion}

{insertion} ~~& world history produces it, the ego, which is its own production once again every day~~[3]~~, since it must eat, drink & clothe itself; the citations in "its own &c" like the polemics of the holy Max against Hess and others more remote are proving how he is also produced intellectually by world history.~~ {end insertion}

---

1. The editors of *Jahrbuch 2003* give the original word order in this phrase as: eats & drinks, {clothes} himself; vol. 2, p. 230, ref. 25.20 l.

2. According to the editors of *Jahrbuch 2003*, this passage was inserted later than the previous one; vol. 2, pp. 230–31, ref. 25.21 l.

3. The editors of *Jahrbuch 2003* give the original word order as: every day once again; vol. 2, p. 230, ref. 25.21 l [right-hand column].

Second page on printer's sheet '9' (in Engels's sequence), numbered '21' by Marx

to rise up against Napoleon & thus become the real basis of the glorious wars of liberation of 1813. It follows from this that the conversion from history to world history is by no means a mere act of the **world spirit's** "self-consciousness" or of any metaphysical spectre at all, but rather a wholly material, empirically verifiable act, an act to which every individual affords the proof as he comes and goes, eats, drinks & clothes himself.

Second page on printer's sheet '9' (in Engels's sequence), numbered '21' by Marx

In history up to now it is just as much an empirical fact that with the extension of their activities to ~~world history~~ the world-historical, disaggregated individuals have become more and more enslaved ~~to a power growing ever more massive to a power which has grown ever more massive~~ to a power alien to them (which burden they ~~then also~~ then also conceive as trickery by the so-called world spirit &c){,} a power which has grown ever more massive & reveals itself in the last instance as the world market.[1] But it is just as empirically grounded that with the overthrow ~~& the dissolution~~ of the existing condition of society by the communist revolution (of which & more below) the transformation of private identical with this, property the power so mysterious to the German theoreticians is thus dissolved & is the liberation of ~~the~~ every single individual. Disaggregated individuals are only freed in this way from the different national & local constraints, put into practical **(including** connection with the production

"On the production of consciousness"

---

1. The editors of *Jahrbuch 2003* identify this as Marx's emphasis. Apparat p. 231 ref. 25.33 l.

Second page on printer's sheet '9' (in Engels's sequence), numbered '21' by Marx

In history up to now it is just as much an empirical fact that with the extension of their activities to the world-historical, disaggregated individuals have become more and more enslaved to a power alien to them (which burden they then also conceive as trickery by the so-called world spirit &c){,} a power which has grown ever more massive & reveals itself in the last instance as the <u>world market</u>.[1] But it is just as empirically grounded that with the overthrow of the existing condition of society by the communist revolution (of which more below) & the transformation of private property identical with this, the power so mysterious to the German theoreticians is dissolved & thus is the liberation of every single individual. Disaggregated individuals are only freed in this way from the different national & local constraints, put into practical connection with the production

"On the production of consciousness"

---

1. Marx's emphasis.

Second page on printer's sheet '9' (in Engels's sequence), numbered '21' by Marx

intellectual production) of the whole world & ~~are capable of enjoying the multifaceted production from the whole earth~~ **put themselves into position to acquire the capacity for enjoying this multifaceted production from the whole earth (~~men's creations~~ creations of men).** <u>All-round</u> natural dependence, this first form of <u>world historical</u> interaction of individuals{,} is changed through

(including intellectual production) of the whole world & **put into position themselves to acquire the capacity for enjoying this multifaceted production from the whole earth (creations of men).** All-round dependence, this first natural form of world historical interaction of individuals{,} is changed through

Third page on printer's sheet '9' (in Engels's sequence), numbered '22' by Marx

this communistic revolution in the regulation and conscious control of these powers, which, generated out of the mutual interactions of men, have up to now imposed on them as thoroughly alien powers & have controlled them. ~~How To this view~~ This view can then be conceived once more speculatively-ideally i.e. fantastically as "self-generation of the species" ("society "as subject") & ~~be been~~ in that way the successive individuals in connection with one another are represented as a single individual which accomplishes the mystery of generating itself. It is evident ~~therefore~~ here that in any case individuals make <u>one another</u>, physically and intellectually, but make themselves ~~even if not in the sense of the~~ neither in the nonsense of the holy Bruno ~~according to which "it lies in the~~
~~(1)   (3 2)~~
~~concept   of the personality["]   in general~~
~~(4 3) (4), limiting itself to setting (where it is~~
~~outstandingly successful) & this limitation,~~
~~which places it (not through itself but neither~~
~~generally nor through its concept) but through~~

this communistic revolution in the regulation and conscious control of these powers, which, generated out of the mutual interactions of men, have up to now imposed on them as thoroughly alien powers & have controlled them. This view can then be conceived once more speculatively-ideally i.e. fantastically as "self-generation of the species" ("society as subject") & in that way the successive individuals in connection with one another are represented as a single individual which accomplishes the mystery of generating itself. It is evident here that in any case individuals make <u>one another</u>, physically and intellectually, but make themselves neither in the nonsense of the holy Bruno nor in the

Third page on printer's sheet '9' (in Engels's sequence), numbered '22' by Marx

~~(5) (6) (7)~~
~~(5)~~
its general being, ~~since~~ that very being ~~is~~
~~(8)~~
~~(6)~~
~~only the result of its~~   internal
~~(9)~~   ~~(10)~~
                              ~~(7)~~
~~self-distinctions, of its activity, again~~   ~~to be~~
                           ~~(11)~~
                           ~~(8)~~
~~transformed {aufzuheben} p. 87, 88;~~
{insertion} **~~(Mr Bruno doesn't get it to a dozen)~~** {end insertion}; nor in the {Stirnerian} sense of the "ego", ~~the one~~ of the "self-made man". ~~It results from the above~~ that for ev{ery}, if, ~~for the communist that so much as there are individuals whose consciousness is communistic then the sooner they the existing~~ with the existing society

Finally from the conception of history developed above we obtain the following results: 1) In the development of the ~~so{cial}~~ forces of production there comes a stage at which the forces of production and means of social interaction are brought forth, which under current relations only cause havoc, which are no longer forces of production but rather forces of destruction (machinery & money) – & coincident with that a class is called forth which ~~outside the~~ has to bear all

{*Stirnerian*} sense of the "ego", of the "self-made man". Finally from the conception of history developed above we obtain the following results: 1) In the development of the forces of production there comes a stage at which the forces of production and means of social interaction are brought forth, which under current relations only cause havoc, which are no longer forces of production but rather forces of destruction (machinery & money) – & coincident with that a class is called forth which has to bear all the burdens

Third page on printer's sheet '9' (in Engels's sequence), numbered '22' by Marx

the burdens of society without enjoying its advantages, which is ousted ~~outside of~~ from society,

Third page on printer's sheet '9' (in Engels's sequence), numbered '22' by Marx

of society without enjoying its advantages,
which is outsted from society,

Fourth page on printer's sheet '9' (in Engels's sequence), numbered '23' by Marx

is ~~comp{elled}~~ forced into the sharpest contradiction with other classes; a class which forms the majority of all members of society & from which proceeds the consciousness of the necessity of a fundamental revolution, the communistic consciousness, which naturally can also form among other classes with the capacity to view the position of that class; 2) that ~~every level of development of soc{iety} productive forces of a particu{lar}) serve as the basis for the rule of a specific class of society,~~ the conditions within which a specific forces of production can be deployed are the conditions of rule of a specific class in society whose social ~~power as the~~ power, proceeding from its property, has its <u>practical</u>-idealistic expression in every case in the form of the state, & therefore ~~at the last stage of civil society~~ every revolutionary struggle is directed against ~~the pre{vious}~~ a class which up to then has been in power; 3) that in all previous revolutions the kind of activity always remains unchanged & it was only a matter of another distribution of that activity in order to effect a new distribution of labour to other per**sons,** while the communistic revolution is directed against the previous <u>kind</u>

That the people are interested in retaining the present state of production.

is forced into the sharpest contradiction with other classes; a class which forms the majority of all members of society & from which proceeds the consciousness of the necessity of a fundamental revolution, the communistic consciousness, which naturally can also form among other classes with the capacity to view the position of that class; 2) that the conditions within which specific forces of production can be deployed are the conditions of rule of a specific class in society whose social power, proceeding from its property, has its practical-idealistic expression in every case in the form of the state, & therefore every revolutionary struggle is directed against a class which up to then has been in power; 3) that in all previous revolutions the kind of activity always remains unchanged & it was only a matter of another distribution of that activity in order to effect a new distribution of labour to other per**sons,** while the communistic revolution is directed against the previous kind of activity, {it} does

That people are interested in retaining the present state of production.

Fourth page on printer's sheet '9' (in Engels's sequence), numbered '23' by Marx

of activity &, {it} does away with <u>labour</u>, ~~which trans{forms} {aufhebt} the moder{n} form of activity under the control of the which to the control of the which the control of the to which the control of the~~ & abolishes {*aufhebt*} the domination of all classes along with the classes themselves because it is achieved through the class which can no longer serve as a class in society, {*insertion*} {which} is already the expression of the dissolution of all classes, nationalities &c within present-day society {*end insertion*} & 4) that a mass alteration of men is necessary, as much as for the mass production of this ~~consc{iousness}~~ communistic consciousness as for the forcing through of the thing itself, which can only proceed in a practical movement, in a <u>revolution</u>; so that the revolution is not only necessary, because the <u>ruling</u> class can be overthrown in no other way, but also because the ~~overthrowing~~ class can only enter into a revolution by ~~destroying~~ getting rid of all the old muck becoming capable of founding society anew.

Fourth page on printer's sheet '9' (in Engels's sequence), numbered '23' by Marx

away with <u>labour</u>, & abolishes {*aufhebt*} the domination of all classes along with the classes themselves, because it is achieved through the class which can no longer serve as a class in society, {which} is already the expression of the dissolution of all classes, nationalities &c within present-day society & 4) that a mass alteration of men is necessary, as much as for the mass production of this communistic consciousness as for the forcing through of the thing itself, which can only proceed in a practical movement, in a <u>revolution</u>; so that the revolution is not only necessary, because the <u>ruling</u> class can be overthrown in no other way, but also because the class can only enter into a revolution by getting rid of all the old muck & becoming capable of founding society anew.

First page on printer's sheet '10' (in Engels's sequence), not numbered by Marx

as well as **Bauer.** While all communists in France, in England & Germany, have long since agreed on the necessity of revolution, the holy Bruno dreams on quietly & opines ~~if the "real humanism" i.e. communism~~ that "real humanism" i.e. communism will take (which has no "the place of spiritualism" place) only for the purpose of gaining him veneration. Then, dreaming on, truly "salvation" would have to have arrived – "making earth heaven & heaven earth (the ~~theologian~~ learned divine will never be able to get over heaven). Then joy & bliss sound in heavenly harmonies from age to age." (p. 140)[1] The holy father of the church will be ever so surprised when Judgement Day breaks over him on which all this comes to pass – a day whose red dawn ~~is,~~ **is** the reflection of among burning cities in the sky, while the "heavenly harmonies" ~~in the form~~ the melodies of the Marseillaise & Carmagnole, with obligatory cannonade, ~~ring~~ echo in his ears & for which the guillotine ~~strikes;~~ **strikes** the beat, while the villainous "mass" ~~screams~~

Holy Family

---

1. Bruno Bauer, "Characteristik Ludwig Feuerbachs", *Wigands Vierteljahrschrift*, vol. 3, October 1845.

First page on printer's sheet '10' (in Engels's sequence), not numbered by Marx

While all communists in France, as well as in England & Germany, have long since agreed on the necessity of revolution, the holy Bruno dreams on quietly & opines that "real humanism" i.e. communism will take "the place of spiritualism" (which has no place) only for the purpose of gaining him veneration. Then, dreaming on, truly "salvation" would have to have arrived – "making earth heaven & heaven earth (the learned divine will never be able to get over heaven). Then joy & bliss sound in heavenly harmonies from age to age." (p. 140)[1] The holy father of the church will be ever so surprised when Judgement Day breaks over him on which all this comes to pass – a day whose red dawn **is** the reflection of burning cities in the sky, while among the "heavenly harmonies" the melodies of the Marseillaise & Carmagnole, with obligatory cannonade, echo in his ears & for which the guillotine **strikes** the beat, while the villanous "mass" **roars**

Bauer.

Holy Family

---

1. Bruno Bauer, "Characteristik Ludwig Feuerbachs", *Wigands Vierteljahrschrift*, vol. 3, October 1845.

First page on printer's sheet '10' (in Engels's sequence), not numbered by Marx

roars ça ira, ça ira & transforms {*aufhebt*} "self-consciousness" ~~à la lanterne~~ by means of a lamppost. ~~The holy Bruno has the least of reasons to sketch an edifying picture of "joy" & bliss from age to age". The "adherents to the Feuerbachian religion of love" appear to have their own conception of this "joy & bliss" when they speak of a revolution where one arrives at things wholly other than "heavenly harmonies".~~ ~~And although they are rather well acquainted with the holy man they still forego~~ **We forego** the pleasure ~~concerning~~ of construing the situation ~~of the hol{y}~~ of Saint Bruno on Judgement Day ~~some specu{lative}~~ a priori. It ~~would be~~ **is** also really difficult to discern whether the prolétaires en révolution ~~were to be understood~~ **must be understood** as "substance", which rebels against self-consciousness, as "mass", which wants to **of spirit**, overturn critique, or as "emanation" which however still lacks the {bodily} consistency necessary to digest

First page on printer's sheet '10' (in Engels's sequence), not numbered by Marx

ça ira, ça ira & transforms {*aufhebt*} "self-consciousness" by means of a lamppost. **We forego** the pleasure of construing the situation of Saint Bruno on Judgement Day a priori. It **is** also really difficult to discern whether the prolétaires en révolution **must be understood** as "substance", which rebels against self-consciousness, as "mass", which wants to overturn the critique, or as "emanation" **of spirit**, which however still lacks the {bodily} consistency necessary to digest

Second page on printer's sheet '10' (in Engels's sequence), numbered '24' by Marx

Bauer-ish thought.

~~This concept{ion}~~ This conception of history rests therefore on explicating the actual process of production, & to be sure, proceeding from the material production of life as such, & grasping the form of social interaction connected with that ~~production~~ mode of production & produced by it, therefore **conceiving of** civil society {*bürgerliche Gesellschaft*} in its various stages ~~& in its practical-idealist mirror image, the state, how the total pro{ducts}, various products & forms of consciousness, religion, philosophy, morals &c &c {are} to be explained. from which {is} to be explained & to which {is} to be attributed to be conceived as the foundation of all history & to be explained from this as well as from its practical-idealistic mirror, how all the different theoretical products & forms of consciousness, religion, philosophy, morals &c &c {are} to be explained from it & to be attributed to it to be conceived as the basis of all history & to be represented in action as the state, how all the different theoretical products & forms of consciousness, religion, philosophy, morals &c &c {are} to be explained & {are}~~

Feuerbach

Bauer-ish thought.

This conception of history rests therefore on explicating the actual process of production, & to be sure, proceeding from the material production of life as such, & grasping the form of social interaction connected with that mode of production & produced by it, therefore **conceiving of** civil society {*bürgerliche Gesellschaft*} in its various stages **as the**

Feuerbach

Second page on printer's sheet '10' (in Engels's sequence), numbered '24' by Marx

~~to be attributed to it~~ **as the foundation of all history & also representing it in action as the state, how all the different theoretical products & forms of consciousness, religion, philosophy, morals &c &c {are} to be explained from it and their process of formation {is} to be traced from them {civil society and the state}, where then naturally the ~~inter{action}~~ matter in its totality (and therefore the interaction of these different factors on one another) can be represented.** It does not have to search for a category in every period, like the idealist conception of history, but rather remains constantly standing on the actual <u>bedrock</u> of history, does not explain praxis from the idea, ~~rather~~ explains the formation of ideas from material praxis, & correspondingly comes to the conclusion that all forms and products of consciousness cannot be dissolved through intellectual critique, through ~~proof~~ dissolution into "self-consciousness" or transformation into "apparitions", "spectres", "spooks" &c but only through the practical overthrow of the real ~~rela{tion}~~ social relations from which these idealist flummeries are proceeding – that not critique but revolution is the driving

Second page on printer's sheet '10' (in Engels's sequence), numbered '24' by Marx

foundation of all history & also representing it in action as the state, how all the different theoretical products & forms of consciousness, religion, philosophy, morals &c &c {are} to be explained from it and their process of formation {is} to be traced from them {civil society and the state}, where then naturally the matter in its totality (and therefore the interaction of these different factors on one another) can be represented. It does not have to search for a category in every period, like the idealist conception of history, but rather remains constantly standing on the actual <u>bedrock</u> of history, does not explain praxis from the idea, explains the formation of ideas from material praxis, & accordingly comes to the conclusion that all forms and products of consciousness cannot be dissolved through intellectual critique, through dissolution into "self-consciousness" or transformation into "apparitions", "spectres", "spooks" &c but only through the practical overthrow of the real social relations from which these idealist flummeries are proceeding – that not critique but revolution is the driving force of history,

Second page on printer's sheet '10' (in Engels's sequence), numbered '24' by Marx

force of history, also of religion, philosophy & other kinds of theory. ~~Proceeding further~~ It demonstrates that history does not end by being dissolved into "self-consciousness" as "mind from mind", rather that in it at each stage there is to hand a material result, a sum of productive forces, {*insertion*} **a historically created relation to nature and of individuals to one another** {*end insertion*}, which is handed down to each generation from its ~~earlier~~ forebears, a mass of productive forces , capital resources & circumstances which is modified to be sure, on the one hand, by the new generation, but also, on the other hand, {the mass of productive forces &c} prescribes to it {every generation} its own conditions of life & gives to it a specific development, a special character – therefore that circumstances make men just as much as

also of religion, philosophy & other kinds of theory. It demonstrates that history does not end by being dissolved into "self-consciousness" as "mind from mind", rather that in it at each stage there is to hand a material result, a sum of productive forces, **a historically created relation to nature and of individuals to one another**, which is handed down to each generation from its forebears, a mass of productive forces, capital resources & circumstances which is modified to be sure, on the one hand, by the new generation, but also, on the other hand, {the mass of productive forces &c} prescribes to it {every generation} its own conditions of life & gives to it a specific development, a special character – therefore that circumstances make men just as much as

men make circumstances. This sum of
productive forces, capital resources &
social forms of interaction, which
every individual &
 every generation ~~given~~
finds to hand, is the real ground of what
the philosophers have represented as
"substance" & "essence of man",
what they
 have apotheosised & attacked, a
real ground which is not in the least
disturbed in its effects and influences on
the development of men by these
philosophers, as "self-consciousness" and
"ego", revolting against it. These
conditions of life to hand for the different
generations also decide whether or not the
revolutionary convulsion recurring
periodically in history will be strong enough to
overthrow the basis of all that exists, & if
these material elements of a total changeover
are not to hand, {*insertion*} **namely the current forces of production, on the one**

men make circumstances. This sum of productive forces, capital resources & social forms of interaction, which every individual & every generation finds to hand, is the real ground of what the philosophers have represented as "substance" & "essence of man", what they have apotheosised & attacked, a real ground which is not in the least disturbed in its effects and influences on the development of men by these philosophers, as "self-consciousness" and "ego", revolting against it. These conditions of life to hand for the different generations also decide whether or not the revolutionary convulsion recurring periodically in history will be strong enough to overthrow the basis of all that exists, & if these material elements of a total changeover are not to hand, **namely the current forces of production, on the one hand, and on the**

Third page on printer's sheet '10' (in Engels's sequence), numbered '25' by Marx

hand, and on the other hand, the formation of a revolutionary mass, which not only revolts against particular conditions of present-day ~~social inter{action}~~ society but against the "production of life" itself, ~~against – their general~~ the "whole activity" on which it was based – {*end insertion*} then it is all the same for practical development whether the idea of that changeover has been proclaimed a hundred times already – as the history of communism stands in evidence.

The whole previous conception of history has either left this real basis of history ~~by~~ wholly & completely unexamined, or it has considered it only as a marginal~~, which has no connection at all with the course of history~~ matter, which has no connection at all with the course of history. {*insertion*} ~~{History} so treated}~~ Hence history had always to be written according to a reference point lying outside it; the real production of

Third page on printer's sheet '10' (in Engels's sequence), numbered '25' by Marx

other hand, the formation of a revolutionary mass, which not only revolts against particular conditions of present-day society but against the "production of life" itself, – the "whole activity" on which it was based – then it is all the same for practical development whether the <u>idea</u> of that changeover has been proclaimed a hundred times already – as the history of communism stands in evidence.

The whole previous conception of history has either left this real basis of history wholly & completely unexamined, or it has considered it only as a marginal matter, which has no connection at all with the course of history. Hence history had always to be written according to a reference point lying outside it; the real life appears as unhistorical, while the historical appears as something separated from ordinary life, over and above the worldly. With this the relation of man to nature was excluded from history, thus producing the opposition of nature & history. {end insertion} Hence they have ~~seen the~~ been able to see in history only high-level political & state actions & religious & generally theoretical struggles, & in particular with each historical epoch they had ~~ta{ken}~~ to share in the illusion of that epoch. **E.g. if an epoch conceives itself to be defined purely through "political" or "religious" motives,** {insertion} **although "religion" and "politics" are only forms of their actual motive,** {end insertion} **then the writer of its history accepts this view. The "conception", the "representation" of these specific men concerning their actual praxis, is transformed into** ~~the actual defining and active essence~~ **the sole defining and active power** which

Third page on printer's sheet '10' (in Engels's sequence), numbered '25' by Marx

production of life appears as unhistorical, while the historical appears as something separated from ordinary life, over and above the worldly. With this the relation of man to nature was excluded from history, thus producing the opposition of nature & history. Hence they have been able to see in history only high-level political & state actions & religious & generally theoretical struggles, & in particular with each historical epoch they had <u>to share in the illusion of that epoch</u>. **E.g. if an epoch conceives itself to be defined purely through "political" or "religious" motives, although "religion" and "politics" are only forms of their actual motive, then the writer of its history accepts this view. The "conception", the "representation" of these specific men concerning their actual praxis, is transformed into the sole defining and active power** which controls & defines the

Third page on printer's sheet '10' (in Engels's sequence), numbered '25' by Marx

controls & defines the praxis of these men. When the crude form in which the division of labour occurs among the Indians & Egyptians calls forth the caste-system among these peoples in ~~to the~~ their state & their religion, then the historian ~~act{ually}~~ believes that the caste-system

praxis of these men. When the crude form in which the division of labour occurs among the Indians & Egyptians calls forth the caste-system among these peoples in their state & their religion, then the historian believes that the caste-system

Fourth page on printer's sheet '10' (in Engels's sequence), numbered '26' by Marx

is the power which has produced this crude social form. While the French and the English ~~themselves~~ at least keep to the political illusion, which still borders on actuality, the Germans occupy themselves in the realm of "pure mind" & make religious illusion into the driving force of history. ~~Hegel is the conseque{tly} the last~~ The Hegelian philosophy of history is the last consequence of the whole of German historiography brought to its "purest expression", which does not deal with actual, nor even political interests, but with pure thoughts, ~~which~~ **hence then {it} must appear even to the holy Bruno as a series of "thoughts", of which one gobbles up the other and finally disappears into "self-consciousness", and** ~~wholly~~ **even more consequentially** the course of history must appear to the holy Max Stirner, who does not know anything at all about actual history, as mere "histories of knights, thieves & ghosts", ~~against which he~~ visions before which he naturally knows how to shrive himself only through "unholiness". This conception is actually religious, it assumes that religious man is the original man from which in its image of things all history proceeds &

So-called <u>objective</u> historiography consisted precisely in conceiving of ~~mater{ial}~~ historical relations separated from activity. Reactionary character.

Fourth page on printer's sheet '10' (in Engels's sequence), numbered '26' by Marx

is the power which has produced this crude social form. While the French and the English at least keep to the political illusion, which still borders on actuality, the Germans occupy themselves in the realm of "pure mind" & make religious illusion into the driving force of history. The Hegelian philosophy of history is the last consequence of the whole of German historiography brought to its "purest expression", which does not deal with actual, nor even political interests, but with pure thoughts, **hence then {it} must appear even to the holy Bruno as a series of "thoughts", of which one gobbles up the other and finally disappears into "self-consciousness", and even more consequentially** the course of history must appear to the holy Max Stirner, who does not know anything at all about actual history, as mere "histories of knights, thieves & ghosts", visions before which he naturally knows how to shrive himself only through "unholiness". This conception is actually religious, it assumes that religious man is the original man from which all history proceeds & in its image of things

So-called <u>objective</u> historiography consisted precisely in conceiving of ~~mater{ial}~~ historical relations separated from activity. Reactionary character.

Fourth page on printer's sheet '10' (in Engels's sequence), numbered '26' by Marx

puts the production of religious fantasy in place of the actual production of the means of life & of life itself. This whole conception of history, including ~~the consequent~~ its dissolution & the scruples & misgivings arising from it, is a ~~wholly~~ merely <u>national</u> affair for the Germans & has only <u>local</u> interest for Germany, as for example the important question in much recent discussion: how exactly one "proceeds from the realm of God into the realm of man", as if this "realm of God", to which they are now seeking the way, had ever existed anywhere other than in the imagination, & ~~as if~~ the learned gentlemen were not continually living in the "realm of man" without knowing it – & as if the [1] scientific {*wissenschaftlich*} pastime, for it is

nothing more   than that   , of explaining the curiosities of this theoretical castle in the air

the opposite,
did not lie in precisely
that one demonstrates their formation

---

1. The editors of *Jahrbuch 2003* give the preceding state of the following phrases as: ~~not the height of scientific pastimes could be more than a scientific pastime to explain and demonstrate the curiosities of this theoretical castle in the air from its actual earthly relations even in individual cases~~; vol. 2, p. 236, ref. 33.33–40 l.

Fourth page on printer's sheet '10' (in Engels's sequence), numbered '26' by Marx

puts the production of religious fantasy in place of the actual production of the means of life & of life itself. This whole conception of history, including its dissolution & the scruples & misgivings arising from it, is a merely <u>national</u> affair for the Germans & has only <u>local</u> interest for Germany, as for example the important question in much recent discussion: how exactly one "proceeds from the realm of God into the realm of man", as if this "realm of God", to which they are now seeking the way, had ever existed anywhere other than in the imagination, & the learned gentlemen were not continually living in the "realm of man" without knowing it – & as if the scientific {*wissenschaftlich*} pastime, for it is nothing more than that, of explaining the curiosities of this theoretical castle in the air did not lie in precisely **the opposite,** that one demonstrates their formation from actual

Fourth page on printer's sheet '10' (in Engels's sequence), numbered '26' by Marx

from actual earthly relations. [1]{*insertion*}
With these Germans it is generally a matter of
always dissolving the nonsense to hand into
{*insertion continues overleaf*}

---

1. The editors of *Jahrbuch 2003* note that this passage, running between Marx's pages 26 and 27, was written down later than the passage above; vol. 2, p. 236, ref. 33.40–34.24 l.

Fourth page on printer's sheet '10' (in Engels's sequence), numbered '26' by Marx

earthly relations. With these Germans it is generally a matter of always dissolving the nonsense to hand <u>into</u>

First page on printer's sheet '11' (in Engels's sequence), numbered '27' by Marx

some other kind of whim, i.e. of presupposing that this whole nonsense has a special <u>sense</u> which can be recovered, while it is really only a matter of explaining ~~this explanation the~~ these theoretical phrases
~~the removal~~
~~in the consciousness of the~~ from the actual relations in existence. The actual, practical dissolution of these phrases, the removal of this conception from the
        as has already been consciousness of men,
said,
 is accomplished by altering circumstances, not by making theoretical ~~proofs~~ deductions. For the mass of men, i.e. the proletariat, ~~the~~ these theoretical conceptions do not exist and therefore do not need to be dissolved for them, & if ~~they~~ this mass ever had even a few theoretical conceptions, e.g. religion, these ~~long~~ have now long been dissolved by circumstances. {end insertion}

 ~~The nationality~~
The purely national character of these questions & solutions is moreover shown by the fact that these theoreticians believe in all seriousness that figments of the imagination like "the god-man", "man" &c have presided

First page on printer's sheet '11' (in Engels's sequence), numbered '27' by Marx

some other kind of whim, i.e. of presupposing that this whole nonsense has a special <u>sense</u> which can be recovered, while it is really only a matter of explaining these theoretical phrases from the actual relations in existence. The actual, practical dissolution of these phrases, the removal of this conception from the consciousness of men, as has already been said, is accomplished by altering circumstances, not by making theoretical deductions. For the mass of men, i.e. the proletariat, these theoretical conceptions do not exist and therefore do not need to be dissolved for them, & if this mass ever had even a few theoretical conceptions, e.g. religion, these have now long been dissolved by circumstances.

The purely national character of these questions & solutions is moreover shown by the fact that these theoreticians believe in all seriousness that figments of the imagination like "the god-man", "man" &c have presided

First page on printer's sheet '11' (in Engels's sequence), numbered '27' by Marx

over individual epochs of history – the holy Bruno even goes so far as to maintain only "critique and critics"–have made history" – &, when they devote themselves to historical constructions they skip over everything earlier in ~~all~~ the greatest haste & proceed from "Mongol-dom" at once to truly "content-ful" history, namely the history of the ~~Deut{sche}~~ Hallische {Jahrbücher} and Deutsche Jahrbücher & the dissolution of the Hegelian school into a general squabble. All other nations, all real events are forgotten, the Theatrum {*sic*} mundi is limited to the Leipzig book fair, and the mutual bickering of "critique", of "man" & of "the ego". If perhaps for once theories are applied to actually considering historical themes, as e.g. the eighteenth century, ~~this also results in~~ they give only a history of ideas torn away from the facts & practical developments which are their ground, & even these merely with a view to presenting this period as an unfulfilled prior stage ~~like Joh{n the Baptist}~~, as the still immature precursor of the truly historical period, i.e. the period of the ~~Berlin~~ German philosophical struggles of 1840/44. To this purpose, that of writing an introductory history so as to let the brilliance of an

First page on printer's sheet '11' (in Engels's sequence), numbered '27' by Marx

over individual epochs of history – the holy Bruno even goes so far as to maintain only "critique and critics have made history" – &, when they devote themselves to historical constructions they skip over everything earlier in the greatest haste & proceed from "Mongol-dom" at once to truly "content-ful" history, namely the history of the Hallische {Jahrbücher} and Deutsche Jahrbücher & the dissolution of the Hegelian school into a general squabble. All other nations, all real events are forgotten, the Theatrum {sic} mundi is limited to the Leipzig book fair, and the mutual bickering of "critique", of "man" & of "the ego". If perhaps for once theories are applied to actually considering historical themes, as e.g. the eighteenth century, they give only a history of ideas torn away from the facts & practical developments which are their ground, & even these merely with a view to presenting this period as an unfulfilled prior stage, as the still immature precursor of the truly historical period, i.e. the period of the German philosophical struggles of 1840/44.
To this purpose, that of writing an introductory history so as to let the brilliance of an

First page on printer's sheet '11' (in Engels's sequence), numbered '27' by Marx

unhistorical persona & its fantasies shine all the brighter, it follows then that all the actual historical events, even the actual historical incursions of politics into history, do not get a mention, & hence this results in a tale resting not on research but on constructions & literary gossip – such as was produced by the holy Bruno in his now forgotten history of the 18th century. These pompous & highfalutin thought-peddlars, who believe themselves to be infinitely exalted over all national prejudices, are thus in practice far more national than ~~our~~ the beer-swilling philistines who dream of a united Germany. They do not recognise the acts of other nations as historical, they live within the bounds of Germany

First page on printer's sheet '11' (in Engels's sequence), numbered '27' by Marx

unhistorical persona & its fantasies shine all the brighter, it follows then that all the actual historical events, even the actual historical incursions of politics into history, do not get a mention, & hence this results in a tale resting not on research but on constructions & literary gossip – such as was produced by the holy Bruno in his now forgotten history of the 18th century.[1] These pompous & highfalutin thought-peddlars, who believe themselves to be infinitely exalted over all national prejudices, are thus in practice far more national than the beer-swilling philistines who dream of a united Germany. They do not recognise the acts of other nations as historical, they live within the bounds of Germany

---

1. Bruno Bauer, *Geschichte der Politik, Cultur un Aufklärung des achtzehnten Jahrhunderts* (Berlin, 19XX).

Second page on printer's sheet '11' (in Engels's sequence), numbered '28' by Marx

& for Germany; they ~~have~~ turn~~ed~~ the Rheinlied into a religious anthem & conquer Alsace & Lorraine by robbing French philosophy instead of the French state, Germanising French ideas instead of French ~~departements~~ provinces. Herr Venedey is a cosmopolitan compared to ~~Br{uno}~~ the holy Bruno & Max, ~~they pro{claim}~~ who in the ~~domination~~ world domination of theory proclaim world domination for Germany. ~~In order then Let us return then, after this inevitable digression, to the holy Bruno & his world historical struggle~~ **Bauer. After** ~~he~~ **Bruno**[1] has therefore urged a few weighty~~,~~ words on Feuerbach, he envisions the battle between him and the "ego". The first way ~~that he~~ through which he shows interest in this struggle is solemn smiling three times over. "The critic proceeds inexorably, certain of victory & victorious on his way. One defames him: he <u>smiles</u>. One calls him a heretic: he <u>smiles</u>. The old world embarks on a crusade against him: he <u>laughs</u>". That the critic goes his own way, or his own ways, is nothing

Feuerbach.

[2]It is also clear from these arguments how thoroughly Feuerbach is deceiving himself when (Wigands Vierteljahrschrift, 1845, vol. 2), under the qualification "common man", he declares himself a communist, {*insertion*} **transformed into a predicate "<u>of</u>" man,** {*end insertion*} hence he believes the word communist, which in today's world indicates an adherent of a specific revolutionary party, can be changed back into a mere category. Feuerbach's whole ~~proof~~ deduction concerning the relation of men to one another only consists in showing that men

---

1. The editors of *Jahrbuch 2003* suggest that this alteration by Marx was made when the text was later marked for copying out; vol. 2, p. 192, ref. Z.1.

2. The editors of *Jahrbuch 2003* suggest that these passages in the right-hand column were written down later than Marx's alterations to text in the left-hand column; vol. 2, p. 238, ref. 36.21–39.20 r.

Second page on printer's sheet '11' (in Engels's sequence), numbered '28' by Marx

& for Germany; they turn the Rheinlied into a religious anthem & conquer Alsace & Lorraine by robbing French philosophy instead of the French state, Germanising French ideas instead of French provinces. Mr Venedey is a cosmopolitan compared to the holy Bruno & Max, who in the world domination of theory proclaim world domination for Germany. **Bauer. After Bruno** has therefore urged a few weighty words on Feuerbach, he envisions the battle between him and the "ego". The first way through which he shows interest in this struggle is solemn smiling three times over. "The critic proceeds inexorably, certain of victory & victorious on his way. One defames him: he smiles. One calls him a heretic: he smiles. The old world embarks on a crusade against him: he smiles". That the critic goes his own way, or his own, ways, is nothing new – my ways are not your

Feuerbach.

It is also clear from these arguments how thoroughly Feuerbach is deceiving himself when (Wigands Vierteljahrschrift, 1845, vol. 2), under the qualification "common man", he declares himself a communist, **transformed into a predicate "of" man,** hence he believes the word communist, which in today's world indicates an adherent of a specific revolutionary party, can be changed back into a mere category. Feuerbach's whole deduction concerning the relation of men to one another only consists in showing that men have need

Second page on printer's sheet '11' (in Engels's sequence), numbered '28' by Marx

new – my ways are not your ways, my thoughts not your thoughts, my ways are theological ways & I am too timid to change to others, so says the critic. The crit(ic) holy Bruno – so his it is therefore noted, proceeds on his ways, but he takes them not as others do, he takes a critical gait, he performs this important task with "smiling". "He smiles more laugh-lines onto his face than you would find in the world map with two Indias. The girl will slap him in the face & when she does that he will smile & consider it great art" – like Shakespeare's Malvolio. The holy Bruno bestirs not a finger to separate the two opponents, he knows a better way of getting rid of them, he leaves them – divide et impera – to their own dispute. He sets Feuerbach the "man" against the "ego" p. 124, & the "ego" against Feuerbach (p. 126ff)[1]; he knows that they are themselves as embittered with each other like

have need of one another & <u>always have had</u>. He wants to establish a consciousness of that fact, hence like the rest of the theorists he only wants to produce a true consciousness of what is currently in existence an *existing* fact, whereas for the actual communist it is a matter of overthrowing the existing state of things. We fully realise moreover very well that Feuerbach, by striving to produce consciousness of just <u>that</u> fact, is going as far as theorists can generally go without ceasing to be a theorist & a philosopher. It is typical, however, that the holy Bruno & Max take the Feu(erbachian) Feuerbach's conception of the communist for in place of the actual communist, & which the

in part
they do   to be able to fight against communism as "mind from mind", as a philosophical category, as an equal opponent – & in the case of the holy Bruno from still more pragmatic interests. As an example of the recognition & at the same time misrecognition of the current situation, which Feuerbach still common shares with our opponents, let us

---

1. Both numerical references are to Bruno Bauer, "Charakteristic Ludwig Feuerbachs," *Wigandsvierteljahrschrift*, vol. 3, October 1845.

ways, my thoughts not your thoughts, my ways are theological ways & I am too timid to change to others, so says the critic. The holy Bruno – so it is therefore noted, proceeds on his ways, but he takes them not as others do, he takes a critical gait, he performs this important task with "smiling". "He smiles more lines onto his face than you would find in the world map with two Indias. The girl will slap him in the face & when she does that he will smile & consider it great art" – like Shakespeare's Malvolio. The holy Bruno bestirs not a finger to separate his two opponents, he knows a better way of getting rid of them, he leaves them – divide et impera – to their own dispute. He sets Feuerbach, the "man" p. 124 against the "ego", & the "ego" against Feuerbach (p. 126ff)[1]; he knows that they are embittered with each other like of one another & <u>always have had</u>. He wants to establish a consciousness of that fact, hence like the rest of the theorists he only wants to produce a true consciousness of an *existing* fact, whereas for the actual communist it is a matter of overthrowing the existing state of things. We fully realise moreover that Feuerbach, by striving to produce consciousness of just <u>that</u> fact, is going as far as theorists can generally go without ceasing to be a theorist & a philosopher. It is typical, however, that the holy Bruno & Max take Feuerbach's conception of the communist in place of the actual communist, which they do in part to be able to fight against communism as "mind from mind", as a philosophical category, as an equal opponent – & in the case of the holy Bruno from still more pragmatic interests. As an example of the recognition & at the same time misrecognition of the current situation, which Feuerbach still shares with our opponents, let us recall the

---

1. Both numerical references are to Bruno Bauer, "Charakteristic Ludwig Feuerbachs," *Wigandsvierteljahrschrift*, vol. 3, October 1845.

Second page on printer's sheet '11' (in Engels's sequence), numbered '28' by Marx

recall the point in the Philosophy of the Future[1] where he works out how the existence of a thing or of man can be at the same time its essence, how the specific relations for existence{,} mode of life & activity of ~~a human~~ an animal or human individual can be the same as that within which its "essence" feels itself fulfilled. Here ~~of~~ every exception ~~is called~~ is expressly conceived as an unhappy accident, an abnormality which cannot be altered. Hence if millions of proletarians are in no way feeling fulfilled, if their "being"

---

1. Ludwig Feuerbach, *Grundsätze der Philosophie der Zukunft* [Principles of the philosophy of the future] (Zürich, Winterthur, 1843).

Second page on printer's sheet '11' (in Engels's sequence), numbered '28' by Marx

point in the Philosophy of the Future where he works out how the existence of a thing or of man can be at the same time its essence, how the specific relations for existence{,} mode of life & activity of an animal or human individual can be the same as that within which its "essence" feels itself fulfilled. Here every exception is expressly conceived as an unhappy accident, an abnormality which cannot be altered. Hence if millions of proletarians are in no way feeling fulfilled, if their "being"

the pair of [Kil]kenny cats in Ireland who ate each other up so completely that in the end only their tails were left. Over these tails the holy **St.** Bruno has made the judgement that they are "substance", henceforth damned for all eternity. ~~Here~~ Finally Mr Bruno calms himself with the **the critic** thought that to him no critique could be hurtful ~~since~~ "**because he** is **(p. 124)**[1] ~~"~~the critic himself."

After the holy man has finished off **Feuerbach & Stirner**[2] completely in ~~this~~ {the} indicated way, after he has further "**cut off** every avenue" for the "ego", he ~~now~~ turns his attention to the alleged consequences of Feuerbach, the German communists. The holy father must naturally take up the present opportunity to put things right with its communism & its theoretical representatives in Germany as needed **& thereby to be able to dispose of them.** ~~which for him~~ **This was all the more necessary for him because** ~~the~~ **chastisement {was} recorded in**

does not correspond in the remotest way to their "essence", then according to the passage cited, this would be an unavoidable misfortune to be borne quietly. These millions of proletarians or communists think quite differently on this subject, & will prove this in their own time when they will bring their "being" into accord with their "essence" in practice, through a revolution. In such cases Feuerbach therefore never speaks of the human world but rather he flees every time external into nature, & to be sure into the nature which has not yet been brought under human control. But with each new invention, each advance of industry a new patch is detached from this terrain, & the soil, from which grow the ~~proof~~ examples for similar Feuerbachian propositions, is thus becoming ever smaller. The "essence" of a fish is its "being", water, keeping to the one proposition. The "essence" of a freshwater fish is the water of a river. But this ceases to be the "essence", it becomes for him no more than a passing medium of existence, as soon as that river is made subject to industry, as soon as it is

---

1. Bruno Bauer, "Charakteristik Ludwig Feuerbachs," *Wigandsvierteljahrschrift*, vol. 3, October 1845.

2. The editors of *Jahrbuch 2003* state that the word order was originally: Stirner & Feuerbach; vol. 2, p. 193, ref. Z. 52–53.

the pair of Kilkenny cats in Ireland who ate each other up so completely that in the end only their tails were left. Over these tails the holy St. Bruno has made the judgement that they are "substance", henceforth damned for all eternity. Finally Herr Bruno calms himself with the thought that to him the critic no critique could be hurtful "because he is the critic himself." (p. 124)[1]

After the holy man has finished off Feuerbach & Stirner completely in {the} indicated way, after he has further "**cut off** every avenue" for the "ego", he turns his attention to the alleged consequences of Feuerbach, the German communists. The holy father must naturally take up the present opportunity to put things right with communism & its theoretical representatives in Germany as needed **& thereby to be able to dispose of them. This was all the more necessary for him because his brainwork and also chastisement {were} recorded in**

does not correspond in the remotest way to their "essence", then according to the passage cited, this would be an unavoidable misfortune to be borne quietly. These millions of proletarians or communists think quite differently on this subject, & will prove this in their own time when they will bring their "being" into accord with their "essence" in practice, through a revolution. In such cases Feuerbach therefore never speaks of the human world but rather he flees every time into external nature, & to be sure into the nature which has not yet been brought under human control. But with each new invention, each advance of industry a new patch is detached from this terrain, & the soil, from which grow the examples for similar Feuerbachian propositions, is thus becoming ever smaller. The "essence" of a fish is its "being", water, keeping to the one proposition. The "essence" of a freshwater fish is the water of a river. But this ceases to be the "essence", it becomes for him no more than a passing medium of existence, as soon as that river is made subject to industry, as soon as it is

---

1. Bruno Bauer, "Charakteristik Ludwig Feuerbachs," *Wigandsvierteljahrschrift*, vol. 3, October 1845.

Third page on printer's sheet '11' (in Engels's sequence), numbered '29' by Marx

~~undersigned we~~ his brainwork and also the "holy family" ~~had made use of communism specially the opposed to "critical criticism" as last most extreme point of German theory~~.

~~as one of the levels~~
The first impression which the "holy family" makes on the distinguished father of the church is one of deep sadness & of a serious, petty bourgeois melancholy. The sole good aspect of the book – that it "demonstrates ⸺what Feuerbach had to become & how his philosophy is able to position itself if it wants to fight against critique –"² **(p. 138)**¹ that it therefore united in an unforced way the obligation with the ability & the desire, – yet does not make up for all the saddening aspects. ~~The Feu{erbachian}~~ **The lamentation of the holy Bruno is was on this is like the lamentation of the old Jehovah, who throughout all four greater & twelve lesser prophets to his holy people Israel lamenting after his holy wayward people Israel so that they do not completely desert him.** The polluted by dye and other waste, navigated by steamships, as soon as its water is diverted into canals ~~which one draws~~ in which simple drainage can withdraw the medium of existence from the fish. This explanation that any such contradiction in terms is an inevitable abnormality is fundamentally no different from the consolation which the holy Max Stirner offers to the discontented, that to wit ~~the abnormality~~ this contradiction {is} their own contradiction, that {*insertion*} this bad condition is their own bad condition {*end insertion*} whereby they should be able either to reassure themselves, keep their own disgust to themselves, or avail themselves of indignation against it in some fantastic way – & just as little different from the holy Bruno's allegation that these unfortunate circumstances come from the fact that those concerned remain stuck fast in the muck of "substance", have not advanced to "absolute self-consciousness" & have not recognised those bad circumstances as spirit of their spirit.

---

1. Bruno Bauer, "Charakteristik Ludwig Feuerbachs," *Wigandsvierteljahrschrift*, vol. 3, October 1845.
2. Marx's emphasis in the foregoing passage; *Jahrbuch 2003*, vol. 2, p. 194, ref. Z. 73, Z. 74.

Third page on printer's sheet '11' (in Engels's sequence), numbered '29' by Marx

necessary for him because his brainwork and also chastisement {were} recorded in the "holy family". The first impression which the "holy family" makes on the distinguished father of the church is one of deep sadness & of a serious, petty bourgeois melancholy. The sole good aspect of the book – that it "demonstrates what Feuerbach <u>had</u> to become & how his philosophy <u>is able</u> to position itself if it <u>wants</u> to fight against critique –" **(p. 138)**[1] that it therefore united in an unforced way the obligation with the ability & the desire, – yet does not make up for all the saddening aspects. The Feuerbachian philosophy, polluted by dye and other waste, navigated by steamships, as soon as its water is diverted into canals in which simple drainage can withdraw the medium of existence from the fish. This explanation that any such contradiction in terms is an inevitable abnormality is fundamentally no different from the consolation which the holy Max Stirner offers to the discontented, that to wit this contradiction {is} their own contradiction, that this bad condition is their own bad condition whereby they should be able either to reassure themselves, keep their own disgust to themselves, or avail themselves of indignation against it in some fantastic way – & just as little different from the holy Bruno's allegation that these unfortunate circumstances come from the fact that those concerned remain stuck fast in the muck of "substance", have not advanced to "absolute self-consciousness" & have not recognised those bad circumstances as spirit of their spirit.

---

1. Marx's emphasis in this passage; *Jahrbuch 2003*, vol. 2, p. 194, ref. Z. 73, Z. 74.

Third page on printer's sheet '11' (in Engels's sequence), numbered '29' by Marx

Feuerbachian philosophy, here set out wholly arbitrarily, "must not & can not understand the critic – it must not and cannot know & recognise critique in its development – it must not & cannot know that the critique

Third page on printer's sheet '11' (in Engels's sequence), numbered '29' by Marx

here set out wholly arbitrarily, "must not &
cannot understand the critic – it must not and
cannot know & recognise critique in its
development – it must not & cannot know
that the critique

Fourth page on printer's sheet '11' (in Engels's sequence), not numbered by Marx

as opposed to all transcendence is a never-
ending fighting & winning, a continuous
destroying & creating, the sole creating &
and producing {entity}. It must not & cannot
know how the critic has worked & still works
to get the transcendental powers, which have
hitherto oppressed men & not let them breathe
                              (!)
& come to life, to posit & to <u>make into</u>[1] what
they <u>actually are</u>, as mind from mind, as inner
                    (!)
from within, as native   from and in the
homeland, as products & creations of self-
consciousness. It must not & cannot know
how solely & by himself the critic has broken
down religion in its totality, the state in its
                        p. 138, 39.[2]
various guises, because &c &c &c"
Is this not exactly like the old Jehovah
who pursues his runaway people, which has
found more joy in the agreeable gods of the
heathens: Hear me Israel, & close not your
ears, Judah! Am I not the Lord thy God
who led thee forth from the land of Egypt into
the land flowing with milk & honey – and

---

1. Marx's emphasis; *Jahrbuch 2003*, vol. 2, p. 194, ref. Z. 97.

2. Bruno Bauer, "Charakteristik Ludwig Feuerbachs," *Wigandsvierteljahrschrift*, vol. 3, October 1845.

Fourth page on printer's sheet '11' (in Engels's sequence), not numbered by Marx

as opposed to all transcendence is a never-ending fighting & winning, a continuous destroying & creating, the sole creating & and producing {entity}. It must not & cannot know how the critic has worked & still works to get the transcendental powers, which have hitherto oppressed men & not let them breathe & come to life, to posit & to <u>make into</u>[1] (!) what they <u>actually are</u>, as mind from mind, as inner from within, as native (!) from and in the homeland, as products & creations of self-consciousness. It must not & cannot know how solely & by himself the critic has broken down religion in its totality, the state in its various guises, because &c &c &c" **p. 138, 39.**[2] Is this not exactly like the old Jehovah who pursues his runaway people, which has found more joy in the agreeable gods of the heathens: Hear me Israel, & close not your ears, Judah! Am I not the Lord thy God who led thee forth from the land of Egypt into the land flowing with milk & honey – and

---

1. Marx's emphasis; *Jahrbuch 2003*, vol. 2, p. 194, ref. Z. 97.
2. Bruno Bauer, "Charakteristik Ludwig Feuerbachs," *Wigandsvierteljahrschrift*, vol. 3, October 1845.

Fourth page on printer's sheet '11' (in Engels's sequence), not numbered by Marx

behold you have from your youth done that which is evil to me, & have angered me with your handiwork, & have turned your back on me & respected not what I have taught you well, & have done abominations in ~~the~~ my house that have polluted it, & have instituted ~~their~~ the rule of Baal (Feuerbach?) in the valley of Ben Hinnom, for which I gave you no warrant & never foresaw that you could do such horror; & have sent you my servant Jeremiah to whom my word has gone out from the thirteenth year of King Josiah, the son of Amon, up to the present day, & he has preached to you for three & twenty years with diligence, but never have you wanted to hear. Thus spake the lord God {*der Herr Herr*}: who has ever heard ~~such a terrible thing as~~ the like, that the maiden Israel doth such an abomination? For the rain water {*text breaks off*}

Fourth page on printer's sheet '11' (in Engels's sequence), not numbered by Marx

behold you have from your youth done that which is evil to me, & have angered me with your handiwork, & have turned your back on me & respected not what I have taught you well, & have done abominations in my house that have polluted it, & have instituted the rule of Baal (Feuerbach?) in the valley of Ben Hinnom, for which I gave you no warrant & never foresaw that you could do such horror; & have sent you my servant Jeremiah to whom my word has gone out from the thirteenth year of King Josiah, the son of Amon, up to the present day, & he has preached to you for three & twenty years with diligence, but never have you wanted to hear. Thus spake the lord God {*der Herr Herr*}: who has ever heard the like, that the maiden Israel doth such an abomination? For the rain water {*text breaks off*}

First page on printer's sheet '20' (in Engels's sequence), not numbered by Marx

{…} therefore Protestantism is the truth of hierarchy hence the true hierarchy. – However, since only the true hierarchy[1] deserves the name, it is clear that the hierarchy of the middle ages must be a "delicate" one, which is as easily proved to him as in the above Hegelian citations and a hundred others where spirit's incomplete rule in the middle ages was demonstrated, which he only needed to copy out & ~~in which~~ through which his whole "ego"[2] activity came to exist, replacing the word "spirit's rule" by "hierarchy". He did not even need ~~to dr{aw}~~ to work the simple syllogism through which spirit's rule was badly transformed into hierarchy, after it was subsumed under the German theoretical mode, the effect transposed with the causal term & everything e.g. ~~to use theological terms, which~~ reverting into the categories of theology, which ~~itself from theology~~ had proceeded from theology ~~—speculation~~ & still function as the highest ~~of their~~ of principles for these

---

1. Marx's emphases in this passage.
2. Marx's emphasis here.

First page on printer's sheet '20' (in Engels's sequence), not numbered by Marx

{...} therefore Protestantism is the truth of
hierarchy hence the true hierarchy. – However,
since only the true hierarchy[1] deserves the
name, it is clear that the hierarchy of the
middle ages must be a "delicate" one, which is
as easily proved to him as in the above
Hegelian citations and a hundred others where
spirit's incomplete rule in the middle ages was
demonstrated, which he only needed to copy
out & through which his whole "ego"[2]
activity came to exist, replacing the
word "spirit's rule" by "hierarchy". He did not
even need to work the simple syllogism
through which spirit's rule was
badly transformed into hierarchy, after it was
subsumed under the German theoretical mode,
the effect transposed with the causal term &
everything e.g. reverting into the categories of
theology, which had proceeded
from theology & still function as
the highest of principles for these

---

1. Marx's emphases in this passage.
2. Marx's emphasis here.

First page on printer's sheet '20' (in Engels's sequence), not numbered by Marx

theoreticians. – e.g. Hegelian speculation, Straussean pantheism pp – a masterpiece which was really top of the list in 1842. From the above citation it also follows that 1) Hegel
1)
  understood the French revolution as a new and more complete phase of this rule of spirit, 2) ~~the rul{ers}~~ saw in the philosophers the rulers of the nineteenth century world, & 3) ~~the~~[1] maintained that today only abstract ideas ~~rule~~ are of any use among men, & 4) that according to him honour, ~~state, family~~ family,
                                    , property
                         , civil order
state, entrepreneurship
pp are understood as "~~the~~ godly & ~~the~~ holy" {and} as "religious things"
                        – {*insertion*} & 5) that ethical life is presented as ~~the complete spiritualisation of the world~~ worldwide holiness or sanctified worldliness, as the highest & last form of spirit's rule over the world.{*end insertion*} All these things we find again ~~already~~ literally in Stirner.

Hereafter there would be nothing more to say & demonstrate in connection with Stirner's hierarchy except why ~~he~~ Saint Max has copied out Hegel – a fact, for the

---

1. Also deleted by Marx.

First page on printer's sheet '20' (in Engels's sequence), not numbered by Marx

theoreticians. – e.g. Hegelian speculation, Straussean pantheism pp – a masterpiece which was really top of the list in 1842. From the above citation it also follows that Hegel 1) understood the French revolution as a new and more complete phase of this rule of spirit, 2) saw in the philosophers the rulers of the nineteenth century world, 3) maintained that today only abstract ideas are of any use among men, 4) that according to him honour, family, state, entrepreneurship, civil order, property, pp are understood as "godly & holy" {and} as "religious things" – & 5) that ethical life is presented as worldwide holiness or sanctified worldliness, as the highest & last form of spirit's rule over the world. All these things we find again literally in Stirner.

Hereafter there would be nothing more to say & demonstrate in connection with Stirner's hierarchy except why Saint Max has copied out Hegel – a fact, for the

explanation of which, however, material facts
are necessary, ~~the~~ &

First page on printer's sheet '20' (in Engels's sequence), not numbered by Marx

explanation of which, however, material facts
are necessary, &

Second page on printer's sheet '20' (in Engels's sequence), numbered 30 by Marx

which therefore is clear already only for those who are acquainted with the Berlin atmosphere. Another question is how the Hegelian ~~understanding~~ conception of spirit's rule came into existence, & concerning that ~~will in any case for here for the German theoreticians a few words will be cited~~, **see above p**

In every epoch the ideas of the dominant class are the dominant ideas, i.e. the class which is the dominant <u>material</u> power over ~~history~~ society is at the same time the dominant <u>intellectual</u> power. The class which has the means of material production at its disposal consequently also deploys the means of intellectual production, so that the ideas of those lacking the means of intellectual production are on average subordinated. The dominant ideas are nothing more than the ~~ideological~~ ideal expression of the dominant material relations, the dominant material relations put into ideas; hence {these are ideas} of the relations which make one class the dominant one, therefore {these are} the ideas of their dominance. The individuals who make up the dominant class possess consciousness among other things and

which therefore is clear already only for those who are acquainted with the Berlin atmosphere. Another question is how the Hegelian conception of spirit's rule came into existence, & concerning that, **see above p**

In every epoch the ideas of the dominant class are the dominant ideas, i.e. the class which is the dominant <u>material</u> power over society is at the same time the dominant <u>intellectual</u> power. The class which has the means of material production at its disposal consequently also deploys the means of intellectual production, so that the ideas of those lacking the means of intellectual production are on average subordinated. The dominant ideas are nothing more than the ideal expression of the dominant material relations, the dominant material relations put into ideas; hence {these are ideas} of the relations which make one class the dominant one, therefore {these are} the ideas of their dominance. The individuals who make up the dominant class possess consciousness among other things and

Third page on printer's sheet '20' (in Engels's sequence), numbered 31 by Marx

labour, so that within this class one part operates as the thinkers of that class, the active, conceptualising ideologists, who make the production of the illusions of that class about itself their main source of livelihood, while the others' relationship with these thoughts & illusions is more passive & receptive, because they are in actuality the active members of that class & have less time to produce illusions about that & thoughts about themselves. Within that class this ~~division of~~ splitting up can even develop into a certain opposition & enmity between the two, but which at any practical collision, where the class ~~as such~~ itself is endangered, this automatically ceases, even the appearance vanishes that the dominant ideas were not the ideas of the dominant class & might have a power distinct from the power of that class. The existence of revolutionary ideas in a specific epoch already presupposes the existence of a revolutionary class, about which presuppositions the

Third page on printer's sheet '20' (in Engels's sequence), numbered 31 by Marx

labour, so that within this class one part operates as the thinkers of that class, the active, conceptualising ideologists, who make the production of the illusions of that class about itself their main source of livelihood, while the others' relationship with these thoughts & illusions is more passive & receptive, because they are in actuality the active members of that class & have less time to produce illusions about that & thoughts about themselves. Within that class this splitting up can even develop into a certain opposition & enmity between the two, but which at any practical collision, where the class itself is endangered, this automatically ceases, even the appearance vanishes that the dominant ideas were not the ideas of the dominant class & might have a power distinct from the power of that class. The existence of revolutionary ideas in a specific epoch already presupposes the existence of a revolutionary class, about which presuppositions the

Third page on printer's sheet '20' (in Engels's sequence), numbered 31 by Marx

necessary things have already been said above (p   )

If, when understanding the course of history, one detaches the thoughts of the dominant class from the dominant class, thus making them independent, one in that way maintains the view that in an epoch such & such thoughts are dominant, without bothering oneself about the ~~modes~~ conditions of production and about the producers of those ideas, {insertion}[1] so one therefore leaves aside the individuals and world conditions lying at the basis of the ideas, {end insertion} hence one can say e.g. that during the time when the aristocracy was dominant the ~~ideas~~ concepts of honour, loyalty &c dominated, during the domination of the bourgeoisie the concepts freedom, equality &c dominated. {insertion} ~~The dominant class itself as a rule has the idea that these dominate its concepts, & are distinguished from the dominant ideas of other classes only in that of earlier epochs, that they present them as eternal truths~~ {end insertion} ~~These "dominant ideas" will have~~ a ~~form~~ the more ~~in order more general and comprehensive,~~ the more the dominant class finds it necessary to present its interest as of all members of society ~~that of the whole society~~   The dominant class as a rule imagines this. This conception of history, which is common to all historians, particularly since the 18th century, will necessarily

---

1. The editors of *Jahrbuch 2003* state that this insertion was written down later than the insertion in the next passage.

Third page on printer's sheet '20' (in Engels's sequence), numbered 31 by Marx

necessary things have already been said above
(p   )

If, when understanding the course of
history, one detaches the thoughts of the
dominant class from the dominant class, thus
making them independent, one in that way
maintains the view that in an epoch such &
such thoughts are dominant, without bothering
oneself about the conditions of
production and about the producers of those
ideas, so one therefore leaves aside the
individuals and world conditions
lying at the basis of the ideas,
hence one can say e.g. that during the time
when the aristocracy was dominant the
concepts of honour, loyalty &c
dominated, during the domination of the
bourgeoisie the concepts freedom, equality &c
dominated. The dominant
class as a rule imagines this. This conception
of history, which is common to all historians,
particularly since the 18th century, will necessarily

Fourth page on printer's sheet '20' (in Engels's sequence), numbered 32 by Marx

come up against the phenomenon that ideas which are more and more abstract become dominant, i.e. ideas which more and more take the form of universality. This means that for each new class that takes the place of the one
                                 now
that was previously dominant, it is
necessary, in order for it ~~to assert~~ to achieve its objectives, for its interest to be represented as
                                common interest
the ~~{interest} of the whole~~   of
all members of society, i.e. expressed ideally: to give to its ideas the form of universality, to
                           , universally
present them as the only rational
applicable
                  ones. The revolutionising class comes on the scene at the outset because it stands opposed to a <u>class</u>, not as a class but as a representative of the whole of society, it appears as the whole mass of society opposing the one dominant class. It can do this because at the beginning its interest in actual fact still largely coincides with the common interest of
                          {and} under
all other non-dominant classes,
pressure of relations hitherto
                      its interest has

(The universality corresponds 1) to the class versus the medieval estate, 2) competition, world interrelations, etc.   **gross**
                        3) the
numerical strength of the dominant class: 4) the illusion of the <u>common</u> interest. At the outset this illusion {is} true. 5) the delusion of the ideologists and the division of labour.)

come up against the phenomenon that ideas which are more and more abstract become dominant, i.e. ideas which more and more take the form of universality. This means that for each new class that takes the place of the one that was previously dominant, it is now necessary, in order for it to achieve its objectives, for its interest to be represented as the common interest of all members of society, i.e. expressed ideally: to give to its ideas the form of universality, to present them as the only rational, universally applicable ones. The revolutionising class comes on the scene at the outset because it stands opposed to a <u>class</u>, not as a class but as a representative of the whole of society, it appears as the whole mass of society opposing the one dominant class. It can do this because at the beginning its interest in actual fact still largely coincides with the common interest of all other non-dominant classes, {and} under pressure of relations hitherto its interest has

(The universality corresponds 1) to the class versus the medieval estate, 2) competition, world interrelations, etc. 3) the gross numerical strength of the dominant class: 4) the illusion of the <u>common</u> interest. At the outset this illusion {is} true. 5) the delusion of the ideologists and the division of labour.)

not yet been able to develop as the particular interest of a particular class ~~& consequently~~. Its victory therefore also benefits many individuals of other classes which have not yet come to be dominant, but only in so far as it puts these individuals in position to raise themselves into the dominating class. When the French bourgeoisie overthrew the dominance of the ~~feud{al}~~ aristocracy it thereby made it possible for many proletarians to raise themselves out of the proletariat, but only in so far as they became bourgeois. Each new class therefore only achieves its objective on a broader basis than that of the class previously dominant, whereas later the confrontation between the non-dominant class and the currently dominant one then develops ever more sharply & thoroughly. These two factors cause the ongoing struggle against the new dominant class to be waged once again ~~from~~ in an ever sharper, more radical negation of the preceding social conditions than all

Fourth page on printer's sheet '20' (in Engels's sequence), numbered 32 by Marx

not yet been able to develop as the particular interest of a particular class.
Its victory therefore also benefits many individuals of other classes which have not yet come to be dominant, but only in so far as it puts these individuals in position to raise themselves into the dominating class. When the French bourgeoisie overthrew the dominance of the aristocracy it
thereby made it possible for many proletarians to raise themselves out of the proletariat, but only in so far as they became bourgeois. Each new class therefore only achieves its objective on a broader basis than that of the class previously dominant, whereas later the confrontation between the non-dominant class and the currently dominant one then develops ever more sharply & thoroughly. These two factors cause the ongoing struggle against the new dominant class to be waged once again in an ever sharper, more radical negation of the preceding social conditions than all

First page on printer's sheet '21' (in Engels's sequence), numbered 33 by Marx

previous classes, striving for dominance, were able to do.

This whole appearance, as if the dominance of a specific class ~~is not~~ is only the dominance of certain ideas, naturally ceases as soon as the dominance of classes ceases in general to be the form of the social order, as soon as it is therefore no longer necessary to represent a particular interest ~~practically as everything social, theoretically~~ as universal {*insertion*} or "the universal" as dominating. {*end insertion*}

Once the dominating ideas have been separated from the dominating individuals {*insertion*} **and above all from the relations which proceed from a given stage of the mode of production** {*end insertion*} & in that way arriving at the conclusion that ideas always dominate in history, it ~~{is} no longer difficult~~ is very easy to abstract from these different ideas themselves "the[1] ideas" {or} **the idea etc.** as that which is dominating in history & hence to understand all these ~~different~~ individual ideas ~~as~~ & concepts as

It also follows naturally then that all relations of men can be derived from the concept of man, from the representation of man, from the essence of man, the man.

---

1. Marx's emphasis.

previous classes, striving for dominance, were able to do.

This whole appearance, as if the dominance of a specific class is only the dominance of certain ideas, naturally ceases as soon as the dominance of classes ceases in general to be the form of the social order, as soon as it is therefore no longer necessary to represent a particular interest as universal or "the universal" as dominating.

Once the dominating ideas have been separated from the dominating individuals **and above all from the relations which proceed from a given stage of the mode of production** & in that way arriving at the conclusion that ideas always dominate in history, it is very easy to abstract from these different ideas themselves "the[1] ideas" {or} **the idea etc.** as that which is dominating in history & hence to understand all these individual ideas & concepts as

        It also follows naturally then that all relations of men can be derived from the concept of man, from the representation of man, from the essence of man, the man.

---

1. Marx's emphasis.

First page on printer's sheet '21' (in Engels's sequence), numbered 33 by Marx

"self-specifications" of the concept developing itself in history. Speculative philosophy has done just this. At the end of the History of Philosophy Hegel himself confesses that he "has considered only the progress of the concept" & has presented "the true theodicy[1]" in history. (p. 446) One can only look back again to the ~~representatives~~ producers of "the concept", to the theoreticians, ideologists & philosophers, and then come to the conclusion , the thinkers as such
that the philosophers
have at all times been
dominant in history – a conclusion which, as we ~~see~~ saw, {that} was also expressed by Hegel. {*insertion*} **Hence the whole gimmick of proving the hegemony of spirit in history (hierarchy in Stirner's work) is reducible to the following 3 ~~change(s)~~ steps.** {*end insertion*}
[2] The adoption of the Hegelian ~~domination~~ world domination of philosophy & its transformation into a hierarchy through ~~Stir{ner}~~ Saint Max ~~is~~ gets, by means of our saints' {Max and Bruno's} wholly uncritical

---

1. Marx's emphasis.
2. *Jahrbuch 2003* Apparat p. 202, left. The passage was separated by Marx from the rest of the text with a horizontal line and struck through vertically; the editors of *Jahrbuch 2003* state that it was written down later than the other insertion on this sheet.

First page on printer's sheet '21' (in Engels's sequence), numbered 33 by Marx

"self-specifications" <u>of the</u> concept developing itself in history. Speculative philosophy has done just this. At the end of the History of Philosophy Hegel himself confesses that he "has considered only the progress <u>of the concept</u>" & has presented "the true <u>theodicy</u>[1]" in history. (p. 446) One can only look back again to the producers of "the concept", to the theoreticians, ideologists & philosophers, and then come to the conclusion that the philosophers, the thinkers as such have at all times been dominant in history – a conclusion which, as we saw,{that} was also expressed by Hegel. **Hence the whole gimmick of proving the hegemony of spirit in history (hierarchy in Stirner's work) is reducible to the following 3 steps.**

[2]The adoption of the Hegelian world domination of philosophy & its transformation into a hierarchy through Saint Max ~~is~~ gets, by means of our saints' {Max and Bruno's} wholly uncritical

---

1. Marx's emphasis.
2. *Jahrbuch 2003* Apparat p. 202, left. The passage was separated by Marx from the rest of the text with a horizontal line and struck through vertically; the editors of *Jahrbuch 2003* state that it was written down later than the other insertion on this sheet.

First page on printer's sheet '21' (in Engels's sequence), numbered 33 by Marx

gullibility ~~to a point~~ and through

First page on printer's sheet '21' (in Engels's sequence), numbered 33 by Marx

gullibility and through

a "holy" or unholy ignorance, to a point where they are satisfied with "looking through" history (i.e. looking through ~~Hegelian hi(story)~~ Hegelian historical matters) without "knowing" many "things" about it. Anyway he has indeed to take care that as soon as he has "learned" enough basics – no longer "abolishing & dissolving" (p. 96), hence sticking to the "busyness of the beetles" – that he does not "go further" and "abolish and dissolve" his own ignorance.

<u>Firstly.</u> N° 1. One must detach the ideas of the rulers, who rule on an empirical basis, under empirical conditions & as material individuals, from them, & thereby recognise the domination of ideas or illusions in history.

<u>Secondly.</u> N° 2. One must ~~this under these ruling ideas~~ bring order to this rule of ideas, establish a ~~ideas logical~~ mystical connection among the ruling ideas as they succeed one another, which ~~can happen~~ is brought ~~only~~ thereby to the point where one understands them as "self-specifications of

Second page on printer's sheet '21' (in Engels's sequence), numbered 34 by Marx

a "holy" or unholy ignorance, to a point where they are satisfied with "looking through" history (i.e. looking <u>through</u> Hegelian historical matters) without "knowing" many "things" about it. Anyway he has indeed to take care that as soon as he has "learned" enough basics – no longer "abolishing & dissolving" (p. 96), hence sticking to the "busyness of the beetles" – that he does not "go further" and "abolish and dissolve" his own ignorance.

N° 1. One must detach the ideas of the rulers, who rule on an empirical basis, under empirical conditions & as material individuals, from them, & thereby recognise the domination of ideas or illusions in history.

N° 2. One must bring order to this rule of ideas, establish a mystical connection among the ruling ideas as they succeed one another, which is brought thereby to the point where one understands them as "self-specifications of "the concept". {*insertion*} (This is possible precisely because these ideas actually connect with one another by means of their empirical basis.) {*further insertion*} **and because, understood as mere ideas they turn into self-distinguishing distinctions, produced by thinking.**) {*end further insertion*} {*end insertion*}

~~Thirdly.~~ N° 3. To get rid of the ~~mystery of this~~ mystical appearance of this "self-specifying concept", one transforms it or ~~to~~ into a person – "self-consciousness" – ~~appear properly materialistic,~~ into a series of persons who represent the concept in history, into "thinkers", "philosophers", **ideologists** who Man: the "thinking human spirit". are again understood as the makers of history, **, as those who rule.** as "the Guardian Council" With this, one has removed all the materialistic elements from history & can gently give speculative thought its head. **If, like Hegel, one constructs for the first and the contemporary time all of history world in its full scope,** ~~as was the case with~~ ~~Hegel~~ **Hegel in both respects** then this is not

This historical method, which ruled in and why Germany, it ruled so prominently, must be explained from its connection with the ~~ideological consciousness~~ illusions of the ideologists generally, e.g. the illusions of the jurists, politicians (even from the practical statesmen amongst them), from the dogmatic daydreams and distortions of

Second page on printer's sheet '21' (in Engels's sequence), numbered 34 by Marx

"the concept". (This is possible precisely because these ideas actually connect with one another by means of their empirical basis) **and because, understood as mere ideas they turn into self-distinguishing distinctions, produced by thinking.)**

N° 3. To get rid of the mystical appearance of this "self-specifying concept", one transforms it into a person – "self-consciousness" – or into a series of persons who represent the concept in history, into "thinkers", "philosophers", **ideologists** who are again understood as the makers of history, as "the Guardian Council", **as those who rule.** With this, one has removed all the materialistic elements from history & can gently give speculative thought its head. **If, like Hegel, one constructs for the first time all of history and the contemporary world in its full scope then this is not**

<u>Man</u>: the "thinking human spirit".

This historical method, which ruled in Germany, and why it ruled so prominently, must be explained from its connection with the illusions of the ideologists generally, e.g. the illusions of the jurists, politicians (even from the practical statesmen amongst them), from the dogmatic daydreams and distortions of these guys, which is simply

Second page on printer's sheet '21' (in Engels's sequence), numbered 34 by Marx

possible without comprehensive positive knowledge, without at least going into empirical history at certain points, ~~and without a great~~ without great energy and deep insight. On the other hand, if one is going to be satisfied

these guys, which is simply self-evident from their practical position in life, ~~and~~ their employment and

                              the division of labour.

Second page on printer's sheet '21' (in Engels's sequence), numbered 34 by Marx

possible without comprehensive positive knowledge, without at least going into empirical history at certain points, without great energy and deep insight. On the other hand, if one is going to be satisfied self-evident from their practical position in life, their employment and the division of labour.

with exploiting and converting a readily available traditional ~~historical~~ construction for one's own purposes & demonstrating this "proper" understanding ~~only~~ in individual examples (e.g. Negroes & Mongolians, Catholics & Protestants, the French Revolution pp), ~~there is~~ -- & our eager {Stirner} does this contra the holy {Hegel} – then for this no knowledge of history is **necessary. The result of this whole exploitation** ~~must~~ **is necessarily** ~~be as~~ **comic** as we have previously found with Saint Max ~~& will still be finding & will still be finding~~, {and is} **at its funniest when jumping from the past into the most immediate present, &** ~~otherwise~~ **like the example we have already** ~~had~~ **found with "whimsy"**[1] ~~and will still be finding further examples~~.

Concerning actual hierarchy in the middle ages we merely remark here that this did not exist for the people, for the great mass of mankind. For the great mass there existed only feudalism, & {there} is hierarchy only in so far as it is itself either feudal or anti-feudal (within feudalism). Feudalism itself has entirely empirical relations with its foundation.

---

1. See CW 5: p. 176 note a.

with exploiting and converting a readily available traditional construction for one's own purposes & demonstrating this "proper" understanding in individual examples (e.g. Negroes & Mongolians, Catholics & Protestants, the French Revolution pp), -- & our eager {Stirner} does this contra the holy {Hegel} – then for this no knowledge of history is **necessary. The result of this whole exploitation is necessarily comic** as we have previously found with Saint Max {and is} **at its funniest when jumping from the past into the most immediate present like the example we have already found with "whimsy".**[1]

Concerning actual hierarchy in the middle ages we merely remark here that this did not exist for the people, for the great mass of mankind. For the great mass there existed only feudalism, & {there} is hierarchy only in so far as it is itself either feudal or anti-feudal (within feudalism). Feudalism itself has entirely empirical relations with its foundation.

---

1. See CW 5: p. 176 note a.

Hierarchy and its ~~struggle~~ struggles with feudalism (the struggles of the ideologists of one class against the class itself) are only the ideological expression of feudalism & of the itself, struggles developing within feudalism of which once again the struggles of the feudally organised nations are a part. ~~Hence hierarchy = ical form of feudalism. Feudalism + political~~ **Hierarchy is the ideal form of feudalism; feudalism {is} the political** form of the medieval relations of production and **interchange** ~~(i.e. of the mutual relation of the individuals in their most immediate material actuality~~ **(i.e. of the mutual relation of the individuals in their most immediate, material actuality)** ~~hence the representation of which in the last instance hence in the last instance the real basis within the two dominating as well as feudalism's.~~ Only from , material the representation of ~~the~~ this practical, relation therefore can ~~hierarchy as well as only~~ the struggle of feudalism

Hierarchy and its struggles with feudalism (the struggles of the ideologists of one class against the class itself) are only the ideological expression of feudalism & of the struggles developing within feudalism itself, of which once again the struggles of the feudally organised nations are a part. **Hierarchy is the ideal form of feudalism; feudalism {is} the political** form of the medieval relations of production and **interchange (i.e. of the mutual relation of the individuals in their most immediate, material actuality).** Only from the representation of this practical, material relation therefore can the struggle of feudalism

Fourth page on printer's sheet '21' (in Engels's sequence), numbered 35 by Marx

be explained; with this representation the previously mentioned conception of history self-destructs, it takes the illusions of the middle ages to be true and credible – namely the illusions that serve the king & pope in their struggles with one another.
While ~~one in ordinary life~~ in ordinary life every shopkeeper knows very well how to distinguish between what someone pretends to be, & what he actually is, yet our writing of history has still not arrived at this trivial insight. It takes every epoch at its word, what it says & imagines about itself.

Since Saint Max ~~says nothing about real, historical the hierarchy than that it has been a very "weakish" one about which nothing is said except to be reduced we have with the above already said too much about hierarchy and said which by the way has not taken place regarding Stirner's Will. One could perhaps allow the worthy "noble" egoist Stirner the one comprehensive real concept of that object, instead of the above indications concerning the real concept, as soon as he "appropriates" the object & no longer satisfies himself with phrases from Hegel's~~

be explained; with this representation the
previously mentioned conception of history
self-destructs, it takes the illusions of the
middle ages to be true and credible – namely
the illusions that serve the king & pope in their
struggles with one another.
While in ordinary life every shopkeeper knows
very well how to distinguish between what
someone pretends to be, & what he actually
is, yet our writing of history has still
not arrived at this trivial insight. It takes
every epoch at its word, what
it says & imagines about itself.
Since Saint Max merely reduces Hegel's

Fourth page on printer's sheet '21' (in Engels's sequence), numbered 35 by Marx

~~abstractions concerning hierarchy & the middle ages.~~ **merely reduces Hegel's abstractions of the middle ages a{nd} hierarchy to "pompous words and miserable ideas" there is no reason** ~~to speak~~ **to go further** ~~of~~ **into real, historical hierarchy**. It is obvious from ~~the above instructions for constructing a hierarchy à la Stirner~~ **the above** that one can even reverse the trick & grasp Catholicism not only as precursor but also as negation of the true hierarchy; hence Catholicism = negation of spirit, non-spirit, sensuousness, & from this proceeds the great pronouncement of our Jacques le bonhomme, that ~~Jesuitism~~ the Jesuits "have rescued us from the <u>arrival</u> & disappearance of sensuousness" (p 118) What would have become of "us" if the "disappearance" of sensuousness ~~would~~ had taken place we do not know. ~~It is not~~ The whole material development ~~which {commenced} with~~ since the sixteenth century did not rescue "us" from the "arrival" of sensuousness, rather the opposite, any further development of sensuousness does not exist for Stirner – it is the Jesuits who have brought everything to this point. Compare Hegel's Philosophy of History on this p. 425.

Fourth page on printer's sheet '21' (in Engels's sequence), numbered 35 by Marx

abstractions of the middle ages a{nd} hierarchy to "pompous words and miserable ideas" there is no reason to go further into real, historical hierarchy. It is obvious from **the above** that one can even reverse the trick & grasp Catholicism not only as precursor but also as negation of the true hierarchy; hence Catholicism = negation of spirit, non-spirit, sensuousness, & from this proceeds the great pronouncement of our Jacques le bonhomme, that the <u>Jesuits</u> "have rescued us from the <u>arrival</u> & disappearance of sensuousness" (p 118) What would have become of "us" if the "disappearance" of sensuousness had taken place we do not know. The whole material development since the sixteenth century did not rescue "us" from the "arrival" of sensuousness, rather the opposite,
any further development of sensuousness does not exist for Stirner – it is the Jesuits who have brought everything to this point. Compare Hegel's Philosophy of History on this p. 425.

Fourth page on printer's sheet '21' (in Engels's sequence), numbered 35 by Marx

~~Now we come to the hierarchy of the holy Max. Since he~~ **Since St. Max** transfers the old rule of knights into modern times, ~~he only brings the~~ he has by that means grasped ~~the dec{ades}~~ modern times as "knightdom"; & since he grasps this knightly rule transferred into modern times once more in distinction from the old knightly rule of the middle ages, he presents it as rule of the ideologists, as "schoolmasterdom". Hence knightdom = ~~intel{lectual}~~ hierarchy as intellectual dominance.

Since St. Max transfers the old rule of knights into modern times, he has by that means grasped modern times as "knightdom"; & since he grasps this knightly rule transferred into modern times once more in distinction from the old knightly rule of the middle ages, he presents it as rule of the ideologists, as "schoolmasterdom". Hence knightdom = hierarchy as intellectual dominance.

First page on printer's sheet '84' (in Engels's sequence), numbered 40 by Marx

... is found. From the first {consideration} it follows that a developed division of labour & extensive trade is presupposed; from the second {consideration}, the locality. For the first, individuals must be brought together, for the second, they are themselves instruments of production alongside the given instruments of production. Here we therefore encounter the distinction between natural instruments of production and the instruments of production created by civilisation. *Agricultural land* **(water etc.)** can be considered a natural instrument of production. In the first case, with the natural instrument of production, individuals are subordinated to nature, in the second case, subordinated to ~~the~~ a labour-product. In the first case, property (landed property) also appears as immediate, natural domination ~~of prop{erty}~~, in the second, as the domination of labour, specifically of accumulated labour, of capital. The first case presupposes that individuals cohere together through some kind of bond, whether ~~as~~ family, tribe , the land itself pp, the second case that they are independent of one another & ~~cohere~~

First page on printer's sheet '84' (in Engels's sequence), numbered 40 by Marx

... is found. From the first {consideration} it follows that a developed division of labour & extensive trade is presupposed; from the second {consideration}, the locality. For the first, individuals must be brought together, for the second, they are themselves instruments of production alongside the given instruments of production. Here we therefore encounter the distinction between natural instruments of production and the instruments of production created by civilisation. *Agricultural land* **(water etc.)** can be considered a natural instrument of production. In the first case, with the natural instrument of production, individuals are subordinated to nature, in the second case, subordinated to a labour-product. In the first case, property (landed property) also appears as immediate, natural domination, in the second, as the domination of labour, specifically of accumulated labour, of capital. The first case presupposes that individuals cohere together through some kind of bond, whether family, tribe, the land itself pp, the second case that they are independent of one another &

First page on printer's sheet '84' (in Engels's sequence), numbered 40 by Marx

relate to one another only through exchange. ~~The first case~~ In the first case, exchange is mainly an exchange between men & nature, an exchange in which the labour of one is ~~exchanged~~ swapped for the products of the other; in the second case, exchange between ~~ordin{ary}~~ men themselves predominates. In the first case, average human intelligence is adequate, physical and intellectual activity are still not separated; in the second case, the division between intellectual & physical labour must already be realised in practice. In the first case, the domination of the property-holder~~s~~ over the non-property-holder can rest ~~through~~ on ~~purely~~ personal relationships, on a kind of community; in the second case ~~they themselves~~ it must have taken on a material form in something else, money. In the first case, ~~{one} finds~~ small-scale industry comes into existence, albeit defined by the use of the natural instrument of production, ~~in the second case~~ & so without the division of labour among different individuals; in the second case, industry works only in & through the division of labour.

First page on printer's sheet '84' (in Engels's sequence), numbered 40 by Marx

relate to one another only through exchange. In the first case, exchange is mainly an exchange between men & nature, an exchange in which the labour of one is swapped for the products of the other; in the second case, exchange between men themselves predominates. In the first case, average human intelligence is adequate, physical and intellectual activity are still not separated; in the second case, the division between intellectual & physical labour must already be realised in practice. In the first case, the domination of the property-holders over the non-property-holder can rest on personal relationships, on a kind of community; in the second case it must have taken on a material form in something else, money. In the first case, small-scale industry comes into existence, albeit defined by the use of the natural instrument of production, & so without the division of labour among different individuals; in the second case, industry works only in & through the division of labour.

Second page on printer's sheet '84' (in Engels's sequence), numbered 41 by Marx

Hitherto we have proceeded from the instruments of production & have already shown here the necessity of private property for certain stages of industry. In *industrie extractive*[1] ~~labour coincides~~ private property still wholly coincides with labour; in small-scale industry & all agriculture up to now property is ~~necessarily~~ the necessary consequence of the instruments of production to hand; in large-scale industry ~~occurs~~ the contradiction between the instrument of production & private property is its very product, for the creation of which {contradiction} ~~if~~ it {industry} ~~is~~ must already be highly developed. Therefore only with it {industry} is the transformation of private property possible.

The most significant division between material & intellectual labour is the separation of city & countryside. The opposition between city & countryside commences with the transition from barbarism to civilisation, from   , from the locality to the
tribal life into the state
nation,
              & persists throughout the whole history

---

1. For example, hunting, fishing, mining; see CW 5, p. 592, n. 28.

Second page on printer's sheet '84' (in Engels's sequence), numbered 41 by Marx

Hitherto we have proceeded from the instruments of production & have already shown here the necessity of private property for certain stages of industry. In *industrie extractive*[1] private property still wholly coincides with labour; in small-scale industry & all agriculture up to now property is the necessary consequence of the instruments of production to hand; in large-scale industry the contradiction between the instrument of production & private property is its very product, for the creation of which {contradiction} it {industry} must already be highly developed. Therefore only with it {industry} is the transformation of private property possible.

The most significant division between material & intellectual labour is the separation of city & countryside. The opposition between city & countryside commences with the transition from barbarism to civilisation, from tribal life into the state, from the locality to the nation & persists throughout the whole history

---

1. For example, hunting, fishing, mining; see CW 5, p. 592, n. 28.

Second page on printer's sheet '84' (in Engels's sequence), numbered 41 by Marx

of civilisation up to the present day (the Anti-Corn Law League). – With the city there arises at the same time the necessity of administration, police, taxation etc., in short of {*insertion*} the community & hence politics in general.{*end insertion*} Here ~~we first see the two great classes~~ we first see the division of the population into two great classes, which rests directly on the division between labour & the instruments of production ~~of the prev{ious}~~. The city is already in fact the concentration of ~~produ{ction}~~ population, of instruments of production, of capital, of pleasures, of needs, while the countryside brings into view precisely the opposite fact, isolation & disaggregation. The opposition between city & countryside can only exist within the bounds of private property. It is the crudest expression of the subordination of the individual to {*insertion*} the division of labour, to {*end insertion*} a specific activity forced upon him, a subordination which makes the one into a stunted city-animal, makes the other into a stunted country-animal & every day produces afresh the opposition of interests between the two. Here labour is again the main factor, the power *over* individuals, & as long as this exists private property also has

Second page on printer's sheet '84' (in Engels's sequence), numbered 41 by Marx

of civilisation up to the present day (the Anti-Corn Law League). – With the city there arises at the same time the necessity of administration, police, taxation etc., in short of the community & hence politics in general. Here we first see the division of the population into two great classes, which rests directly on the division between labour & the instruments of production. The city is already in fact the concentration of population, of instruments of production, of capital, of pleasures, of needs, while the countryside brings into view precisely the opposite fact, isolation & disaggregation. The opposition between city & countryside can only exist within the bounds of private property. It is the crudest expression of the subordination of the individual to the division of labour, to a specific activity forced upon him, a subordination which makes the one into a stunted city-animal, makes the other into a stunted country-animal & every day produces afresh the opposition of interests between the two. Here labour is again the main factor, the power *over* individuals, & as long as this exists private property also has

Second page on printer's sheet '84' (in Engels's sequence), numbered 41 by Marx

to exist. The transformation of the opposition
between city & countryside is one of the first

Second page on printer's sheet '84' (in Engels's sequence), numbered 41 by Marx

to exist. The transformation of the opposition
between city & countryside is one of the first

Third page on printer's sheet '84' (in Engels's sequence), numbered 42 by Marx

conditions of community, a condition which once again depends on a mass of material presuppositions & ~~with which~~ which cannot be fulfilled by a mere act of will, as anyone can see at a glance (these conditions have still to be set out {here}). The separation between city & countryside can also be understood as the separation between capital & landed property, as the beginning of an existence & development of capital independent of landed property, {the beginning} of property ~~of which that~~ that has its basis simply in labour & in exchange.

~~Now we come to our example.~~ In the cities, which were not preserved intact from earlier historical periods but were ~~only~~ formed anew by emancipated serfs, the particular labour of any one of them was his sole property apart from the small capital he brought with him, consisting almost entirely of the necessary hand tools. Competition among the runaway serfs who were continually arriving in the city, ~~the necessity~~ the continuing war of the countryside against the cities & hence the necessity for an organised municipal armed force, the bond of common

conditions of community, a condition which once again depends on a mass of material presuppositions & which cannot be fulfilled by a mere act of will, as anyone can see at a glance (these conditions have still to be set out {here}). The separation between city & countryside can also be understood as the separation between capital & landed property, as the beginning of an existence & development of capital independent of landed property, {the beginning} of property that has its basis simply in labour & in exchange.

In the cities, which were not preserved intact from earlier historical periods but were formed anew by emancipated serfs, the particular labour of any one of them was his sole property apart from the small capital he brought with him, consisting almost entirely of the necessary hand tools. Competition among the runaway serfs who were continually arriving in the city, the continuing war of the countryside against the cities & hence the necessity for an organised municipal armed force, the bond of common property in a

Third page on printer's sheet '84' (in Engels's sequence), numbered 42 by Marx

property in a particular kind of labour, {*insertion*} {*further insertion*} the necessity of common buildings for selling their commodities at a time when craftsmen were simultaneously traders, & the consequent exclusion of those without status from these buildings {*end further insertion*}, the opposition of interests between the individual crafts themselves, the necessity of protection ~~against~~ for their ~~with time~~ hard-won skills {*end insertion*} and the feudal organisation of the whole countryside ~~led~~ were the causes of the unification of the labourers in each craft into guilds. {*insertion*} We do not need to go any further here into the manifold modifications of the guild system, which arise through later historical developments. {*end insertion*} The flight of the serfs into the cities ~~came without interruption during the whole of the middle ages~~ took place without interruption during the whole of the middle ages. The serfs, persecuted in the countryside ~~before their lords~~ by their lords, came one by one into the cities where they found an organised ~~commons~~ community against which they were powerless & ~~where~~ within which they had ~~to make do with~~ to subordinate themselves to a status which determined the particular kind of labour, the necessity of common buildings for selling their commodities at a time when craftsmen were simultaneously traders, & the consequent exclusion of those without status from these buildings, the opposition of interests between the individual crafts themselves, the necessity of protection for their hard-won skills and the feudal organisation of the whole countryside were the causes of the unification of the labourers in each craft into guilds. We do not need to go any further here into the manifold modifications of the guild system, which arise through later historical developments. The flight of the serfs into the cities took place without interruption during the whole of the middle ages. The serfs, persecuted in the countryside by their lords, came one by one into the cities where they found an organised community against which they were powerless & within which they had to subordinate themselves to a status which determined the demand for their labour & the

Third page on printer's sheet '84' (in Engels's sequence), numbered 42 by Marx

demand for their labour & the interest of their organised municipal competitors. On arrival the individual labourer could never get much power because if his labour was of the guild type ~~that had to be learned~~ the guildmaster took them over and & organised them according to their interest, or, if their labour ~~in many cases~~ did not have to be learned, hence was not compatible with the guilds, it was rather daily wage labour that was never going to get organised, hence remaining unorganised rabble. The need for daily wage labour in the cities created the rabble. – These cities were true "unions"[1] called into existence by immediate

---

1. A satirical reference to Stirner's voluntary "unions" of "egoists"; see CW 5, p. 592, n. 30.

Third page on printer's sheet '84' (in Engels's sequence), numbered 42 by Marx

interest of their organised municipal competitors. On arrival the individual labourer could never get much power because if his labour was of the guild type that had to be learned the guildmaster took them over and & organised them according to their interest, or, if their labour did not have to be learned, hence was not compatible with the guilds, it was rather daily wage labour that was never going to get organised, hence remaining unorganised rabble. The need for daily wage labour in the cities created the rabble. – These cities were true "unions"[1] called into existence by immediate

---

1. A satirical reference to Stirner's voluntary "unions" of "egoists"; see CW 5, p. 592, n. 30.

Fourth page on printer's sheet '84' (in Engels's sequence), numbered 43 by Marx

need to provide for the protection of property, & to multiply ~~their~~ the means of production & means for defending the individual members. The rabble of these cities was ~~through its~~ devoid of all power because it consisted of individuals alien to one another, coming together one by one, standing unorganised against an organised power armed for battle which surveys them with intent. The journeymen & apprentices in each craft were organised as best suited the interest of the master; ~~they the journeymen of a they were again split up among themselves because once again the journeymen of a different master opposed one another within one and the same craft~~ the patriarchal relation between them and their masters gave to the latter a dual power, on one side in their direct influence on the whole life of the journeyman & then for the journeymen who worked for the same master there was an actual bond holding them together against the journeymen of another master & making divisions between them; & finally the journeymen were already tied to the existing order through the interest which they

Fourth page on printer's sheet '84' (in Engels's sequence), numbered 43 by Marx

need to provide for the protection of property, & to multiply the means of production & means for defending the individual members. The rabble of these cities was devoid of all power because it consisted of individuals alien to one another, coming together one by one, standing unorganised against an organised power armed for battle which surveys them with intent. The journeymen & apprentices in each craft were organised as best suited the interest of the master; the patriarchal relation between them and their masters gave to the latter a dual power, on one side in their direct influence on the whole life of the journeyman & then for the journeymen who worked for the same master there was an actual bond holding them together against the journeymen of another master & making divisions between them; & finally the journeymen were already tied to the existing order through the interest which they

Fourth page on printer's sheet '84' (in Engels's sequence), numbered 43 by Marx

had in becoming masters themselves. While the rabble at least rose up against the whole civic order, this remained ineffective on account of their powerlessness, whereas the journeymen only got to minor acts of resistance within individual guilds, consistent with the guild system itself. {*insertion*} The great uprisings of the middle ages all proceeded from the countryside but in any case remained totally ineffective because of the disaggregation & consequent ignorance of the peasantry. {*end insertion*} –

Capital in these cities was naturally developed ~~specifically medieval estate~~ capital, consisting ~~of a house~~ of housing ~~&~~, hand tools & a naturally developed clientele handed down over generations, & {it} had to be inherited by sons from fathers because of undeveloped economic exchange & insufficient circulation ~~&~~ which made it unrealisable. This capital, unlike modern capital, was not assessable in monetary terms for investment indifferently in this or that venture, but rather it directly coincided with the specific labour of its possessor, was utterly inseparable ~~capital~~ from it & in that way {was} <u>medieval estate</u> capital. –

Fourth page on printer's sheet '84' (in Engels's sequence), numbered 43 by Marx

had in becoming masters themselves. While the rabble at least rose up against the whole civic order, this remained ineffective on account of their powerlessness, whereas the journeymen only got to minor acts of resistance within individual guilds, consistent with the guild system itself. The great uprisings of the middle ages all proceeded from the countryside but in any case remained totally ineffective because of the disaggregation & consequent ignorance of the peasantry. –

Capital in these cities was naturally developed capital, consisting of housing, hand tools & a naturally developed clientele handed down over generations, & {it} had to be inherited by sons from fathers because of undeveloped economic exchange & insufficient circulation which made it unrealisable. This capital, unlike modern capital, was not assessable in monetary terms for investment indifferently in this or that venture, but rather it directly coincided with the specific labour of its possessor, was utterly inseparable from it & in that way {was} <u>medieval estate</u> capital. –

Fourth page on printer's sheet '84' (in Engels's sequence), numbered 43 by Marx

In these cities the ~~lab{our}~~ division of labour was ~~st{ill}~~

In these cities the division of labour was

First page on printer's sheet '85' (in Engels's sequence), numbered 44 by Marx

still very little
as yet developed between the
individual guilds & in the guilds themselves
not at all between the individual labourers.
Every labourer had to be accomplished in a
whole range of tasks, had to be able to make
everything that could be made with his tools;
the limited interrelations of & the weak
, the
connections between individual cities
dearth of population and restricted demand
did
further
not allow division of labour to arise &
hence every man who wanted to become a
master had to be proficient over the whole of
his craft. Hence with the craftsmen of the
middle ages we still find an interest in their
specialised labour & in skilfulness which
could rise as far as a certain narrow sense of
artistry. In that way, however, every medieval
craftsman was wholly wrapped up in his
labour, had a relationship of agreeable
servitude to it & was stood & was much more
subordinated to it than the modern labourer for
whom labour is a matter of indifference.

The next extension in the division of
labour was the separation of production from

First page on printer's sheet '85' (in Engels's sequence), numbered 44 by Marx

as yet still very little developed between the individual guilds & in the guilds themselves not at all between the individual labourers. Every labourer had to be accomplished in a whole range of tasks, had to be able to make everything that could be made with his tools; the limited interrelations of & the weak connections between individual cities, the dearth of population and restricted demand did not allow further division of labour to arise & hence every man who wanted to become a master had to be proficient over the whole of his craft. Hence with the craftsmen of the middle ages we still find an interest in their specialised labour & in skilfulness which could rise as far as a certain narrow sense of artistry. In that way, however, every medieval craftsman was wholly wrapped up in his labour, had a relationship of agreeable servitude to it & was much more subordinated to it than the modern labourer for whom labour is a matter of indifference.

The next extension in the division of labour was the separation of production from

First page on printer's sheet '85' (in Engels's sequence), numbered 44 by Marx

exchange, the formation of a ~~spe{cialised}~~
particular class of merchants, a ~~div{ision}~~
separation which had been handed down in the
                                   (and among
cities that history has preserved
other things with the Jews)
                                   & appeared very
quickly in newly formed ones. Here there is
the possibility of a trade connection going
beyond the ~~immediate~~ nearby surroundings, a
possibility the realisation of which depends on
the existing means of communication, the state
of public safety in the countryside as
conditioned by political relations (in the whole
                       as everyone knows
of the middle ages   merchants
travelled in armed caravans) & on the
rougher or more developed needs of the area
that is open to trade, as ~~conditioned~~
                                    at the time.
conditioned by the level of culture
– With exchange vested in a particular class,
                       by the merchants
with the extension of trade
beyond the immediate purview of the city,
~~with the there enters~~ there arises ~~the connec{tion}~~ at the same time a reciprocity
between production and interchange. The
cities enter ~~exchange from their isolation,~~

First page on printer's sheet '85' (in Engels's sequence), numbered 44 by Marx

exchange, the formation of a particular class of merchants, a separation which had been handed down in the cities that history has preserved (and among other things with the Jews) & appeared very quickly in newly formed ones. Here there is the possibility of a trade connection going beyond the nearby surroundings, a possibility the realisation of which depends on the existing means of communication, the state of public safety in the countryside as conditioned by political relations (in the whole of the middle ages, as everyone knows, merchants travelled in armed caravans) & on the rougher or more developed needs of the area that is open to trade, as conditioned by the level of culture at the time. – With exchange vested in a particular class, with the extension of trade by the merchants beyond the immediate purview of the city, there arises at the same time a reciprocity between production and interchange. The cities enter into relations <u>with one another</u>,

First page on printer's sheet '85' (in Engels's sequence), numbered 44 by Marx

~~as[sociating]~~ into relations <u>with one another,</u> ~~the instruments of production of one~~ new tools are brought from one city into another, & the division between production & exchange soon brings forth a new division of production between

First page on printer's sheet '85' (in Engels's sequence), numbered 44 by Marx

new tools are brought from one city into
another, & the division between production &
exchange soon brings forth a new division of
production between

Second page on printer's sheet '85' (in Engels's sequence), numbered 45 by Marx

the individual towns, each of which soon exploits its leading sector of industry. The initial limitations ~~of every~~ of the locality gradually begin to break down. –

It depends solely on the extension of trade ~~the extent to which~~ whether or not the powers of production secured in a locality, particularly inventions, are lost for later development. As long as there is still no trade proceeding beyond the immediate vicinity, every invention has to be made in each locality ~~anew~~ in particular, & ~~only~~ mere accidents, like incursions of barbarian peoples, ~~wa{rs}~~ even the usual sort of wars, are sufficient to bring a ~~mass~~ country with ~~hard-won~~ developed productive forces & ~~inventions for a long time & again~~ requirements to such a state that it has to start over again from the beginning. In early history every invention had to be made afresh every day, & be made independently in every locality. How little even developed productive forces are safe from complete destruction by their ~~quite~~ proportionate extension of trade is proved by ~~the history of~~ the Phoenicians, whose inventions were lost through the expulsion of their nation from

Second page on printer's sheet '85' (in Engels's sequence), numbered 45 by Marx

the individual towns, each of which soon exploits its leading sector of industry. The initial limitations of the locality gradually begin to break down. –

It depends solely on the extension of trade whether or not the powers of production secured in a locality, particularly inventions, are lost for later development. As long as there is still no trade proceeding beyond the immediate vicinity, every invention has to be made in each locality in particular, & mere accidents, like incursions of barbarian peoples, even the usual sort of wars, are sufficient to bring a country with developed productive forces & requirements to such a state that it has to start over again from the beginning. In early history every invention had to be made afresh every day, & be made independently in every locality. How little even a developed productive forces are safe from complete destruction by their proportionate extension of trade is proved by the Phoenicians, whose inventions were lost through the expulsion of their nation from trade, their conquest by

Second page on printer's sheet '85' (in Engels's sequence), numbered 45 by Marx

trade, ~~& their conquest by Alexander~~ their conquest by Alexander & the subsequent long period of decline ~~of that natio{n}~~. {*insertion*} {It was} just the same in the middle ages – e.g. stained glass production.{*end insertion*} Only when trade has become worldwide & ~~a competitive struggle of all n{ations}~~ on the basis of large-scale industry & all nations are drawn into the competitive struggle is the permanence of hard-won productive forces secured.

 The division of labour between the different cities had as its next consequence the development of manufacturing, where the branch of production had outgrown the guild system. The first flush of manufacturing – in
   and later in Flanders
Italy   – had trade with foreign nations for its historical presupposition. In other countries – e.g. England & France – manufacturing was limited at the beginning to the domestic market. Beyond the presuppositions given above, ~~general~~ manufacturing, also an advanced concentration of population – particularly in the countryside – and of capital, which began to accumulate in individual hands partly in the guilds
     in spite of their

Second page on printer's sheet '85' (in Engels's sequence), numbered 45 by Marx

Alexander & the subsequent long period of decline. {It was} just the same in the middle ages – e.g. stained glass production. Only when trade has become worldwide & on the basis of large-scale industry & all nations are drawn into the competitive struggle is the permanence of hard-won productive forces secured.

The division of labour between the different cities had as its next consequence the development of manufacturing, where the branch of production had outgrown the guild system. The first flush of manufacturing – in Italy and later in Flanders – had trade with foreign nations for its historical presupposition. In other countries – e.g. England & France – manufacturing was limited at the beginning to the domestic market. Beyond the presuppositions given above, manufacturing, also an advanced concentration of population – particularly in the countryside – and of capital, which began to accumulate in individual hands partly in the guilds in spite of their law, partly with the

partly with the merchants
laws,   as presupposed.

Second page on printer's sheet '85' (in Engels's sequence), numbered 45 by Marx

merchants   as presupposed.

Third page on printer's sheet '85' (in Engels's sequence), numbered 46 by Marx

The kind of labour that from the outset presupposed a machine, even if only of the crudest kind, very quickly revealed itself to be the most capable of development. Weaving, previously pursued in the countryside by the peasantry as an ancillary activity in order to procure their necessary clothing, was the first labour to obtain an impetus & further development through the extension of trade. Weaving ~~is~~ was the first & remained by far the leading form of manufacture. The rising population's rising demand for articles of clothing, the initial accumulation & mobilisation of ~~capi{tal}~~ natural capital through accelerated circulation, the demand for luxury products elicited in this way & generally ~~increa{sed}~~ encouraged by the gradual extension of trade, gave to weaving a quantitative & qualitative impetus which tore it away from previous forms of production. ~~To the The~~ Alongside the ~~weaving~~ peasantry, engaged in weaving for their own use, ~~evermore~~ persisting in this & still ~~themselves~~ doing so, there arose a new class of ~~export{ers}~~ weavers in the cities whose cloth

Third page on printer's sheet '85' (in Engels's sequence), numbered 46 by Marx

The kind of labour that from the outset presupposed a machine, even if only of the crudest kind, very quickly revealed itself to be the most capable of development. Weaving, previously pursued in the countryside by the peasantry as an ancillary activity in order to procure their necessary clothing, was the first labour to obtain an impetus & further development through the extension of trade. Weaving was the first & remained by far the leading form of manufacture. The rising population's rising demand for articles of clothing, the initial accumulation & mobilisation of natural capital through accelerated circulation, the demand for luxury products elicited in this way & generally encouraged by the gradual extension of trade, gave to weaving a quantitative & qualitative impetus which tore it away from previous forms of production. Alongside the peasantry, engaged in weaving for their own use, persisting in this & still doing so, there arose a new class of weavers in the cities whose cloth

was destined for the whole of the domestic market
 & oftentimes also for the foreign one. – Weaving, a form of labour demanding little skill for the most part & soon falling into countless branches was resistant ~~to the g{uild}~~ by its very nature to the fetters of the guild. Hence weaving was also mostly carried on in villages & market sites without guild organisation, which gradually turned into cities & indeed soon turned into the most flourishing cities in the country. – With guild-free ~~org{anisation} weaving came~~ manufacture the property system also changed at once. The first step beyond natural-estate capital ~~was the proper{ty} the capital of the the arrival of the merchants~~ took place with
                                            was
the arrival of merchants whose capital mobile from the outset, capital in the modern sense, in so far as ~~this under present relations~~ one can speak of this under the relations existing at the time. The second step ~~was~~ came with manufacture which again mobilised a mass of natural capital & ~~the mass~~ generally increased the mass of mobile capital as opposed to the naturally developed kind. – At the same time manufacture was a refuge for the peasantry from the guilds which excluded

was destined for the whole of the domestic market & oftentimes also for the foreign one. – Weaving, a form of labour demanding little skill for the most part & soon falling into countless branches was resistant by its very nature to the fetters of the guild. Hence weaving was also mostly carried on in villages & market sites without guild organisation, which gradually turned into cities & indeed soon turned into the most flourishing cities in the country. – With guild-free manufacture the property system also changed at once. The first step beyond natural-estate capital took place with the arrival of merchants whose capital was mobile from the outset, capital in the modern sense, in so far as one can speak of this under the relations existing at the time. The second step came with manufacture which again mobilised a mass of natural capital & generally increased the mass of mobile capital as opposed to the naturally developed kind. – At the same time manufacture was a refuge for the peasantry from the guilds which excluded them or paid

Third page on printer's sheet '85' (in Engels's sequence), numbered 46 by Marx

them or paid them badly, as earlier the guild-
cities had served a the peasantry as a refuge

Third page on printer's sheet '85' (in Engels's sequence), numbered 46 by Marx

them badly, as earlier the guild-cities had
served the peasantry as a refuge

Fourth page on printer's sheet '85' (in Engels's sequence), numbered 47 by Marx

from the landowners. ~~With manufacture the relationship of worker to c{apitalist} employer changed in any case. In place of patriarchal~~

~~The~~

With the onset of manufacture there was at the same time a period of vagabondage ,~~end~~ prompted by the dissolution of feudal retinues, the disbanding of armies thrown together to serve kings against their vassals, & by improved agriculture & the transformation of tracts of farmland into grazing for livestock. This shows just how vagabondage exactly coincides with ~~the abo{lition}~~ the dissolution of feudalism. By the thirteenth century isolated episodes of ~~these~~ this kind occur, general and persistent vagabondage only arrives at the end of the ~~17th~~ ~~14th~~ 15th and beginning of the ~~18th~~ ~~15th~~ 16th centuries. ~~The~~ These vagabonds, who were so numerous that Henry VIII of England, among others, had 72,000 of them hanged, were only brought into employment with the greatest difficulty & through extreme necessity, & only after lengthy resistance. The rapid rise of manufactures, particularly in England, absorbed them gradually. –

With manufacture the various nations come

Fourth page on printer's sheet '85' (in Engels's sequence), numbered 47 by Marx

from the landowners.

With the onset of manufacture there was at the same time a period of vagabondage prompted by the dissolution of feudal retinues, the disbanding of armies thrown together to serve kings against their vassals, by improved agriculture & the transformation of tracts of farmland into grazing for livestock. This shows just how vagabondage exactly coincides with the dissolution of feudalism. By the thirteenth century isolated episodes of this kind occur, general and persistent vagabondage only arrives at the end of the 15th and beginning of the 16th centuries. These vagabonds, who were so numerous that Henry VIII of England, among others, had 72,000 of them hanged, were only brought into employment with the greatest difficulty & through extreme necessity, & only after lengthy resistance. The rapid rise of manufactures, particularly in England, absorbed them gradually. –   With manufacture the various nations come

With manufacture there arose at the same time an altered relationship of worker to employer. In the guilds a patriarchal relationship between journeyman & master persisted; in manufacture the money-relationship between labourer & capitalist took its place; a relationship which remained tinged with patriarchalism in the country & in small cities, but which in the larger, more properly manufacturing cities lost all patriarchal colouring much earlier.

& the development of Manufacture production generally received an enormous boost through the ~~end~~ extension of trade that arrived with the discovery of the Americas & with the sea route to the East Indies. The ~~new markets, the~~ products newly imported from there, particularly the mass of gold & silver which went into circulation, ~~& totally changed the positioning of classes opposed to one another~~ totally changed the positioning of classes opposed to one another & dealt a hard blow to ~~landed property~~ feudal landed property and to the labourers, the expeditions by adventurers, ~~the~~ colonisation, & above all the extension of the market to a world market, into a relation of competition, in commercial conflict, which ~~itself in wars, protective tariffs & prohibitions~~ was fought out in wars, protective tariffs & prohibitions, whereas in earlier times nations ~~in a~~ had conducted a harmless exchange with one another in so far as they were in contact. Trade thus took on political significance.

Fourth page on printer's sheet '85' (in Engels's sequence), numbered 47 by Marx

With manufacture there arose at the same time an altered relationship of worker to employer. In the guilds a patriarchal relationship between journeyman & master persisted; in manufacture the money-relationship between labourer & capitalist took its place; a relationship which remained tinged with patriarchalism in the country & in small cities, but which in the larger, more properly manufacturing cities lost all patriarchal colouring much earlier.

Manufacture & the development of production generally received an enormous boost through the extension of trade that arrived with the discovery of the Americas & with the sea route to the East Indies. The products newly imported from there, particularly the mass of gold & silver which went into circulation, totally changed the positioning of classes opposed to one another & dealt a hard blow to feudal landed property and to the labourers, the expeditions by adventurers, colonisation, & above all the extension of the market to a world market, into a relation of competition, in commercial conflict, which was fought out in wars, protective tariffs & prohibitions, whereas in earlier times nations had conducted a harmless exchange with one another in so far as they were in contact. Trade thus took on political significance.

Fourth page on printer's sheet '85' (in Engels's sequence), numbered 47 by Marx

which had now become possible & was
gaining ever more ground day by day,
produced ~~need{s}~~ a new phase of historical

Fourth page on printer's sheet '85' (in Engels's sequence), numbered 47 by Marx

which had now become possible & was
gaining ever more ground day by day,
produced a new phase of historical

First page on printer's sheet '86' (in Engels's sequence), numbered 48 by Marx

development, which in general we won't pursue any further here. Through the colonisation of newly discovered lands the ~~com{petition}~~ commercial conflict among nations obtained new impetus and proportionately greater extension and bitterness.

The extension of trade & manufacture accelerated the accumulation of ~~capital~~ mobile capital, while in the guilds, ~~the~~ which experienced no stimulus to increase their production, natural capital remained stationary or actually declined. Trade & manufacture created the rich commercial class; small businessmen, who no longer dominated the cities as in earlier times but had to submit ~~under~~ to the domination of rich merchants & manufacturers, were concentrated in the guilds. Hence the decline of the guild as soon as it came into contact with manufacture.

Small businessmen.
Middle class.
Rich commercial class.

The relation of nations to each other in their trade took on two different forms during the epoch that we have been talking about. At the outset the limited quantity of gold & silver in circulation resulted in a prohibition on the export of these metals; & industry, made

First page on printer's sheet '86' (in Engels's sequence), numbered 48 by Marx

development, which in general we won't pursue any further here. Through the colonisation of newly discovered lands the commercial conflict among nations obtained new impetus and proportionately greater extension and bitterness.

The extension of trade & manufacture accelerated the accumulation of mobile capital, while in the guilds, which experienced no stimulus to increase their production, natural capital remained stationary or actually declined. Trade & manufacture created the rich commercial class; small businessmen, who no longer dominated the cities as in earlier times but had to submit to the domination of rich merchants & manufacturers, were concentrated in the guilds. Hence the decline of the guild as soon as it came into contact with manufacture.

Small businessmen.
Middle class.
Rich commercial class.

The relation of nations to each other in their trade took on two different forms during the epoch that we have been talking about. At the outset the limited quantity of gold & silver in circulation resulted in a prohibition on the export of these metals; & industry, made

First page on printer's sheet '86' (in Engels's sequence), numbered 48 by Marx

by the
necessary   need to employ the growing
urban population, and mostly imported from
                give up
abroad, could not   privileges which
                chiefly
could be granted   against foreign
                                merely
competition, and, naturally enough, not
against domestic competition. In these original
prohibitions & customs duties the local
privilege for guilds was extended over the
whole nation. {*insertion*} Customs duties
originated from the tributes that the feudal
lords demanded from merchants passing
through their lands as protection payment
against robbery, tributes that were later
imposed by the cities in the same way &
which, with the arrival of the modern state,
were the handiest means for the treasury to
raise money. {*end insertion*} –

The discovery appearance of
American gold & silver on the European
markets, the devel{opment} gradual
development of industry, the rapid boost for
trade & the rise of the non-guild commercial
class & of money generated in this way gave
these measures another significance. The state,
which was no longer every day less and less
able to be without money, now retained the

First page on printer's sheet '86' (in Engels's sequence), numbered 48 by Marx

necessary by the need to employ the growing urban population, and mostly imported from abroad, could not give up privileges which could be granted chiefly against foreign competition, and, naturally enough, not merely against domestic competition. In these original prohibitions the local privilege for guilds was extended over the whole nation. Customs duties originated from the tributes that the feudal lords demanded from merchants passing through their lands as protection payment against robbery, tributes that were later imposed by the cities in the same way & which, with the arrival of the modern state, were the handiest means for the treasury to raise money. –

The appearance of American gold & silver on the European markets, the gradual development of industry, the rapid boost for trade & the rise of the non-guild commercial class & of money generated in this way gave these measures another significance. The state, which was every day less and less able to be without money, now retained the

First page on printer's sheet '86' (in Engels's sequence), numbered 48 by Marx

prohibition on the export of gold & silver out of fiscal considerations; the commercial class, for which this mass of money, newly cast onto the market, was the main object of speculative buying, were completely content ~~and in place of their previous privileges~~ with this; prior privileges became a source of income for the government & were sold for money; in customs law export duties sprang up, which ~~only hemmed industry in~~, presenting only a hindrance to the course of industry,

First page on printer's sheet '86' (in Engels's sequence), numbered 48 by Marx

prohibition on the export of gold & silver out of fiscal considerations; the commercial class, for which this mass of money, newly cast onto the market, was the main object of speculative buying, were completely content with this; prior privileges became a source of income for the government & were sold for money; in customs law export duties sprang up, which, presenting only a hindrance to the course of industry,

Second page on printer's sheet '86' (in Engels's sequence), numbered 49 by Marx

had a purely fiscal purpose. –

The second period began in the middle of the seventeenth century, & continued right up to the end of the eighteenth. Trade ~~had~~ & shipping had spread more quickly than manufacture, which played a secondary role; began to be heavy consumers, colonies ~~the world market that was opening up was bid for by individual nations who struggled for its exploitation~~ through long wars individual nations took their shares in the world market that was opening up. This period begins with the navigation laws[1] and colonial monopolies. Competition among nations was excluded through tariffs, prohibitions, treaties ~~& in the last instance~~ as much as possible, & in the last instance the competitive struggle was pursued and decided through wars (especially sea wars). ~~The sea trade~~ The most powerful nation on the sea, the English, maintained superiority in trade & ~~ind{ustry}~~ manufacture. Here {we see} a concentration in one country already. – Manufacture was continually protected by

---

1. Limiting import/export shipments to/from a country to ships of that country only.

Second page on printer's sheet '86' (in Engels's sequence), numbered 49 by Marx

had a purely fiscal purpose. –

The second period began in the middle of the seventeenth century, & continued right up to the end of the eighteenth. Trade & shipping had spread more quickly than manufacture, which played a secondary role; colonies began to be heavy consumers, through long wars individual nations took their shares in the world market that was opening up. This period begins with the navigation laws[1] and colonial monopolies. Competition among nations was excluded through tariffs, prohibitions, treaties as much as possible, & in the last instance the competitive struggle was pursued and decided through wars (especially sea wars). The most powerful nation on the sea, the English, maintained superiority in trade & manufacture. Here {we see} a concentration in one country already. – Manufacture was continually protected by

---

1. Limiting import/export shipments to/from a country to ships of that country only.

Second page on printer's sheet '86' (in Engels's sequence), numbered 49 by Marx

protective tariffs in the home market ~~& in foreign trade as much as possible by~~ by monopolies in the ~~differential tariffs~~, colonial market & as much as possible in the foreign {market} by differential tariffs. The working up of materials produced in a ~~hom{e}~~ country itself (wool & linen in England, silk in France) was encouraged & that of imported materials downgraded or suppressed (cotton in England). The nation that was dominant in maritime trade & colonial ~~domination~~ power naturally secured for itself the greatest quantitative & qualitative extension of ~~industry~~ manufacture. ~~Small~~ Manufacture ~~can~~ could not in general get by without protection since with the slightest change taking place in another country it ~~under encouraging unencouraging conditions~~ can ~~just~~ lose its markets & be ruined; it can easily be introduced into a country under reasonably encouraging conditions & for that reason just as easily destroyed. At the same time, through the way that it was pursued, particularly in the 18th century in the countryside, it is so interwoven with the living conditions of a no ~~nation~~ great mass of individuals that

the export of raw materials produced locally {was} forbidden (wool in England)

Second page on printer's sheet '86' (in Engels's sequence), numbered 49 by Marx

protective tariffs in the home market, by monopolies in the colonial market & as much as possible in the foreign {market} by differential tariffs. The working up of materials produced in a country itself (wool & linen in England, silk in France) was encouraged & that of imported materials downgraded or suppressed (cotton in England). The nation that was dominant in maritime trade & colonial power naturally secured for itself the greatest quantitative & qualitative extension of manufacture. Manufacture could not in general get by without protection since with the slightest change taking place in another country it can lose its markets & be ruined; it can easily be introduced into a country under reasonably encouraging conditions & for that reason just as easily destroyed. At the same time, through the way that it was pursued, particularly in the 18th century in the countryside, it is so interwoven with the living conditions of a great mass of individuals that no

the export of raw materials produced locally {was} forbidden (wool in England)

Second page on printer's sheet '86' (in Engels's sequence), numbered 49 by Marx

country may risk
their existence by bringing
into
free competition   play. Hence in so far as it
{manufacture} succeeds in exporting, it
depends wholly on the expansion or
contraction of trade & exercises a very limited
and proportional reciprocal effect. Hence its
secondary [role] & hence the ~~dominance~~
influence of [the mer]chants in the eighteenth
century.

Second page on printer's sheet '86' (in Engels's sequence), numbered 49 by Marx

country may risk their existence by bringing free competition into play. Hence in so far as it {manufacture} succeeds in exporting, it depends wholly on the expansion or contraction of trade & exercises a very limited and proportional reciprocal effect. Hence its secondary [role] & hence the influence of [the mer]chants in the eighteenth century.

Third page on printer's sheet '86' (in Engels's sequence), numbered 50 by Marx

More than anyone else it was the merchants and particularly the ship-owners who pressed for state protection and monopolies; the manufacturers ~~got their~~ also demanded & indeed received protection, but continually ranked below the merchants in political significance. The trading cities, especially the seaports, became {somewhat} more civilised & highly bourgeois, while in the factory towns the crudest petty-bourgeois outlook persisted. See Aikin pp[1] The eighteenth century was the century of trade ~~which as~~. Pinto says this explicitly: "Trade is the mania of the century"; and "For some time now the talk is only of trade, navigation and the navy."[2] –

Although significantly accelerated, the movement of capital still remained relatively slow. The fragmentation of the world market into individual sectors, each of which was ~~closed off~~ exploited by a particular nation, the {*insertion*} suppression of competition among the nations themselves, {*end insertion*} the

---

1. John Aikin, *A Description of the Country from Thirty to Forty Miles round Manchester* (London, 1795); cf. CW 5, pp. 71 n. a, 627.
2. Isaac Pinto, *Traité de la circulation et du crédit* (Amsterdam, 1771); cf. CW 5, pp. 71 n. b, 72 n. a, 637.

Third page on printer's sheet '86' (in Engels's sequence), numbered 50 by Marx

More than anyone else it was the merchants and particularly the ship-owners who pressed for state protection and monopolies; the manufacturers also demanded & indeed received protection, but continually ranked below the merchants in political significance. The trading cities, especially the seaports, became somewhat more civilised & highly bourgeois, while in the factory towns the crudest petty-bourgeois outlook persisted. See Aikin pp[1] The eighteenth century was the century of trade. Pinto says this explicitly: "Trade is the mania of the century"; and "For some time now the talk is only of trade, navigation and the navy."[2] –

Although significantly accelerated, the movement of capital still remained relatively slow. The fragmentation of the world market into individual sectors, each of which was exploited by a particular nation, the suppression of competition among the nations themselves, the hitches in

---

1. John Aikin, *A Description of the Country from Thirty to Forty Miles round Manchester* (London, 1795); cf. CW 5, pp. 71 n. a, 627.
2. Isaac Pinto, *Traité de la circulation et du crédit* (Amsterdam, 1771); cf. CW 5, pp. 71 n. b, 72 n. a, 637.

Third page on printer's sheet '86' (in Engels's sequence), numbered 50 by Marx

hitches in production itself & the use of money, ~~from the dev{elopment}still~~ only then developing beyond its first stage, impeded {commercial} circulation. The consequence of this was a haggling, crudely small-minded mentality which still stuck to all the merchants & to the whole business of being in trade. ~~The factory{owners} To be sure~~ In comparison with the manufacturers & above all with the craftsmen, they were certainly high-bourgeois {or} bourgeois {but} in comparison with the merchants & industrialists of the next period they remained ~~minor bour{geois}~~ petty-bourgeois. See A. Smith.[1] –

This period is also distinguished by the abolition of the ban on exporting gold & silver, the rise of currency exchange, of banks, of state debt, of paper money, of speculation in stocks & shares, ~~&~~ of forward-trading ~~generally~~ in all articles, & of the development of the money-system in general. Capital again lost a large part of the natural character still adhering to it.

The concentration of trade & of manufacture in one country, England, ~~through~~

---

1. Adam Smith, *An Inquiry into the Nature and Causes of the Wealth of Nations*, 2 vols (London, 1776); CW 5, pp. 72 n. b, 639.

production itself & the use of money, only then developing beyond its first stage, impeded {commercial} circulation. The consequence of this was a haggling, crudely small-minded mentality which still stuck to all the merchants & to the whole business of being in trade. In comparison with the manufacturers & above all with the craftsmen, they were certainly high-bourgeois {or} bourgeois {but} in comparison with the merchants & industrialists of the next period they remained petty-bourgeois. See A. Smith.[1] –

This period is also distinguished by the abolition of the ban on exporting gold & silver, the rise of currency exchange, of banks, of state debt, of paper money, of speculation in stocks & shares, of forward-trading in all articles, & of the development of the money-system in general. Capital again lost a large part of the natural character still adhering to it.

The concentration of trade & of manufacture in one country, England, which

---

1. Adam Smith, *An Inquiry into the Nature and Causes of the Wealth of Nations*, 2 vols (London, 1776); CW 5, pp. 72 n b, 639.

Third page on printer's sheet '86' (in Engels's sequence), numbered 50 by Marx

~~the quickly~~ which developed without check in the seventeenth century, gradually created for
                    a relative share
this country   in the world market ~~so far as a~~ & with that a demand for the manufactured products of this country that could no longer be satisfied by the industrial forces of production developed up to then. This demand, causing productive forces to grow beyond that point, was the driving force which called forth the third

Third page on printer's sheet '86' (in Engels's sequence), numbered 50 by Marx

developed without check in the seventeenth century, gradually created for this country a relative share in the world market & with that a demand for the manufactured products of this country that could no longer be satisfied by the industrial forces of production developed up to then. This demand, causing productive forces to grow beyond that point, was the driving force which called forth the third

Fourth page on printer's sheet '86' (in Engels's sequence), numbered 51 by Marx

period of private property since the middle ages in that it produced large-scale industry – the turning of elemental productive powers to industrial purposes, machinery & the most other extensive division of labour. The conditions for this new phase already existed in England – freedom of competition throughout the nation, the development of theoretical mechanics {*insertion*} (in France and England mechanics as perfected by Newton ~~in {the} 18{th century}~~ was in general the most popular science) {*end insertion*} pp. (Free competition throughout a nation ~~was won everywhere~~ must be won everywhere by means of a revolution – 1640 & 1688 in England, 1789 in France). Competition soon forced every country {*insertion*} which wanted to retain its historical role {*end insertion*} to protect its manufactures through renewed regulatory tariffs (the old tariff barriers no longer worked in the face of large-scale industry) and soon after to put large-scale industry under a protective regime. In spite of these protective measures large-scale industry universalised

period of private property since the middle ages in that it produced large-scale industry – the turning of elemental productive powers to industrial purposes, machinery & the most extensive division of labour. The other conditions for this new phase already existed in England – freedom of competition throughout the nation, the development of theoretical mechanics (in France and England mechanics as perfected by Newton was in general the most popular science) pp. (Free competition throughout a nation must be won everywhere by means of a revolution – 1640 & 1688 in England, 1789 in France). Competition soon forced every country which wanted to retain its historical role to protect its manufactures through renewed regulatory tariffs (the old tariff barriers no longer worked in the face of large-scale industry) and soon after to put large-scale industry under a protective regime. In spite of these protective measures large-scale industry universalised competition (it is the freedom of

Fourth page on printer's sheet '86' (in Engels's sequence), numbered 51 by Marx

competition {*insertion*} (it is the freedom of trade in practice, a protective tariff is only a palliative for it, a form of resistance *within* the means of free trade) {*end insertion*}, set up communication and the modern world market, took command over trade, ~~& produced rapid economic circulation of capitals which {produced} depend{ence} for that & & central{isation} concentration of capitals~~ transformed all capital into industrial capital & thereby produced rapid economic circulation (the development of the money system) & ~~the~~ centralisation of capital funds. It produced world history for the first time in so far as it made every civilised nation & every individual in them dependent for the satisfaction of their needs on the whole world & abolished the natural up to exclusivity of individual nations that time. It subsumed natural science under capital and took from the division of labour the last semblance of natural development. In general it abolished natural development in so far as this is possible in terms of labour & and {*insertion*} resolved all natural relations into

Through universal competition it forced all individuals to strain their energies to an extreme. It destroyed ideology ~~and where~~, religion, morals &c as much as possible, and where it could not do this, it made them into a palpable lie.

Fourth page on printer's sheet '86' (in Engels's sequence), numbered 51 by Marx

trade in practice, a protective tariff is only a palliative for it, a form of resistance *within* free trade), set up the means of communication and the modern world market, took command over trade, transformed all capital into industrial capital & thereby produced rapid economic circulation (the development of the money system) & centralisation of capital funds. It produced world history for the first time in so far as it made every civilised nation & every individual in them dependent for the satisfaction of their needs on the whole world & abolished the natural exclusivity of individual nations up to that time. It subsumed natural science under capital and took from the division of labour the last semblance of natural development. In general it abolished natural development in so far as this is possible in terms of labour & and resolved all natural relations into money relations. In place of

Through universal competition it forced all individuals to strain their energies to an extreme. It destroyed ideology, religion, morals &c as much as possible, and where it could not do this, it made them into a palpable lie.

Fourth page on printer's sheet '86' (in Engels's sequence), numbered 51 by Marx

money relations.{*end insertion*} In place of naturally developing cities it created large, modern, industrial cities which have sprung up overnight. Wherever it penetrated it destroyed craftwork & all earlier stages of industry in general. It completed the victory of the ci[ty] over the countryside. Its [. . .] is the automatic system. [It pro]duced a mass of pro[ductive] f[orces] for which private prop[erty] became just as much a fetter

Fourth page on printer's sheet '86' (in Engels's sequence), numbered 51 by Marx

naturally developing cities it created large, modern, industrial cities which have sprung up overnight. Wherever it penetrated it destroyed craftwork & all earlier stages of industry in general. It completed the victory of the ci[ty] over the countryside. Its [. . .] is the automatic system. [It pro]duced a mass of pro[ductive] f[orces] for which private prop[erty] became just as much a fetter

First page on printer's sheet '87' (in Engels's sequence), numbered 52 by Marx

as the guild {was} for manufacture & the small-scale country workshop {was} for the developing craft industries. {*insertion*} ~~A great many~~ Under private property these forces of production get only a limited development, and in the majority of cases turn into forces of destruction & a great many of such forces cannot be deployed under private property at all.{*end insertion*} In general it {large-scale industry} produced the same relations between the classes of society everywhere, & in that way abolished the particular features of individual nationalities. And finally while the commercial classes ~~through~~ of every nation ~~through still {having} interests at odds with other nations~~ still retain national interests at odds with one another, ~~creates~~ large-scale industry created a class ~~in all nations~~ which has the same interest in every nation, & through which nationality has already been abolished, {*insertion*} a class which is really rid of the old world in its entirety & stands as opposed to it the same time. For the labourer it makes not only ~~the {relationships}~~ the relationship with the

First page on printer's sheet '87' (in Engels's sequence), numbered 52 by Marx

as the guild {was} for manufacture & the small-scale country workshop {was} for the developing craft industries. Under private property these forces of production get only a limited development, and in the majority of cases turn into forces of destruction & a great many of such forces cannot be deployed under private property at all. In general it {large-scale industry} produced the same relations between the classes of society everywhere, & in that way abolished the particular features of individual nationalities. And finally while the commercial classes of every nation still retain national interests at odds with one another, large-scale industry created a class which has the same interest in every nation, & through which nationality has already been abolished, a class which is really rid of the old world in its entirety & stands as opposed to it the same time. For the labourer it makes not only the relationship with the

First page on printer's sheet '87' (in Engels's sequence), numbered 52 by Marx

capitalist but also labour itself unbearable. {*end insertion*}

It is evident that large-scale industry has not attained the same ~~poi{nt}~~ level of development ~~however in all countries & not every {country} in every locality~~ in every locality. This does ~~uses~~ not hold back the movement of the ~~class~~ proletariat as a class, however, since the proletarians produced by large-scale industry take over leadership of this movement & carry the whole mass along with them & because the workers excluded by large-scale industry are placed in a worse condition of life than the workers in large-scale industry itself. {*insertion*} Countries in which a large-scale industry has developed act in the same way on the more or less non-industrial countries, in so far as these are drawn into ~~while in that way~~ universal competition through world trade. {*end insertion*}

These different forms {of production} are just as much forms for the organisation ~~of prop{erty}~~ of labour & hence of property. In every period a ~~conc{entration}~~ unification of the existing forces of production took place in so far as this became necessary because of demand.

First page on printer's sheet '87' (in Engels's sequence), numbered 52 by Marx

capitalist but also labour itself unbearable.

It is evident that large-scale industry has not attained the same level of development in every locality. This does not hold back the movement of the proletariat as a class, however, since the proletarians produced by large-scale industry take over leadership of this movement & carry the whole mass along with them & because the workers excluded by large-scale industry are placed in a worse condition of life than the workers in large-scale industry itself. Countries in which a large-scale industry has developed act in the same way on the more or less non-industrial countries, in so far as these are drawn into universal competition through world trade.

These different forms {of production} are just as much forms for the organisation of labour & hence of property. In every period a unification of the existing forces of production took place in so far as this became necessary because of demand.

First page on printer's sheet '87' (in Engels's sequence), numbered 52 by Marx

----

The contradiction between the forces of production & the form of trade, which as we have seen has occurred several times in history up to now without ever endangering its ~~true~~ basis must burst out every time into ~~revolution~~ revolutions whereby it ~~reproduces itself together with~~ takes on at the same time different subsidiary the totality of forms such as clashes, clashes between different classes, such as contradiction of consciousness, battle of ideas, political struggle &c. From a narrow point of view one can pick out one of these subsidiary forms & consider it as the ~~real~~ basis of the ~~revolution~~ revolutions, which is all the easier since the individuals from whom the revolutions originated have made up illusions corresponding to their level of development & to the stage of historical itself. development of their own activity

----

Therefore according to our conception, all clashes in history have their origin in the contradiction between the forces of production and the form of

First page on printer's sheet '87' (in Engels's sequence), numbered 52 by Marx

----

The contradiction between the forces of production & the form of trade, which as we have seen has occurred several times in history up to now without ever endangering its basis must burst out every time into revolutions whereby it takes on at the same time different subsidiary forms such as the totality of clashes, clashes between different classes, such as contradiction of consciousness, battle of ideas, political struggle &c. From a narrow point of view one can pick out one of these subsidiary forms & consider it as the basis of the revolutions, which is all the easier since the individuals from whom the revolutions originated have made up illusions corresponding to their level of development & to the stage of historical development of their own activity itself.

Therefore according to our conception, all clashes in history have their origin in the contradiction between the forces of production and the form of

Second page on printer's sheet '87' (in Engels's sequence), numbered 53 by Marx

trade. In general for this contradiction to lead to clashes {in a country} it is not necessary that it be driven to its height. The competition ~~is sufficient~~ with industrially more developed countries that arises from an expanding international trade is sufficient to produce a ~~contradiction~~ similar contradiction even in countries with less developed industry (e.g. the latent proletariat in Germany brought to light by the ~~English~~ competition with English industry).

~~As~~ Competition isolates individuals from one another, not only middle class {*bourgeois*} but ~~also~~ even more the workers {*proletariat*}, in spite of the fact that it brings them together. Hence it is a long time till these individuals ~~are united once more~~ can unite themselves {*insertion*} besides the fact that for this union {*further insertion*} if it is not to be merely local {*end further insertion*} the necessary means, the large-scale industrial cities & the cheap & quick means of communication, must first be produced by large-scale industry,{*end insertion*} & hence every organised power opposed to these isolated individuals, living in relations which daily reproduce the isolation,

Second page on printer's sheet '87' (in Engels's sequence), numbered 53 by Marx

trade. In general for this contradiction to lead to clashes in a country it is not necessary that it be driven to its height. The competition with industrially more developed countries that arises from an expanding international trade is sufficient to produce a similar contradiction even in countries with less developed industry (e.g. the latent proletariat in Germany brought to light by the competition with English industry).

Competition isolates individuals from one another, not only middle class {*bourgeois*} but even more the workers {*proletariat*}, in spite of the fact that it brings them together. Hence it is a long time till these can unite themselves besides the fact that for this union if it is not to be merely local the necessary means, the large-scale industrial cities & the cheap & quick means of communication, must first be produced by large-scale industry & hence every organised power opposed to these isolated individuals, living in relations which daily reproduce the isolation, is only overcome

Second page on printer's sheet '87' (in Engels's sequence), numbered 53 by Marx

is only overcome after long struggles. To demand the opposite would be just like demanding that competition should not exist in a specific historical period ~~&~~ or that individuals should expunge from their brains the relations over ~~over of which which they as isolated individuals have no control~~ which they as isolated individuals have no control.

House-building. With savages it is apparent that each family ~~or already {has} its own~~ has its own cave or hut just as with nomads each family has a separate tent. This distinctively domestic economy becomes still more necessary with the further development of private property. With agricultural peoples the common domestic economy is just as impossible as the common cultivation of the soil. The construction of cities was a great step forward. In all previous periods, however, the transformation {*Aufhebung*} of the distinctively domestic economy, which is inseparable from the transformation {*Aufhebung*} of private property, was impossible already because the material conditions for it were not present. Setting up a

Second page on printer's sheet '87' (in Engels's sequence), numbered 53 by Marx

after long struggles. To demand the opposite would be just like demanding that competition should not exist in a specific historical period or that individuals should expunge from their brains the relations over which they as isolated individuals have no control.

House-building. With savages it is apparent that each family has its own cave or hut just as with nomads each family has a separate tent. This distinctively domestic economy becomes still more necessary with the further development of private property. With agricultural peoples the common domestic economy is just as impossible as the common cultivation of the soil. The construction of cities was a great step forward. In all previous periods, however, the transformation {*Aufhebung*} of the distinctively domestic economy, which is inseparable from the transformation {*Aufhebung*} of private property, was impossible already because the material conditions for it were not present. Setting up a common domestic economy

Second page on printer's sheet '87' (in Engels's sequence), numbered 53 by Marx

common domestic economy presupposes
the development of machinery, the use of
natural forces, & many other productive
forces, e.g. waterworks,

Second page on printer's sheet '87' (in Engels's sequence), numbered 53 by Marx

presupposes the development of machinery,
the use of natural forces, & many other
productive forces, e.g. waterworks,

Third page on printer's sheet '87' (in Engels's sequence), numbered 54 by Marx

gas lighting, steam-heating etc. and {insertion} **the transformation {*Aufhebung*} of city and countryside.** {*end insertion*} Without these conditions the common economy would not itself become a new force of production in turn, {hence} lacking all material basis, resting on a purely theoretical foundation, i.e. being a mere nonsense and consisting only of a monastic economy. – What was possible can be seen in the concentrating movement into cities & in the construction of common buildings for individually defined purposes (prisons, barracks pp). That the transformation {*Aufhebung*} of the distinctively {domestic} economy is inseparable from the transformation {*Aufhebung*} of the family is obvious.

----

[1][The proposition that frequently recurs with Saint Sancho that every man is everything that he is through the state is at bottom just the same as saying that commercial man {*der Bourgeois*} is only a specimen of the commercial species {*Bourgeoisgattung*}; a proposition that the middle *class* {*die Klasse*

With the philosophers the pre-existence of the class

---

1. The square brackets are Marx's.

gas lighting, steam-heating etc. and **the transformation {*Aufhebung*} of city and countryside.** Without these conditions the common economy would not itself become a new force of production in turn, {hence} lacking all material basis, resting on a purely theoretical foundation, i.e. being a mere nonsense and consisting only of a monastic economy. – What was possible can be seen in the concentrating movement into cities & in the construction of common buildings for individually defined purposes (prisons, barracks pp). That the transformation {*Aufhebung*} of the distinctively {domestic} economy is inseparable from the transformation {*Aufhebung*} of the family is obvious.

----

[1][The proposition that frequently recurs with Saint Sancho that every man is everything that he is through the state is at bottom just the same as saying that commercial man {*der Bourgeois*} is only a specimen of the commercial species {*Bourgeoisgattung*}; a proposition that the middle *class* {*die Klasse*

With the philosophers the pre-existence of the class

---

1. The square brackets are Marx's.

der *Bourgeois*} has already existed before the individuals that constitute it.] In the middle ages the citizenry {*die Bürger*} in every city were forced to unite against the nobility in order to defend their lives; the extension of trade, the establishment of communication led ~~to the asso.cia{tion} of unification of more and more cities which had its basis in the similarity of their interests in opposition to the feudal lords~~ individual cities to learn about other cities which had asserted the same interests in the struggle with the same antagonist. From the many local citizenries {*Bürgerschaften*} ~~of every ci{ty}~~ of individual cities the middle *class* {*die Bürgerklasse*} arose only very gradually. Through ~~the unification of those individuals into the common conditions of existence of a class~~ the opposition between the existing relations &
                       by this,
the type of labour conditioned   the conditions of life of ~~the individual~~ the individual citizen {*Bürger*} at the same time turned into conditions which were common ~~& themselves~~ to all of them & independent of each individual. {*insertion*} The citizenry {*Die Bürger*} had created these conditions in so far as they had got rid of feudal bonds, and

Third page on printer's sheet '87' (in Engels's sequence), numbered 54 by Marx

der *Bourgeois*} has already existed before the individuals that constitute it.] In the middle ages the citizenry {*die Bürger*} in every city were forced to unite against the nobility in order to defend their lives; the extension of trade, the establishment of communication led individual cities to learn about other cities which had asserted the same interests in the struggle with the same antagonist. From the many local citizenries {*Bürgerschaften*} of individual cities the middle *class* {*die Bürgerklasse*} arose only very gradually. Through the opposition between the existing relations & the type of labour conditioned by this, the conditions of life of the individual citizen {*Bürger*} at the same time turned into conditions which were common to all of them & independent of each individual. The citizenry {*Die Bürger*} had created these conditions in so far as they had got rid of feudal bonds, and were {in turn} created by

were {in turn} created by them in so far as they were conditioned ~~to these~~ through their opposition to the feudalism they were presented with. {*end insertion*} With the introduction of links between the individual cities common conditions developed into class conditions. The same conditions, the same opposition, the same interests, on the whole and for the most part, had to bring forth equivalent circumstances everywhere. The commercial class {*Die Bourgeoisie*} develops only gradually with these conditions ~~& splits up again according to the division of labour into different fractions~~, splits up again into different fractions & ~~finally draws all existing~~ propertied ~~classes~~ finally absorbs all existing classes into itself, {*insertion*} (while it develops the majority of the existing propertyless & a part of the previously propertied class into a new class, the workers {*Proletariat*}, in proportion to the conversion of ~~the~~ all existing property into industrial or commercial capital. The particular individuals only form a class in so far as

At first it absorbs the branches of labour directly belonging to the state, then all ± {more or less} ideological professions.

Third page on printer's sheet '87' (in Engels's sequence), numbered 54 by Marx

them in so far as they were conditioned through their opposition to the feudalism they were presented with. With the introduction of links between the individual cities common conditions developed into class conditions. The same conditions, the same opposition, the same interests, on the whole and for the most part, had to bring forth equivalent circumstances everywhere. The commercial class {*Die Bourgeoisie*} develops only gradually with these conditions, splits up again into different fractions & finally absorbs all existing propertied classes into itself, (while it develops the majority of the existing propertyless & a part of the previously propertied class into a new class, the workers {*Proletariat*}, in proportion to the conversion of all existing property into industrial or commercial capital. The particular individuals only form a class in so far as

At first it absorbs the branches of labour belonging directly to the state, then all ± {more or less} ideological professions.

they have to undertake a common struggle against ~~a third party~~ another class; otherwise they are by contrast in competition with one another and enemies again. On the other hand the class in turn takes on an independence opposed to the individuals, so they discover that their conditions of life are predetermined, ~~&~~ have their station in life & hence their personal development assigned, are subsumed under it. This is the same phenomenon as the subsumption of particular individuals under the division of labour, & can only be abolished by the transformation {*Aufhebung*} of private property & of labour. How this subsumption of individuals under the class develops at the same time into a subsumption {of individuals} under all kinds of conceptions pp we have already pointed out on numerous occasions. –

If one considers *philosophically* this development of individuals within ~~the give{n}, to them given to them in part considered philosophically in part through the further formation of the given conditions of existence~~ the common conditions of existence of the estates   that follow one another
    & classes

Fourth page on printer's sheet '87' (in Engels's sequence), numbered 55 by Marx

they have to undertake a common struggle against another class; otherwise they are by contrast in competition with one another and enemies again. On the other hand the class in turn takes on an independence opposed to the individuals, so they discover that their conditions of life are predetermined, have their station in life & hence their personal development assigned, are subsumed under it. This is the same phenomenon as the subsumption of particular individuals under the division of labour, & can only be abolished by the transformation {*Aufhebung*} of private property & of labour. How this subsumption of individuals under the class develops at the same time into a subsumption {of individuals} under all kinds of conceptions pp we have already pointed out on numerous occasions. –

If one considers *philosophically* this development of individuals within the common conditions of existence of the estates & classes that follow one another historically

Fourth page on printer's sheet '87' (in Engels's sequence), numbered 55 by Marx

historically &
 within the general conceptions
thereby imposed on these {individuals}, then
one can indeed easily imagine ~~these individuals~~ that the species or man has
developed in these individuals, or that they
{species or man} have developed the men; a
conceit by which history is given some hard
knocks. One can then conceive of these
different estates & classes as specific instances
of the general term, as sub-types of the
species, as phases of development of man.

 This subsumption of individuals under
specific classes cannot be transformed
{*aufgehoben*} until a class has formed which
has no particular class interest to assert against
the ruling class anymore~~, a class~~.
--
 (relations)
The changing of personal powers
into material {ones} through the division of
labour cannot be transformed {*aufgehoben*} in
turn by tackling the general conception of this
from the head, but only by the individuals
gaining control over these material powers
 , & transforming {*aufheben*} the division
again
of labour.
 This ~~cannot happen~~ is not possible
without life in common ~~& the completely free~~

Fourth page on printer's sheet '87' (in Engels's sequence), numbered 55 by Marx

& within the general conceptions thereby imposed on these {individuals}, then one can indeed easily imagine that the species or man has developed in these individuals, or that they {species or man} have developed the men; a conceit by which history is given some hard knocks. One can then conceive of these different estates & classes as specific instances of the general term, as sub-types of the species, as phases of development of man.

This subsumption of individuals under specific classes cannot be transformed {*aufgehoben*} until a class has formed which has no particular class interest to assert against the ruling class anymore.

--

The changing of personal powers (relations) into material {ones} through the division of labour cannot be transformed {*aufgehoben*} in turn by tackling the general conception of this from the head, but only by the individuals gaining control over these material powers again, & transforming {*aufheben*} the division of labour. This is not possible without life in

Fourth page on printer's sheet '87' (in Engels's sequence), numbered 55 by Marx

~~development of the individual the individuals that it implies. In common life it is only~~ Only in a common life can the means exist for every individual

common. Only in a common life can the
means exist for every individual

to develop his capacities in an all-round way, only in a common life ~~the~~ therefore does personal freedom become possible. In previous ~~apparent~~ surrogates for life in common, in the state etc. personal freedom only existed for individuals formed in the relations of the dominating class & only in so far as they were of that class. ~~In the~~ The illusory common life into which individuals were always united up to now ~~as a~~ made itself independent in opposition to them & at the same time ~~a~~, since it was ~~the expression~~ a unification of one class against another, ~~a new~~ {it} ~~became~~ was for the dominated class ~~just a wholly illusory common life~~ not just a completely illusory common life but also a new fetter. In actual common life individuals ~~have~~ attain their freedom in and through their association at the same time. – Individuals have always acted autonomously, naturally however autonomously from within their given historical conditions & relations, not from "pure" individuality as the ideologists understand it. However, in the course of historical development & precisely through the

First page on printer's sheet '88' (in Engels's sequence), numbered 56 by Marx

to develop his capacities in an all-round way, only in a common life therefore does personal freedom become possible. In previous surrogates for life in common, in the state etc. personal freedom only existed for individuals formed in the relations of the dominating class & only in so far as they were of that class. The illusory common life into which individuals were always united up to now made itself independent in opposition to them & at the same time, since it was a unification of one class against another, {it} was for the dominated class not just a completely illusory common life but also a new fetter. In actual common life individuals attain their freedom in and through their association at the same time. – Individuals have always acted autonomously, naturally however autonomously from within their given historical conditions & relations, not from "pure" individuality as the ideologists understand it. However, in the course of historical development & precisely through the

First page on printer's sheet '88' (in Engels's sequence), numbered 56 by Marx

~~historical~~ social relations that have inevitably gained an independence within the division of labour there appears a distinction between the life of every individual, so far as it is personal & in so far as it is subsumed under any branch of labour & the conditions pertaining to it. This is not to be understood as if e.g. the rentier, ~~& the capitalist~~ the capitalist pp have ceased to be persons; rather their personality is conditioned & ~~modified~~ defined wholly through the specific class relations, & the distinction appears only in opposition to another class & for themselves only when they go bankrupt. In the {medieval} estate (and even more in the tribe) this is still hidden, e.g. a nobleman always remains a nobleman, a commoner always a commoner, a quality inseparable ~~of~~ from his individuality, apart from his other relations. The distinction between the personal individual as opposed to the class individual {*insertion*}, the contingency of the conditions of life for the individual{*end insertion*}, only occur with the appearance of the class which is itself a product of the commercial class {*Bourgeoisie*}. Competition and struggle among individuals produces & develops only

First page on printer's sheet '88' (in Engels's sequence), numbered 56 by Marx

social relations that have inevitably gained an independence within the division of labour there appears a distinction between the life of every individual, so far as it is personal & in so far as it is subsumed under any branch of labour & the conditions pertaining to it. This is not to be understood as if e.g. the rentier, the capitalist pp have ceased to be persons; rather their personality is conditioned & defined wholly through the specific class relations, & the distinction appears only in opposition to another class & for themselves only when they go bankrupt. In the {medieval} estate (and even more in the tribe) this is still hidden, e.g. a nobleman always remains a nobleman, a commoner always a commoner, a quality inseparable from his individuality, apart from his other relations. The distinction between the personal individual as opposed to the class individual, the contingency of the conditions of life for the individual, only occur with the appearance of the class which is itself a product of the commercial class {*Bourgeoisie*}. Competition and struggle among individuals produces & develops only this contingency as such. Thus under the dominance of the commercial class {*Bourgeoisieherrschaft*}, individuals are freer than before, conceptually because their conditions of life are unfixed; in actuality they are of course more unfree, because more subjugated beneath material power. The distinction with respect to the medieval estate system clearly arises in the opposition between commercial class {*Bourgeoisie*} and labourers {*Proletariat*}. When the medieval estate of ~~citi{zens}~~ urban citizens {*Bürger*}, the corporate bodies pp emerged in opposition to the landed nobility, their condition of existence – movable property ~~as something which already~~ & craftwork which had a latent existence ~~& ther{efore} took~~ before their separation from feudal restrictions – appeared as something positive, which was made to work against feudal landed property & hence in ~~its~~ their own mode adopted a feudal form at first. Certainly fugitive serfs treated their previous servitude as something contingent to them personally. But in this they were only doing what every class does when it frees this contingency as such. Thus under the dominance of the commercial class {*Bourgeoisieherrschaft*}, individuals are freer conceptually than before, because their conditions of life are unfixed; in actuality they are of course more unfree, because more subjugated beneath material power. The distinction with respect to the medieval estate system clearly arises in the opposition between commercial class {*Bourgeoisie*} and labourers {*Proletariat*}. When the medieval estate of urban citizens {*Bürger*}, the corporate bodies pp emerged in opposition to the landed nobility, their condition of existence – movable property & craftwork which had a latent existence before their separation from feudal restrictions – appeared as something positive, which was made to work against feudal landed property & hence in their own mode adopted a feudal form at first. Certainly fugitive serfs treated their previous servitude as something contingent to them personally. But in this they were only doing what every class does when it frees itself from a fetter,

Second page on printer's sheet '88' (in Engels's sequence), numbered 57 by Marx

itself from a fetter, & so they did not free themselves as a class but rather individually. Moreover they did not break out of the medieval estate system, but rather only formed a new estate & retained their previous mode of working even in the new situation & developed it further by freeing it from its previous fetters, which no longer corresponded to the development already attained. – With ~~the labouring class {Proletariat}~~ the labourers {*Proletariariern*}, on the other hand, their own conditions of life, work ~~for them to{gether}~~ & hence all the conditions of existence of modern society have become something contingent for them, over which ~~they {have} no~~ the individual workers {*Proletarier*} have no control, {*insertion*} **and over which ~~the~~ no organisation *in commercial society* ~~cannot~~ give them control** {*end insertion*} & the ~~oppo{sition}~~ contradiction between the individuality of the particular worker and labour, his conditions of life that are forced upon him, becomes ~~perspicu{ous}~~ obvious to him.

~~Not to for{get}~~
, particularly when he is sacrificed from youth

Second page on printer's sheet '88' (in Engels's sequence), numbered 57 by Marx

& so they did not free themselves as a class but rather individually. Moreover they did not break out of the medieval estate system, but rather only formed a new estate & retained their previous mode of working even in the new situation & developed it further by freeing it from its previous fetters, which no longer corresponded to the development already attained. – With the labourers {*Proletariariern*}, on the other hand, their own conditions of life, work & hence all the conditions of existence of modern society have become something contingent for them, over which the individual workers {*Proletarier*} have no control, **and over which no organisation *in commercial society* can give them control** & the contradiction between the individuality of the particular worker and labour, his conditions of life that are forced upon him, becomes obvious to him,

---

particularly when he is sacrificed from youth

Second page on printer's sheet '88' (in Engels's sequence), numbered 57 by Marx

onwards, & when within his own class he
lacks the chance to arrive at the conditions that
would place him in the other class. –

Second page on printer's sheet '88' (in Engels's sequence), numbered 57 by Marx

onwards, & when within his own class he
lacks the chance to arrive at the conditions that
would place him in the other class. –

Third page on printer's sheet '88' (in Engels's sequence), numbered 58 by Marx

NB. not to be forgotten that the necessity for the serfs to exist, & the impossibility of a large-scale economy, resulting in the assignment of allotments to the serfs, very soon reduced ~~a~~ the obligations of the serfs to the ~~proprie{tors}~~ feudal lords to an average of payments in kind & labour-services, which made it possible for the serf to accumulate movable property & hence facilitated his escape from being the property of his lord {*insertion*} & gave him the prospect of ~~&~~ his advancement as an urban citizen {*Stadtbürger*}, {*end insertion*} also producing gradations among the serfs ~~and so it properly~~. Result that runaway serfs are already half citizens {*Bürger*}. Whereby it is likewise apparent that the enserfed peasants with craftwork skills had the most chance to acquire movable property. –

Thus while the ~~serf{fs}~~ runaway serfs only wanted to develop freely & put to use their conditions of existence already to hand, & hence in the last instance only to arrive at free labour, the labourers {*Proletarier*} have to

Third page on printer's sheet '88' (in Engels's sequence), numbered 58 by Marx

NB. not to be forgotten that the necessity for the serfs to exist, & the impossibility of a large-scale economy, resulting in the assignment of allotments to the serfs, very soon reduced the obligations of the serfs to the feudal lords to an average of payments in kind & labour-services, which made it possible for the serf to accumulate movable property & hence facilitated his escape from being the property of his lord & gave him the prospect of his advancement as an urban citizen {*Stadtbürger*}, also producing gradations among the serfs. Result that runaway serfs are already half citizens {*Bürger*}. Whereby it is likewise apparent that the enserfed peasants with craftwork skills had the most chance to acquire movable property. –

Thus while the runaway serfs only wanted to develop freely & put to use their conditions of existence already to hand, & hence in the last instance only to arrive at free labour, the labourers {*Proletarier*} have to transform

Third page on printer's sheet '88' (in Engels's sequence), numbered 58 by Marx

transform {*aufheben*} labour, {*insertion*} in order to put to use personally {*end insertion*} their own condition of existence up to now,{*insertion*} which at the same time is that {condition of existence} of the whole of society {*further insertion*} up to the present {*end further insertion*} {*end insertion*}. Thus they also find themselves in direct opposition to the ~~society {which has} up to now a connecti{on}~~ form in which the individuals of a society gave themselves a collective expression up to now, to the state, & they have to overthrow the state in order to ~~come to dominance~~ realise their individuality.

It follows from the whole previous discussion above that ~~the individuals who free themselves in every historical epoch only develop further the conditions of existence already to hand that they have been given~~ ~~the collectivity~~ the collective relation into which the individuals of a class & which are entering, was conditioned by their collective interests against others, was always a collectivity to which these individuals belonged only as average individuals, only in so far as they lived within the conditions of existence of their class, a

Third page on printer's sheet '88' (in Engels's sequence), numbered 58 by Marx

{*aufheben*} labour, in order to put to use personally their own condition of existence up to now, which at the same time is that {condition of existence} of the whole of society up to the present. Thus they also find themselves in direct opposition to the form in which the individuals of a society gave themselves a collective expression up to now, to the state, & they have to overthrow the state in order to realise their individuality.

It follows from the whole previous discussion above that the collective relation into which the individuals of a class are entering & which was conditioned by their collective interests against others, was always a collectivity to which these individuals belonged only as average individuals, only in so far as they lived within the conditions of existence of their class, a relation in which they had a part

Third page on printer's sheet '88' (in Engels's sequence), numbered 58 by Marx

~~collectivity~~ relation in which they had a part not ~~however~~ as individuals but as members of a class. With the collectivity of revolutionary labourers {*Proletarier*}, on the other hand, who

Third page on printer's sheet '88' (in Engels's sequence), numbered 58 by Marx

not as individuals but as members of a class.
With the collectivity of revolutionary
labourers {*Proletarier*}, on the other hand,
who

Fourth page on printer's sheet '88' (in Engels's sequence), numbered 59 by Marx

take their conditions of existence under control [&]¹ {those of} all the members of society, it is exactly the reverse; individuals take their part in it as individuals. It is precisely the unification of individuals (presupposing the current development of productive forces, of course) which provides the conditions ~~which {?} to the free development & activity of the individuals~~ for the free development and activity of individuals, ~~ne{eds}~~ under their {own} control, conditions which up to now were left to fortuity and chance & had made themselves independent of and opposed to particular individuals precisely because of their separateness as individuals, {*insertion*} because of their necessary unification effected by the division of labour & because their separateness had become an alien bond to them.{*end insertion*} Up to now unification was a{n} ²{*insertion*} in no way arbitrary one {*further insertion*} as is represented e.g. in the social contract ~~a~~ {*end further insertion*} but a necessary {*end insertion*} unification

---

1. The square brackets are Engels's.
2. The editors of *Jahrbuch 2003* suggest that this insertion was written down later than the previous one.

Fourth page on printer's sheet '88' (in Engels's sequence), numbered 59 by Marx

take their conditions of existence under control [&]¹ {those of} all the members of society, it is exactly the reverse; individuals take their part in it as individuals. It is precisely the unification of individuals (presupposing the current development of productive forces, of course) which provides the conditions for the free development and activity of individuals under their {own} control, conditions which up to now were left to fortuity and chance & had made themselves independent of and opposed to particular individuals precisely because of their separateness as individuals, because of their necessary unification effected by the division of labour & because their separateness had become an alien bond to them. Up to now unification was a{n} in no way arbitrary one as is represented e.g. in the social contract but a necessary unification

---

1. The square brackets are Engels's.

Fourth page on printer's sheet '88' (in Engels's sequence), numbered 59 by Marx

¹{*insertion*} (compare e.g. the formation of the North American states & the ~~repu{blies}~~ South American republics) {*end insertion*} of these conditions, within which individuals then had the benefit of fortuity and chance. This right, to be able to please oneself ~~undisturbed onself with fortuity and chance~~ with fortuity and chance, undisturbed within certain conditions, has been known up to now as ~~politi{cal}~~ personal freedom. – These conditions of existence are naturally only the forces of production & forms of exchange of any given time. –
Communism distinguishes itself from all previous movements in that it overturns the basis of all previous production relations & relations of exchange, & for the first time ~~when with consciousness~~ self-consciously considers all naturally arising preconditions up to now
    as human creations, strips away
          power
their naturalness & subjects them to the
of
 united ~~p{ower}~~ individuals. Its ~~organisations~~ organisation is ~~simply~~ therefore essentially economic, the material ~~organisation~~

---

1. The editors of *Jahrbuch 2003* suggest that this insertion was written down later than the previous one.

(compare e.g. the formation of the
North American states & the South American
republics) of these conditions, within which
individuals then had the benefit of fortuity and
chance. This right, to be able to please oneself
with fortuity and chance, undisturbed within
certain conditions, has been known up to now
as personal freedom. – These conditions of
existence are naturally only the forces of
production & forms of exchange of any given
time. –
Communism distinguishes itself from all
previous movements in that it overturns the
basis of all previous production relations &
relations of exchange, & for the first time
self-consciously considers all naturally arising
preconditions up to now as human creations,
strips away their naturalness & subjects them
to the power of united individuals. Its
organisation is therefore essentially economic,
the material realisation of the conditions of

realisation of the conditions of this unification; it makes current conditions into the conditions of unification. The mode of existence which communism creates is precisely the actual basis for making it impossible that anything should exist independently of individuals ~~&~~ ~~yet~~, insofar as what exists is in any case only a product of the previous interrelations of individuals themselves. Thus the communists ~~relate to~~ deal practically with the conditions produced by production & exchange up to now as non-organic, without in that way imagining that it was the plan or intention of preceding generations to provide them with material, & without believing that these conditions were non-organic for the individuals creating them.

Fourth page on printer's sheet '88' (in Engels's sequence), numbered 59 by Marx

this unification; it makes current conditions into the conditions of unification. The mode of existence which communism creates is precisely the actual basis for making it impossible that anything should exist independently of individuals, insofar as what exists is in any case only a product of the previous interrelations of individuals themselves. Thus the communists deal practically with the conditions produced by production & exchange up to now as non-organic, without in that way imagining that it was the plan or intention of preceding generations to provide them with material, & without believing that these conditions were non-organic for the individuals creating them.

First page on printer's sheet '89' (in Engels's sequence), numbered 60 by Marx

The distinction between what is personal to the individual & what is contingent to the individual is not a conceptual distinction but rather a historical fact. This distinction has a different significance at different times, e.g. the medieval estate as something contingent to the individual in the 18th century, also the family, more or less. It is not a distinction that we have to make for each era but rather each era makes the distinction itself out of the different elements that it finds to hand, & to be sure not according to a concept but rather forced by the material interactions of life. What appears as contingent to a later era in contradistinction to an earlier one, hence also among the elements taken over from the earlier era, is a form of exchange which corresponded to a specific development of productive forces. The relation of the productive forces to the form of exchange is the relation of the form of exchange to the ~~self-activity~~ **activity or engagement** of the individuals. [1](The fundamental form of this ~~self-activity~~ **engagement** is naturally material, on which all other {forms}, intellectual,

---

1. Marx's parentheses around this passage.

First page on printer's sheet '89' (in Engels's sequence), numbered 60 by Marx

The distinction between what is personal to the individual & what is contingent to the individual is not a conceptual distinction but rather a historical fact. This distinction has a different significance at different times, e.g. the medieval estate as something contingent to the individual in the 18th century, also the family, more or less. It is not a distinction that we have to make for each era but rather each era makes the distinction itself out of the different elements that it finds to hand, & to be sure not according to a concept but rather forced by the material interactions of life. What appears as contingent to a later era in contradistinction to an earlier one, hence also among the elements taken over from the earlier era, is a form of exchange which corresponded to a specific development of productive forces. The relation of the productive forces to the form of exchange is the relation of the form of exchange to the **activity or engagement** of the individuals. [1](The fundamental form of this **engagement** is naturally material, on which all other {forms},

---

1. Marx's parentheses around this passage.

First page on printer's sheet '89' (in Engels's sequence), numbered 60 by Marx

political, religious etc., depend. The varying shape of material life is naturally dependent in every case on the needs that have already been developed, & the ~~development~~ production ~~or~~ as well as the satisfaction of these needs is itself a historical process which does not take place with sheep or dogs {*insertion*} (Stirner's factitious main argument *against* humanity) {*end insertion*}, although sheep and dogs in their present form are certainly, albeit in spite of themselves, the products of a historical process.) The ~~conditions~~ **conditions** under which individuals interact with one another, so long as the contradiction has not yet surfaced, are conditions appertaining to their individuality, in no way external for them, conditions under which these specific individuals, existing under specific ~~conditions~~ relations, can alone produce their material life & whatever goes together with that, therefore the conditions are also {those of} their self-engagement & are produced by that self-engagement. The specific condition under which they produce, as long as the contradiction has not yet arisen, thus

Production of the form of exchange itself.

First page on printer's sheet '89' (in Engels's sequence), numbered 60 by Marx

intellectual, political, religious etc., depend. The varying shape of material life is naturally dependent in every case on the needs that have already been developed, & production as well as the satisfaction of these needs is itself a historical process which does not take place with sheep or dogs (Stirner's factitious main argument *against* humanity), although sheep and dogs in their present form are certainly, albeit in spite of themselves, the products of a historical process.) The **conditions** under which individuals interact with one another, so long as the contradiction has not yet surfaced, are conditions appertaining to their individuality, in no way external for them, conditions under which these specific individuals, existing under specific relations, can alone produce their material life & whatever goes together with that, therefore the conditions are also {those of} their self-engagement & are produced by that self-engagement. The specific condition under which they produce, as long as the contradiction has not yet arisen, thus

Production of the form of exchange itself.

corresponds to their actual circumstances, to their limited being, the limitations of which only become evident with the onset of the contradiction & hence only exists for those who come later. Then this condition appears contingently as a fetter, & ~~then becomes a~~ then the consciousness that it is a fetter is also projected onto the earlier era. – These different conditions, which appear at first as ~~condition~~ conditions of self-engagement, later as its fetters, form for the whole of historical development a connected series of forms of interaction whose connection consists in the replacement of the earlier form of interaction, which has become a fetter, with a new one corresponding to more developed forces of production ~~corresponding & hence to the~~ & hence to the advancing mode through which individuals engage themselves. Since these conditions correspond at the same time to each level of development of the productive forces, their history is equally the history of the developing forces of production taken on by every new generation & hence ~~a~~ the history of the ~~power development~~ development of the

corresponds to their actual circumstances, to their limited being, the limitations of which only become evident with the onset of the contradiction & hence only exists for those who come later. Then this condition appears contingently as a fetter, & then the consciousness that it is a fetter is also projected onto the earlier era. – These different conditions, which appear at first as conditions of self-engagement, later as its fetters, form for the whole of historical development a connected series of forms of interaction whose connection consists in the replacement of the earlier form of interaction, which has become a fetter, with a new one corresponding to more developed forces of production & hence to the advancing mode through which individuals engage themselves. Since these conditions correspond at the same time to each level of development of the productive forces, their history is equally the history of the developing forces of production taken on by every new generation & hence the history of the development of the powers of the individuals

Second page on printer's sheet '89' (in Engels's sequence), numbered 61 by Marx

powers of ~~these~~ the individuals themselves.

Since this development proceeds naturally, i.e. is not subordinated to a collective plan of freely united individuals, it thus arises out of different localities, tribes, nations, branches of labour &c, each of which starts developing independently ~~with~~ of the other & only by and by forms a relationship with the other~~, furthermore only proceeds~~. Furthermore this proceeds only very slowly; ~~&~~ the different stages ~~are~~ & interests are never completely resolved, but only subordinated to the commanding interests & drag alongside them for centuries. {*insertion*} It follows from this that even within a nation individuals have wholly different developmental formations, quite apart from ~~his~~ their comparative wealth, & that ~~which {is} already in~~ an earlier interest, after a form of interaction belonging to a later one has ~~long ago~~ already displaced its particular form of interaction, remains for long afterwards in possession of a traditional power in the illusory collectivity (state, law) that has become ~~always~~ independently opposed to individuals, a power which in the last instance is only broken by a revolution. {*end insertion*} This explains why ~~it appears~~ in relation to single instances, themselves.

Since this development proceeds naturally, i.e. is not subordinated to a collective plan of freely united individuals, it thus arises out of different localities, tribes, nations, branches of labour &c, each of which starts developing independently of the other & only by and by forms a relationship with the other. Furthermore this proceeds only very slowly; the different stages & interests are never completely resolved, but only subordinated to the commanding interests & drag alongside them for centuries. It follows from this that even within a nation individuals have wholly different developmental formations, quite apart from their comparative wealth, & that an earlier interest, after a form of interaction belonging to a later one has already displaced its particular form of interaction, remains for long afterwards in possession of a traditional power in the illusory collectivity (state, law) that has become independently opposed to individuals, a power which in the last instance is only broken by a revolution. This explains why in relation to single instances,

Third page on printer's sheet '89' (in Engels's sequence), numbered 62 by Marx

which afford a more general summing up, consciousness can at times appear further advanced than the empirical relations which coincide with it, so that ~~it the~~ in the conflicts of a later epoch one can invoke earlier theoreticians as authorities. – On the other hand, in countries such as North America, starting from scratch ~~at an already developed historical epoch~~ in an already developed historical epoch, development {*insertion*} rushes quickly ahead. Such countries have {*end insertion*} no other natural preconditions ~~than the~~ besides the individuals ~~which form it~~ who settled there, & who were prompted to do this by the forms of ~~rela{tion}~~ interaction in the old countries which did not correspond to their needs. Thus they started with the most advanced individuals of the old countries & hence with the developed forms of interaction ~~already~~ corresponding to those individuals, but before this form of interaction could take hold in the old countries. This is the case with all colonies in so far as they are not purely military or trading posts.   Carthage{,} the Greek colonies & Iceland in the 11th & 12th century

Third page on printer's sheet '89' (in Engels's sequence), numbered 62 by Marx

which afford a more general summing up, consciousness can at times appear further advanced than the empirical relations which coincide with it, so that in the conflicts of a later epoch one can invoke earlier theoreticians as authorities. – On the other hand, in countries such as North America, starting from scratch in an already developed historical epoch, development rushes quickly ahead. Such countries have no other natural preconditions besides the individuals who settled there, & who were prompted to do this by the forms of interaction in the old countries which did not correspond to their needs. Thus they started with the most advanced individuals of the old countries & hence with the developed forms of interaction corresponding to those individuals, but before this form of interaction could take hold in the old countries. This is the case with all colonies in so far as they are not purely military or trading posts. Carthage{,}the Greek colonies & Iceland in the 11th & 12th century

Third page on printer's sheet '89' (in Engels's sequence), numbered 62 by Marx

~~&c~~ provide examples of this. A similar relation arises from conquest when a form of interaction already developed on other soil is brought over complete to a conquered country; while in its homeland it was still burdened with ~~nature{al}~~ interests & relations from ~~an~~ earlier epochs, here it can & must be established completely & without hindrance, {*insertion*} if only to assure the enduring power of the conquerors {*end insertion*}. (England ~~after the con{quest}~~ & Naples after the Norman conquest, where they received the ~~complete{d}~~ most complete form of feudal organisation) –

[1][The fact of conquest appears to contradict this whole conception of history. Up to now war, pillage, murderous violence, robbery pp have been made into the driving force of history. We can only restrict ourselves here to the chief points & so offer only the ~~example~~ most striking example, the destruction of an old ~~feu{dal}~~ civilisation by a barbarian people, & the consequent formation, from a fresh start, of a new structure of society. (Rome & the barbarians, feudalism &

---

1. Engels's square bracket.

Third page on printer's sheet '89' (in Engels's sequence), numbered 62 by Marx

provide examples of this. A similar relation arises from conquest when a form of interaction already developed on other soil is brought over complete to a conquered country; while in its homeland it was still burdened with interests & relations from earlier epochs, here it can & must be established completely & without hindrance, if only to assure the enduring power of the conquerors. (England & Naples after the Norman conquest, where they received the most complete form of feudal organisation) –

[1][The fact of conquest appears to contradict this whole conception of history. Up to now violence, war, pillage, murderous robbery pp have been made into the driving force of history. We can only restrict ourselves here to the chief points & so offer only the most striking example, the destruction of an old civilisation by a barbarian people, & the consequent formation, from a fresh start, of a new structure of society. (Rome & the barbarians, feudalism & Gaul, the Byzantine

---

1. Engels's square bracket.

Gaul, the Byzantine Empire and the Turks)

Empire and the Turks)

With the conquering barbarian peoples war itself, as indicated above, is still a regular form of interaction which is exploited all the more vigorously the more the increase in population creates the need for new means of production in conjunction with the traditional crude mode of production, the only one possible for it.
In Italy, on the other hand, through the concentration of landed property {*insertion*} & indebtedness (caused not only by buy-up but also by inheritance, since with gross indulgence and infrequent marriage the older generations gradually died out & their property fell into the hands of a few) & its conversion into pasturage (which ~~the~~ was caused not only by the usual economic factors applicable today but by the import of plundered & tribute grain & the ~~related~~ consequent shortfall in consumers for Italian corn) {*end insertion*} the free population almost disappeared, ~~&~~ slaves themselves constantly died off & always had to be replaced with new ones. Slavery remained the basis of all production ~~& gets~~. The plebeians, standing between freemen & slaves, never got

Fourth page on printer's sheet '89' (in Engels's sequence), numbered 63 by Marx

With the conquering barbarian peoples war itself, as indicated above, is still a regular form of interaction which is exploited all the more vigorously the more the increase in population creates the need for new means of production in conjunction with the traditional crude mode of production, the only one possible for it. In Italy, on the other hand, through the concentration of landed property (caused not only by buy-up & indebtedness but also by inheritance, since with gross indulgence and infrequent marriage the older generations gradually died out & their property fell into the hands of a few) & its conversion into pasturage (which was caused not only by the usual economic factors applicable today but by the import of plundered & tribute grain & the consequent shortfall in consumers for Italian corn) the free population almost disappeared, slaves themselves constantly died off & always had to be replaced with new ones. Slavery remained the basis of all production. The plebeians, standing between freemen & slaves, never got beyond riffraff beyond riffraff {*Lumpenproletariat*}. Indeed Rome never amounted to more than a city & had an almost purely political connection with the provinces which could be broken again by political means, naturally enough.

There is nothing more common than the conception that history up to now consists only of *taking*. The barbarians *took* the Roman Empire, and the fact of this take-over is used to explain the transition from the ancient world to feudalism. This barbarian take-over raises the issue whether the nation which is taken over has developed the productive forces of industry, as is the case with modern nations, or whether their productive forces rest for the most part merely on their unification & ~~on working together themselves, so far as this is possible~~ on the collectivity. Taking is further conditioned by the object taken over. The wealth on paper of a banker cannot be taken at all without the taker's submission to the conditions of production and social interaction in the country taken over. {It is} just the same with the whole industrial capital of a modern industrial country. And finally, taking very soon comes to an end, & if there is nothing

{*Lumpenproletariat*}. Indeed Rome never amounted to more than a city & had an almost purely political connection with the provinces which could be broken again by political means, naturally enough.

There is nothing more common than the conception that history up to now consists only of *taking*. The barbarians *took* the Roman Empire, and the fact of this take-over is used to explain the transition from the ancient world to feudalism. This barbarian take-over raises the issue whether the nation which is taken over has developed the productive forces of industry, as is the case with modern nations, or whether their productive forces rest for the most part merely on their unification & on the collectivity. Taking is further conditioned by the object taken over. The wealth on paper of a banker cannot be taken at all without the taker's submission to the conditions of production and social interaction in the country taken over. {It is} just the same with the whole industrial capital of a modern industrial country. And finally, taking very soon comes to an end, & if there is nothing

Fourth page on printer's sheet '89' (in Engels's sequence), numbered 63 by Marx

more to be taken, production must begin. From this necessity to produce, which very soon asserts itself,

Fourth page on printer's sheet '89' (in Engels's sequence), numbered 63 by Marx

more to be taken, production must begin. From this necessity to produce, which very soon asserts itself,

First page on printer's sheet '90' (in Engels's sequence), numbered 64 by Marx

it follows that the form of collectivity taken over by the conquerors as they settle down must correspond to the stage of development of the productive forces found there, or ~~must~~ if this is not the case at the outset, {the form of collectivity} must change in accordance with the productive forces. This explains the fact ~~that~~ which has been remarked on everywhere
     in the period
that   after migration the servant was master, & the conqueror took on the language, culture and customs of the ~~romanised~~ conquered. – Feudalism was by no means transferred complete from Germany but rather ~~originated~~ it had its origin on the conquerors' side ~~only through~~ in the military organisation of the army during the conquest itself & this only developed after the conquest through the effect of the forces of production to hand in the conquered countries. How far this form was conditioned by the forces of production is shown by the failed attempts to establish an alternative ~~forms~~ form deriving from nostalgia for ancient Rome (Charlemagne pp) –

     to be continued

First page on printer's sheet '90' (in Engels's sequence), numbered 64 by Marx

it follows that the form of collectivity taken over by the conquerors as they settle down must correspond to the stage of development of the productive forces found there, or if this is not the case at the outset, {the form of collectivity} must change in accordance with the productive forces. This explains the fact which has been remarked on everywhere that in the period after migration the servant was master, & the conqueror took on the language, culture and customs of the conquered. – Feudalism was by no means transferred complete from Germany but rather it had its origin on the conquerors' side in the military organisation of the army during the conquest itself & this only developed after the conquest through the effect of the forces of production to hand in the conquered countries. How far this form was conditioned by the forces of production is shown by the failed attempts to establish an alternative form deriving from nostalgia for ancient Rome (Charlemagne pp) –

    to be continued

First page on printer's sheet '90' (in Engels's sequence), numbered 64 by Marx

----

In large-scale industry & competition the entire conditions of existence of individuals are amalgamated into the two simplest forms: private property & labour. With money every form of interaction & interaction itself is ~~not to~~ for individuals.
premised as contingent
{*insertion*} Thus money already implies that all previous interaction was only the interaction of individuals under specific conditions, not that of individuals as individuals. These conditions are reduced to two – accumulated labour or private property, or actual labour. If one or both of these ceases, then interaction comes to a standstill. The modern economists themselves, e.g. Sismondi, Cherbuliez &c oppose the association of individuals to the association of capitalists. {*end insertion*} On the other hand the individuals are themselves completely subordinated to the division of labour & by that means brought into the most complete dependence on one another. Private property, in so far as it is in opposition to labour within labour itself, ~~appears as the~~ develops out of the
&
necessity to accumulate, ~~the~~ is in the

First page on printer's sheet '90' (in Engels's sequence), numbered 64 by Marx

----

In large-scale industry & competition the entire conditions of existence of individuals are amalgamated into the two simplest forms: private property & labour. With money every form of interaction & interaction itself is premised as contingent for individuals. Thus money already implies that all previous interaction was only the interaction of individuals under specific conditions, not that of individuals as individuals. These conditions are reduced to two – accumulated labour or private property, or actual labour. If one or both of these cease, then interaction comes to a standstill. The modern economists themselves, e.g. Sismondi, Cherbuliez &c oppose the association of individuals to the association of capitalists. On the other hand the individuals are themselves completely subordinated to the division of labour & by that means brought into the most complete dependence on one another. Private property, in so far as it is in opposition to labour within labour itself, develops out of the necessity to accumulate, & is in the beginning still a collective form,

First page on printer's sheet '90' (in Engels's sequence), numbered 64 by Marx

beginning ~~however~~ still a collective form, however ~~gradually~~ in its further development getting closer and closer to the modern form of private property. At the outset the division of labour already implies the division of the *conditions* of labour{,} tools and materials & hence the splitting up of accumulated capital among different proprietors {*insertion*}, & hence the split between capital & labour, & the different forms of property itself. {*end insertion*} The more the division of labour ~~forms~~ develops

First page on printer's sheet '90' (in Engels's sequence), numbered 64 by Marx

however in its further development getting closer and closer to the modern form of private property. At the outset the division of labour already implies the division of the *conditions* of labour{,} tools and materials & hence the splitting up of accumulated capital among different proprietors, & hence the split between capital & labour, & the different forms of property itself. The more the division of labour develops

& the more accumulation grows, the more sharply this fragmentation develops. Labour itself can only take place within the premise of this fragmentation.

(Personal energy of ~~nations~~ the individuals of a particular nation – Germans and Americans – energy even from racial crosses – hence German cretinism – in France, England &c foreign peoples transplanted to an already developed ground, in America to a wholly new ground, in Germany the indigenous population remains stationary and quiescent.)

Here two facts come to the fore. First, the forces of production appear as wholly independent of individuals and removed from them, as a world of their own alongside the individuals, the reason for which is that the individuals, to whom these forces belong, exist fragmentedly and in opposition to one another, while these forces on the other hand are only real forces in the interaction & interconnection of these individuals. Thus on the one hand there is a totality of the forces of production which have taken on a material form, as it

Second page on printer's sheet '90' (in Engels's sequence), numbered 65 by Marx

& the more accumulation grows, the more sharply this fragmentation develops. Labour itself can only take place within the premise of this fragmentation.

(Personal energy of the individuals of a particular nation – Germans and Americans – energy even from racial crosses – hence German cretinism – in France, England &c foreign peoples transplanted to an already developed ground, in America to a wholly new ground, in Germany the indigenous population remains stationary and quiescent.)

Here two facts come to the fore. First, the forces of production appear as wholly independent of individuals and removed from them, as a world of their own alongside the individuals, the reason for which is that the individuals, to whom these forces belong, exist fragmentedly and in opposition to one another, while these forces on the other hand are only real forces in the interaction & interconnection of these individuals. Thus on the one hand there is a totality of the forces of production which have taken on a material form, as it

Second page on printer's sheet '90' (in Engels's sequence), numbered 65 by Marx

were, & are for the individuals themselves no longer the powers of individuals but rather of private property, & hence of individuals only in so far as they are owners of private property. In no earlier period have ~~these~~ the forces of production taken on this form, indifferent to the interaction of individuals *as* individuals, because their interaction itself was still such a limited one. On the other hand opposed to these forces of production are the majority of individuals ~~to whom~~ from whom these powers were stripped away & who have become abstract individuals, robbed of all the actual content of life, but who are only put by those means into a position to enter into relations with one another *as individuals*. The sole connection that is still between them and the forces of production & their own existence, labour, has lost all appearance of self-activity for them & only sustains their life

were, & are for the individuals themselves no longer the powers of individuals but rather of private property, & hence of individuals only in so far as they are owners of private property. In no earlier period have the forces of production taken on this form, indifferent to the interaction of individuals *as* individuals, because their interaction itself was still such a limited one. On the other hand opposed to these forces of production are the majority of individuals from whom these powers were stripped away & who have become abstract individuals, robbed of all the actual content of life, but who are only put by those means into a position to enter into relations with one another *as individuals*. The sole connection that is still between them and the forces of production & their own existence, labour, has lost all appearance of self-activity for them & only sustains their life

Third page on printer's sheet '90' (in Engels's sequence), numbered 66 by Marx

& the more accumulation grows, the more sharply this fragmentation develops. Labour itself can only take place within the premise of this fragmentation.

(Personal energy of ~~nations~~ the individuals of a particular nation – Germans and Americans – energy even from racial crosses – hence German cretinism – in France, England &c foreign peoples transplanted to an already developed ground, in America to a wholly new ground, in Germany the indigenous population remains stationary and quiescent.)

Here two facts come to the fore. First, the forces of production appear as wholly independent of individuals and removed from them, as a world of their own alongside the individuals, the reason for which is that the individuals, to whom these forces belong, exist fragmentedly and in opposition to one another, while these forces on the other hand are only real forces in the interaction & interconnection of these individuals. Thus on the one hand there is a totality of the forces of production which have taken on a material form, as it

Third page on printer's sheet '90' (in Engels's sequence), numbered 66 by Marx

& the more accumulation grows, the more sharply this fragmentation develops. Labour itself can only take place within the premise of this fragmentation.

(Personal energy of the individuals of a particular nation – Germans and Americans – energy even from racial crosses – hence German cretinism – in France, England &c foreign peoples transplanted to an already developed ground, in America to a wholly new ground, in Germany the indigenous population remains stationary and quiescent.)

Here two facts come to the fore. First, the forces of production appear as wholly independent of individuals and removed from them, as a world of their own alongside the individuals, the reason for which is that the individuals, to whom these forces belong, exist fragmentedly and in opposition to one another, while these forces on the other hand are only real forces in the interaction & interconnection of these individuals. Thus on the one hand there is a totality of the forces of production which have taken on a material form, as it

Third page on printer's sheet '90' (in Engels's sequence), numbered 66 by Marx

were, & are for the individuals themselves no longer the powers of individuals but rather of private property, & hence of individuals only in so far as they are owners of private property. In no earlier period have ~~these~~ the forces of production taken on this form, indifferent to the interaction of individuals *as* individuals, because their interaction itself was still such a limited one. On the other hand opposed to these forces of production are the majority of individuals ~~to whom~~ from whom these powers were stripped away & who have become abstract individuals, robbed of all the actual content of life, but who are only put by those means into a position to enter into relations with one another *as individuals*. The sole connection that is still between them and the forces of production & their own existence, labour, has lost all appearance of self-activity for them & only sustains their life

Third page on printer's sheet '90' (in Engels's sequence), numbered 66 by Marx

were, & are for the individuals themselves no longer the powers of individuals but rather of private property, & hence of individuals only in so far as they are owners of private property. In no earlier period have the forces of production taken on this form, indifferent to the interaction of individuals *as* individuals, because their interaction itself was still such a limited one. On the other hand opposed to these forces of production are the majority of individuals from whom these powers were stripped away & who have become abstract individuals, robbed of all the actual content of life, but who are only put by those means into a position to enter into relations with one another *as individuals*. The sole connection that is still between them and the forces of production & their own existence, labour, has lost all appearance of self-activity for them & only sustains their life

Fourth page on printer's sheet '90' (in Engels's sequence), numbered 67 by Marx

& hence there resulted only a new set of constraints. Their instrument of production became their property, however they themselves remained subordinated to the division of labour & to their own instrument of production. In all appropriations up to now a mass of individuals remained subordinated to a single instrument of production; in the appropriation done by the labourers {*Proletarier*} a mass of instruments of production must be subordinated to every
        & property to all.
individual   Modern universal social interaction cannot be subordinated to individuals other than by being subordinated to all. – The appropriation is further conditioned by the mode & manner through which it must be carried out. ~~These~~ It can only be carried out through a unification which again can only be a universal one through the ~~univers{al}~~ character of the labouring class {*Proletariat*} itself, & through a revolution in which,
       on the one hand, ~~in order to over{throw}~~ the power of the
        mode of production & mode of social
previous

Fourth page on printer's sheet '90' (in Engels's sequence), numbered 67 by Marx

& hence there resulted only a new set of constraints. Their instrument of production became their property, however they themselves remained subordinated to the division of labour & to their own instrument of production. In all appropriations up to now a mass of individuals remained subordinated to a single instrument of production; in the appropriation done by the labourers {*Proletarier*} a mass of instruments of production must be subordinated to every individual & property to all. Modern universal social interaction cannot be subordinated to individuals other than by being subordinated to all. – The appropriation is further conditioned by the mode & manner through which it must be carried out. It can only be carried out through a unification which again can only be a universal one through the character of the labouring class {*Proletariat*} itself, & through a revolution in which, on the one hand, the power of the previous mode of production & mode of social interaction &

Fourth page on printer's sheet '90' (in Engels's sequence), numbered 67 by Marx

interaction &   is overthrown
      social structure
&, on the other hand, there is a development of
the universal character & the strength of the
labouring class {*Proletariats*} necessary to
carry through the appropriation, moreover the
labouring class {*Proletariat*} strips off
everything that still adheres to it from ~~the~~ its
previous position in society.

    Only at this stage does self-
engagement coincide with the material life
which corresponds to the development of
individuals into total individuals & the
stripping off of all that has grown up naturally;
& then the transformation of labour into self-
engagement is in correspondence with the
transformation of social interaction that was
previously conditioned into the social
interaction of individuals as such. With the
appropriation of the total productive forces by
the united individuals private property ceases
to exist. While in history up to now a
particular condition always appeared as
contingent, now the isolation of individuals
themselves, the particular private livelihood of
every individual himself, has become
contingent.

    The individuals who are no longer

Fourth page on printer's sheet '90' (in Engels's sequence), numbered 67 by Marx

social structure is overthrown &, on the other hand, there is a development of the universal character & the strength of the labouring class {*Proletariats*} necessary to carry through the appropriation, moreover the labouring class {*Proletariat*} strips off everything that still adheres to it from its previous position in society.

Only at this stage does self-engagement coincide with the material life which corresponds to the development of individuals into total individuals & the stripping off of all that has grown up naturally; & then the transformation of labour into self-engagement is in correspondence with the transformation of social interaction that was previously conditioned into the social interaction of individuals as such. With the appropriation of the total productive forces by the united individuals private property ceases to exist. While in history up to now a particular condition always appeared as contingent, now the isolation of individuals themselves, the particular private livelihood of every individual himself, has become contingent.

The individuals who are no longer

subordinated to the division of labour have been conceived by the philosophers as an ideal under the term "man", & the whole process which we have discussed has been understood by them as a process of development "of man", such that at every historical stage "man" was substituted for individuals up to that point & was represented as the driving force of history. The whole process was understood as the process of self-alienation of "man" & this was essentially a matter of shifting the average **self-alienation** individual of a later stage into the earlier one & later consciousness into earlier individuals. Through this inversion, which from the outset abstracts from actual conditions, it was possible to transform all of history into a process of development of consciousness. -- --

Commercial society {*bürgerliche Gesellschaft*} comprises the whole material social interaction of individuals within a specific stage of development of the productive forces. It comprises the whole commercial and industrial life of a stage & thus far goes ~~from~~ beyond the state & the nation, although on the other hand externally it

First page on printer's sheet '91' (in Engels's sequence), numbered 68 by Marx

subordinated to the division of labour have been conceived by the philosophers as an ideal under the term "man", & the whole process which we have discussed has been understood by them as a process of development "of man", such that at every historical stage "man" was substituted for individuals up to that point & was represented as the driving force of history. The whole process was understood as the process of self-alienation of "man" & this was essentially a matter of shifting the average individual of a later stage into the earlier one & later consciousness into earlier individuals. Through this inversion, which from the outset abstracts from actual conditions, it was possible to transform all of history into a process of development of consciousness. -- --

self-alienation

Commercial society {*bürgerliche Gesellschaft*} comprises the whole material social interaction of individuals within a specific stage of development of the productive forces. It comprises the whole commercial and industrial life of a stage & thus far goes beyond the state & the nation, although on the other hand externally it

First page on printer's sheet '91' (in Engels's sequence), numbered 68 by Marx

has to function as nationality, internally it has to structure itself as the state. The word commercial society {*bürgerliche Gesellschaft*} appeared in the eighteenth century when property relations had already worked themselves away from the classical & medieval collectivity. Commercial society as such is developed only with the commercial classes {*Bourgeoisie*}; the social organisation developed directly ~~on~~ from production & social interaction which at all times forms the basis of the state & of the rest of the idealistic superstructure ~~can just as well be~~ has from then on been designated by the same word. –

Relation of the state and law to property. – The first form of property, both in the classical world and in the middle ages, is family property, defined for the Romans mainly by war and for the

First page on printer's sheet '91' (in Engels's sequence), numbered 68 by Marx

has to function as nationality, internally it has to structure itself as the state. The word commercial society {*bürgerliche Gesellschaft*} appeared in the eighteenth century when property relations had already worked themselves away from the classical & medieval collectivity. Commercial society as such is developed only with the commercial classes {*Bourgeoisie*}; the social organisation developed directly from production & social interaction which at all times forms the basis of the state & of the rest of the idealistic superstructure has from then on been designated by the same word. –

Relation of the state and law to property. – The first form of property, both in the classical world and in the middle ages, is family property, defined for the Romans mainly by war and for the

Germans by cattle-rearing. {*insertion*} With ancient peoples (partic{ularly} Rome & Sparta) family property appears as state property, because a number of cities families live together in a city, & the right of the individual {appears} as mere possession, which is limited, as with family property generally, only to mova{ble} landed property. Landed property properly so called commenced, for ancient as for modern peoples, with la{nded} movable property. –

& communal life {*Gemeinwesen*} (Slavery

dominium ex jure Quiritum)[1] {*end insertion*} In the case of peoples coming out of the middle ages it family property is developed through different stages – feudal landed property, corporate movable property, manufacturing capital – up to modern capital, conditioned by large-scale industry and universal competition, pure private property which has stripped off all semblance of communal life {*Gemeinwesen*} & has excluded the all influ{ence} action of the state from the development of property. To this modern private property corresponds the

---

1. Rights of ownership according to Roman law.

Second page on printer's sheet '91' (in Engels's sequence), numbered 69 by Marx

Germans by cattle-rearing. With ancient peoples family property appears as state property, because a number of families live together in a city, & the right of the individual {appears} as mere possession, which is limited, as with family property generally, only to landed property. Landed property properly so called commenced, for ancient as for modern peoples, with movable property. – (Slavery & communal life {*Gemeinwesen*} *dominium ex jure Quiritum*)[1] In the case of peoples coming out of the middle ages family property is developed through different stages – feudal landed property, corporate movable property, manufacturing capital – up to modern capital, conditioned by large-scale industry and universal competition, pure private property which has stripped off all semblance of communal life {*Gemeinwesen*} & has excluded action of the state from the development of property. To this modern private property corresponds the modern state,

---

1. Rights of ownership according to Roman law.

Second page on printer's sheet '91' (in Engels's sequence), numbered 69 by Marx

modern state, which is gradually purchased for themselves by the owners of private property through taxation, ~~is~~ completely delivered into their hands through state indebtedness & whose ~~material~~ existence has become wholly dependent on the commercial credit which the owners of private property, the commercial class {*Bourgeoisie*} extend to it, on state bonds which rise & fall on the exchange. The commercial class {*Bourgeoisie*}, because it is a *class*, ~~was~~ is no longer a *medieval estate*, hence {it is} forced to organise itself nationally, not {just} locally any more, & to give a general form to its typical interests.[1] Through the emancipation of private property from communal life {*Gemeinwesen*}, the state has become a particular interest alongside & outside commercial society {*bürgerliche Gesellschaft*}; however it is nothing more than the form of organisation which the commercial class {*Bourgeoisie*}, externally as well as internally, necessarily takes on ~~for commun{al}~~ for the mutual guarantee of its property & its interests. The independence of the state arises in modern times only in

---

1. The sentence was originally written down after the following sentence. *Jahrbuch 2003* Apparat p. 267, ref. 94.26–95.1 l.

which is gradually purchased for themselves by the owners of private property through taxation, completely delivered into their hands through state indebtedness & whose existence has become wholly dependent on the commercial credit which the owners of private property, the commercial class {*Bourgeoisie*} extend to it, on state bonds which rise & fall on the exchange. The commercial class {*Bourgeoisie*}, because it is a *class*, is no longer a *medieval estate*, hence {it is} forced to organise itself nationally, not {just} locally anymore, & to give a general form to its typical interests.[1] Through the emancipation of private property from communal life {*Gemeinwesen*}, the state has become a particular interest alongside & outside commercial society {*bürgerliche Gesellschaft*}; however it is nothing more than the form of organisation which the commercial class {*Bourgeoisie*}, externally as well as internally, necessarily takes on for the mutual guarantee of its property & its interests. The independence of the state arises in modern times only in countries where the medieval

---

1. The sentence was originally written down after the following sentence. *Jahrbuch 2003* Apparat p. 267, ref. 94.26–95.1 l.

Second page on printer's sheet '91' (in Engels's sequence), numbered 69 by Marx

countries where the medieval estates have not yet completely developed into classes, where the medieval estates, ~~overturned~~ abolished in the more progressive countries, still play a role & a mixture exists in which no part of the population can therefore bring itself to dominance over the rest. This is ~~only~~ especially the case in Germany. The most complete example of the modern state is North

Second page on printer's sheet '91' (in Engels's sequence), numbered 69 by Marx

estates have not yet completely developed into classes, where the medieval estates, abolished in the more progressive countries, still play a role & a mixture exists in which no part of the population can therefore bring itself to dominance over the rest. This is especially the case in Germany. The most complete example of the modern state is North

Third page on printer's sheet '91' (in Engels's sequence), numbered 70 by Marx

America. The more recent French, English & American writers are ~~also~~ all agreed that the state only exists for the sake of private property so this has been taken over into everyday consciousness.

Since the state is the form in which the individuals of a dominating class make good their common interests {*insertion*} & {in which} the whole of commercial society {*bürgerliche Gesellschaft*} is summed up as an epoch, {*end insertion*} it follows that ~~everything~~ all common ~~to~~ are institutions facilitated by the state, {and} take on a political form. Hence the illusion that law rests on free will & to be sure on *free* will torn away from its real basis. In just the same way again rightful justice is reduced to positive law.

The rights of private individuals develop from the dissolution of organic communal life at the same time as private property. With the Romans the development of ~~the rights of private individuals~~ private property & the rights of private individuals further industrial & remained without

America. The more recent French, English & American writers are all agreed that the state only exists for the sake of private property so this has been taken over into everyday consciousness.

Since the state is the form in which the individuals of a dominating class make good their common interests & {in which} the whole of commercial society {*bürgerliche Gesellschaft*} is summed up as an epoch, it follows that all common institutions are facilitated by the state, {and} take on a political form. Hence the illusion that law rests on free will & to be sure on *free* will torn away from its real basis. In just the same way again rightful justice is reduced to positive law.

The rights of private individuals develop from the dissolution of organic communal life at the same time as private property. With the Romans the development of private property & the rights of private individuals remained without further industrial

Third page on printer's sheet '91' (in Engels's sequence), numbered 70 by Marx

commercial consequences because their whole mode of production remained the same ~~& this~~ (Usury!) ~~development was not brought about by a development through the expanstion of industry & trade. With~~ With modern peoples, where the feudal form of communal life {*feudale Gemeinwesen*} was dissolved by industry & trade, a new phase, capable of further development, began with ~~the development~~ the inception of private property & the rights of private individuals. The very first city which ~~itself developed~~ conducted an extensive maritime trade in the middle ages, Amalfi, also developed maritime law. As soon as industry & trade, at first in Italy & later in other countries, developed private property further, highly developed Roman rights for private individuals were immediately adopted again & elevated to authority. Later, when the commercial class {*Bourgeoisie*} had achieved enough power for princes to take up its interests in order to destroy the feudal nobility by using the commercial classes {*Bourgeoisie*}, the proper development of the rights of private individuals began in all countries, in France in the 16th century – which went forward in all

Third page on printer's sheet '91' (in Engels's sequence), numbered 70 by Marx

& commercial consequences because their whole mode of production remained the same With modern peoples, where the feudal form of communal life {*feudale Gemeinwesen*} was dissolved by industry & trade, a new phase, capable of further development, began with the inception of private property & the rights of private individuals. The very first city which conducted an extensive maritime trade in the middle ages, Amalfi, also developed maritime law. As soon as industry & trade, at first in Italy & later in other countries, developed private property further, highly developed Roman rights for private individuals were immediately adopted again & elevated to authority. Later, when the commercial class {*Bourgeoisie*} had achieved enough power for princes to take up its interests in order to destroy the feudal nobility by using the commercial classes {*Bourgeoisie*}, the proper development of the rights of private individuals began in all countries, in France in the 16th century – which went forward in all

(Usury!)

countries, except England, on the basis of Roman law. Even in England Roman legal principles had to be adopted for the further development of the rights of private individuals (particularly with respect to movable property). – (It is not to be forgotten that law no more has its own history than does religion.)

With the rights of private individuals the existing property relations are declared to be the result of the general will. The jus utendi et abutendi[1] expresses, on the one hand, that private property has become entirely independent of communal life {*Gemeinwesen*}, & on the other hand, the illusion that private property itself is founded on the mere ~~undef{ined}~~ private will to dispose of a thing arbitrarily. In practice the abuti has very definite economic limitations for the holder of private property ~~so long as~~ if he does not want to see his property and thus his jus abutendi pass into other hands, since anyway the thing, considered in relation to his will, is not really a thing, but only becomes a

Relation for the philosophers = idea. **They only know the relation of "*man*" to himself and hence for them all actual relations turn into ideas.**

---

1. Property right of use and disposal.

countries, except England, on the basis of Roman law. Even in England Roman legal principles had to be adopted for the further development of the rights of private individuals (particularly with respect to movable property). – (It is not to be forgotten that law no more has its own history than does religion.)

With the rights of private individuals the existing property relations are declared to be the result of the general will. The jus utendi et abutendi[1] expresses, on the one hand, that private property has become entirely independent of communal life {*Gemeinwesen*}, & on the other hand, the illusion that private property itself is founded on the mere private will to dispose of a thing arbitrarily. In practice the abuti has very definite economic limitations for the holder of private property if he does not want to see his property and thus his jus abutendi pass into other hands, since anyway the thing, considered in relation to his will, is not really a thing, but only becomes a thing, actual

***Relation for the philosophers = idea.* They only know the relation of "*man*" to himself and hence for them all actual relations turn into ideas.**

---

1. Property right of use and disposal.

Fourth page on printer's sheet '91' (in Engels's sequence), numbered 71 by Marx

thing, actual property, in social interaction
, & independently of the law.
                   (a *relation*
which the philosophers term an idea). This   **To the will however the will {becomes**
juridical illusion, which reduces law and right   **an?}** ***actual*** **{thing}**
                            in the
{*Recht*} to mere will, necessarily leads,
further development of property relations,
                       to
the result that someone is able to have legal
title to a thing without actually having the
thing. If, e.g. the ~~ground~~ rent for a parcel of
land disappears because of competition then
its proprietor indeed holds his legal title to it,
~~but~~ including the jus utendi et abutendi.
However, ~~his property benefits him is usable for him for nothing~~ he can do nothing with it,
as owner of landed property he owns nothing
if he does not have sufficient capital elsewhere
to put ~~the~~ his land to cultivation. This illusion
of the jurists also explains the fact that for
    & for every legal code
them   it is altogether
contingent that individuals enter into relations
with one another e.g. contracts, ~~& the fact that for the content of the con{tracts}~~ & the fact
that these relations are taken to be such that
one [can] enter or not as one likes[1],

---

1. The editors of the *Jahrbuch 2003* text render an earlier state of this passage as follows (continuing to ||72|):

This illusion of the jurists also explains the fact that all relations into ~~the~~ which individuals enter among themselves ~~for~~ {appear} to them {the jurists} as
           contingent
entirely   arbitrary relations, which one [can] enter or not enter, which {are} therefore entirely founded on the individual arbitrary [wil]l

property, in social interaction, &
independently of the law. (a *relation* which
the philosophers term an idea). This juridical
illusion, which reduces law and right
{*Recht*} to mere will, necessarily leads,
in the further development of property
relations, to the result that someone is able to
have legal title to a thing without actually
having the thing. If, e.g. the rent for a parcel of
land disappears because of competition then
its proprietor indeed holds his legal title to it,
including the jus utendi et abutendi.
However, he can do nothing with it, as owner
of landed property he owns nothing if he does
not have sufficient capital elsewhere to put
his land to cultivation. This illusion of the
jurists also explains the fact that for them &
for every legal code it is altogether contingent
that individuals enter into relations with one
another e.g. contracts, & the fact that these
relations are taken to be such that one [can]
enter or not as one likes,

To the will however the will {becomes an?} *actual* **{thing}**

First page on printer's sheet '92' (in Engels's sequence), numbered 72 by Marx

& whose content [res]ts entirely on the arbitrary individual [wil]ls of the contracting parties. – Whenever, through the development of industry & trade, new forms of [commercial int]eraction have been formed, [e.]g. insurance &c companies, it was necessary every time for the legal system {*Recht*} to include them ~~to the~~ within {existing} ways of acquiring property.

First page on printer's sheet '92' (in Engels's sequence), numbered 72 by Marx

& whose content [res]ts entirely on the arbitrary individual [wil]ls of the contracting parties. – Whenever, through the development of industry & trade, new forms of [commercial int]eraction have been formed, [e.]g. insurance &c companies, it was necessary every time for the legal system {*Recht*} to include them within {existing} ways of acquiring property.

Abbreviation and Bibliography

Abbreviation of Work Cited

CW: Karl Marx and Frederick Engels, *Collected Works* in 50 volumes (London: Lawrence & Wishart, 1975–2004).

Other Works Cited

Berlin, Isaiah. 2013 [1939]. *Karl Marx: His Life and Environment*, 5th ed. Princeton and Oxford: Princeton University Press.
Carver, Terrell. 1998. *The Postmodern Marx*. Manchester: Manchester University Press.
———. 2003. *Engels: A Very Short Introduction*. Oxford: Oxford University Press.
———. 2010. "The *German Ideology* Never Took Place." *History of Political Thought*, 31:1 (spring), 107–28.
Carver, Terrell, and Daniel Blank. 2014. *A Political History of the Editions of Marx and Engels's "German ideology Manuscripts."* New York: Palgrave Macmillan.
Kitching, Gavin, and Nigel Pleasants. 2002. *Marx and Wittgenstein: Knowledge, Morality and Politics*. Milton Park: Routledge.
Leopold, David. 2007. *The Young Karl Marx: German Philosophy, Modern Politics, and Human Flourishing*. Cambridge: Cambridge University Press.
Marx, Karl. 1996. "The Eighteenth Brumaire of Louis Bonaparte." In *Marx: Later Political Writings*, ed. Terrell Carver, pp. 31–127. Cambridge: Cambridge University Press.
Rojahn, Jürgen. 2002. "The Emergence of a Theory: The Importance of Marx's Notebooks Exemplified by Those from 1844." *Rethinking Marxism*, 14:4, 29–46.
Taubert, Inge, Hans Pelger, and Jacques Grandjonc. 1998. "Marx' Erklärung vom 3. April 1847." In *MEGA-Studien*, issue no. 1997/2, ed. Internationale Marx-Engels-Stiftung, Amsterdam, pp. 154–61. Amsterdam: IMES.
Veneziani, Roberto. 2012. "Analytical Marxism." *Journal of Economic Surveys*, 26:4, 649–73.

Index

Page references in *italics* refer to the Analytical Introduction

agricultural land, 208, 209
Aikin, John, 266, 267
Alexander (the Great; king, Macedonia), 238, 239
alienation, *25–8, 30,* 94, 95
  abolition of, 100, 101
Amalfi (city), 374, 375
animal activity, *15*
animals, *28*
Anti-Corn Law League, 214, 215
apparatus criticus, 3, 33

Bauer, Bruno, *7,* 114–16, 127
  on antithesis in history and nature, *9,* 50, 51
  on Feuerbach, 154–7, 160–3
  on Hegelian philosophy, 142, 143
  Hegelianism of, 188–93
  on historians, 150, 151
  on history of 18th century, 152, 153
  on humanism, 124, 125
  philosophism of, *12*
  on producing, 62–4
  "Profile of Ludwig Feuerbach" by, 38–43
  on revolution, 126
Bauer, Edgar, *30*
Bogen (printer's sheets), *2*
bourgeois (middle class), 284, 285
  commercial society structured as state by, 364, 365
  development, during feudalism, of, 290–5
  state indebtedness and, 368, 369
Bruno. *See* Bauer, Bruno

capital
  independent of landed property, 218, 219
  industrial capital, 274, 275
  in medieval cities, 226, 227
  mobile, 244, 245, 254, 255

Carthage, 332–5
caste systems, 140–3
Catholicism, 204, 205
Cherbuliez, Charles Victor, 346, 347
cities
  countryside and, 212–19
  development of middle class in, 292–5
  division of labour between, 238, 239
  division of labour in, 228–31
  eighteenth-century development of, 266, 267
  industrial, 276, 277
  manufacturing, 250, 251
  serfs and labourers in, 218–25
  trade among, 232–7
  transformation of, 290, 291
civil society, 100–3, 128–31
class struggle, *24–5,* 184, 185
classes. *See* social classes
colonies, 260, 261, 332–5
colonization, 250–5
commercial class, 254, 255, 258, 259, 278, 279, 304, 305
  commercial society structured as state by, 364, 365
  conflicts between proletariat and, 306, 307
  under feudalism, 294, 295
  See also bourgeois
commercial society, 362–5
common lives, 302–5
communism, *21,* 96–101, 320–3
  Bruno Bauer on, 124, 125
  Feuerbach on, 154–7
  as movement to transform current state of affairs, 92, 93
  social activity under, 90, 91
Communist League, *23*
communistic consciousness, 120–3
communistic revolutions, 120–3

Index

communists, 44, 45
community, 214–19
competition, 284–7, 304–7
conquests, 334–9
consciousness, *13–14*, 72–7
   communistic, 120–3
   division of labour and, 78, 79
   national, 80–3
   praxis and, 130, 131
   production of, 110, 111
   self-consciousness and, *21*
A Contribution to the Critique of Political Economy (Marx), *29*
countryside
   city and, 212–21
   transformation of, 290, 291
   uprisings of middle ages in, 226, 227
   victory of cities over, 276, 277

democracy, 92, 93
Deutsche-Zeitschrift für Philosophie 2003 (German philosophy journal), *3*
division of labour, *15*, 78, 79, 208–11
   accumulation and, 348–51
   caste systems as, 140–3
   between cities, 238, 239
   classes based in, 214, 215
   development of classes and, 296, 297
   in family, 84–9
   during industrialization, 272, 273
   under industrialization, 274, 275
   in medieval cities, 228–31
   mental and material, 82, 83
   separation of production from exchange in, 230–5
   social classes and, 88–91
   transformation of, 298, 299
domestic economy, 286–91
"Draft of a Communist Confession of Faith" (Engels), *23*

"Economic and Philosophical Manuscripts of 1844" (Marx), *25, 26, 30*
ego, 116, 117, 134, 135, 150, 151
   Bruno Bauer on, 154, 155
empirical facts, *9–10*
Engels, Friedrich
   Communist League founding declarations by, *23*

   on Feuerbach, *9, 12*
   handwriting of, *3*
   joint works with Marx, *2*
   on "man" and "nature," *10–11*
   on man-nature merger, *12–13*
   pages numbered by, *3*
   on praxis, *19–20*
   on self-consciousness, *5*
England
   development of trade and manufacturing in, 268–71
   feudalism in, 334, 335
   industrialization in, 272, 273
   Roman law in, 376, 377
English (people), 64, 65
epistemology, *20*
exchange, 210, 211
   forms of, 324–7
   separation of production from, 230–3
export duties, 258, 259

family, 68, 69
   division of labour in, 84–9
   Engels on, *16*
   slavery in, 86, 87
   transformation of, 290, 291
   See also *The Holy Family*
family property, 364–7
feudalism, 198–203
   barbarian capture of Roman Empire and, 340, 341
   conflicts between classes under, 306, 307
   customs duties under, 256, 257
   development of classes during, 292–7
   dissolution of, 248, 249
   in Germany, 344, 345
Feuerbach, Ludwig, *7*
   Bruno Bauer on, 38–43, 154–7, 160–3
   Engels on, *9*
   on "Man," 44, 45
   Marx on, *5, 8,* 34, 35
   materialism of, *12,* 58–61
   method of, *11*
   on natural sciences, 52, 53
   on nature, 56, 57
   perception of actuality of, 46, 47, 50, 51
   philosophism of, *12*
   on "Philosophy of the Future," 158, 159

forces of production, *29,* 116, 117, 120, 121, 134–7
  contradictions between forms of trade and, 282–5
  development of, 328, 329
  in material form, 350–7
  modes of social interaction as, 70, 71
forms of trade, 282–5
France, 154, 155, 272, 273
  private property in, 374–7
freedom, 302, 303, 320, 321
French (people), 64, 65
French revolution, 184, 185, 272, 273
  Hegel on, 172, 173

German ideologists, *4*
"German man," 44, 45
Germans, 62–7, 70–3, 142, 143, 354, 355
Germany, 38, 39
  feudalism in, 344, 345
  state in, 370, 371
  united, 152–5
God, 166–9
  realm of, 144, 145
gold and silver
  American, 256, 257
  circulation of, 250, 251, 254, 255
  end of ban on exporting, 268, 269
  prohibition on the export of, 258, 259
ground, *21, 22*
guilds, 220–41
  peasantry excluded from, 244–9
  relationship between journeymen and master under, 250, 251
  weaving outside of, 244, 245

handwriting of Marx and Engels, *3*
Hegel, Georg Wilhelm Friedrich, *18,* 62, 63
  on history, 194–7
  "History of Philosophy" by, 188, 189, 204, 205
  Stirner and, 172–7, 202–5
Hegelian philosophy, 142, 143, 150, 151
  of Bruno Bauer and Stirner, 188–93
Hegelians, *18*
Henry VIII (king, England), 248, 249
hierarchy, 198–205
history, *7, 22,* 64, 65
  antithesis of nature and, *9–10,* 50, 51
  conquests as driving force in, 334–9
  Hegel on, 194–7
  Hegelian philosophy of, 142, 143
  made natural, *30*
  materialist interpretation of, *2*
  prehistory and, *13,* 66, 67
  production tied to, 72, 73, 128, 129, 136–9
  self-consciousness and, 132, 133
  Stirner on, 202–5
  as succession of generations, 104, 105
  as world history, 106–9
"holy family," 162, 163
The Holy Family (Engels and Marx), *2, 25, 30, 34, 35,* 124, 125
human activity, *15*
humans (man)
  classes as phases of development of, 298, 299
  concept of, 186, 187
  consciousness in, *13–14,* 72–7
  exchanges between, 210, 211
  Feuerbach, 44, 45
  loving relationships of, 58, 59
  nature distinct from, *10–12,* 56, 57
  remaking of nature and men by, 102, 103
  struggle with nature, 50, 51
  substituted for individuals, 362, 363

Iceland, 332–5
idealists, *4, 7*
ideas
  of dominant class, 176–87
  empirical basis for, 192–5
  of rulers, 192, 193
ideologists, *8,* 178, 179
industrialization, 272–81
instruments of production, 208, 209, 212, 213
  in city and countryside, 214, 215
intellectual production, *19,* 112, 113
  tied to dominant class, 176–9
inventions, *23–4,* 236–9
Italy, 338–41

Jesuits, 204, 205

labour, 346, 347, 352–5
  material and intellectual, 212, 213
  of weavers, 242–5
labourers. *See* proletariat

land, 208, 209
  capital independent of, 218, 219
language, *14,* 74, 75
law, 378–81
  maritime, 374, 375
  Roman, 376, 377
liberation, *5, 6,* 34–7
loving relationships, 58, 59
Lumpenproletariat, 340, 341

Manifesto of the Communist Party (Marx and Engels), *2, 22*
manufacturing
  development of, 238, 239, 244, 245, 248, 249
  for export, 264, 265
  protective tariffs for, 260–3
  relationship between labourer and capitalist under, 250, 251
maritime law, 374, 375
markets
  English dominance of, 268–71
  world, 250–5
Marx, Karl
  handwriting of, *3*
  joint works with Engels, *2*
  manuscripts left unfinished by, *1*
  on Proudon, *23, 30*
  on "woman question," *12*
material, *20*
materialism, *1, 5, 13*
  Feuerbach's, *12,* 58–61
  idealism versus, *4*
"materialist interpretation of history," *2*
matter/consciousness dichotomy, *29*
Mayer, Gustav, *2*
Mehring, Franz, *7*
merchants
  development of class of, 232, 233
  influence of, 264, 265
  with mobile capital, 244, 245
  state protection for, 266, 267
mice, *2*
middle class (bourgeois). *See* bourgeois
mind/matter dichotomy, *13, 15*
modes of production, *29*
  conjoined with modes of social interaction, 70, 71
money, 210, 211, 346, 347
  development of system of, 268, 269, 274, 275

Naples (Italy), 334, 335
Napoleon Bonaparte, 108, 109
"natural," *16–18*
nature
  antithesis of history and, *9–10,* 50, 51
  distinct from humans, *10–12,* 56, 57
  historicization of, *30*
  remaking of, by men, 102, 103
Newton, Isaac, 272, 273
North America, 320, 321, 332, 333
  modern state in, 370–3

On the Jewish Question (Marx), *25*
"ordinary experience" epistemology, *18*

peasantry, 226, 227
  excluded from guilds, 244–9
personal freedom, 302, 303, 320, 321
philosophers, 46, 47
philosophism, *12*
Phoenicians, *24,* 236–9
Pinto, Isaac, 266, 267
population, 78, 79
The Poverty of Philosophy (Marx), *23*
practical production, *19*
praxis, 138, 139
  consciousness and, 130, 131
  Engels on, *19–20*
prehistory, *13,* 66, 67
"Principles of Communism" (Engels), *23*
private property, 212–19, 276–9, 286, 287, 346–9
  ceases to exist, 360, 361
  forces of production becomes, 356, 357
  modern state and, 366–9, 372–7
production
  history tied to, 72, 73, 128, 129, 136–9
  instruments of, 208, 209, 212–15
  modes of, *29,* 70, 71
  separation of exchange from, 230–3
  See also forces of production
productive forces, 132–5, 276–9
  development of, 328, 329
  forms of exchange specific to, 324, 325
  See also forces of production
proletariat (workers), 100, 101, 184, 185, 308–11
  competition among, 284, 285
  conditions of existence of, 316–19
  conflicts between commercial class and, 306, 307

development of, as class, 280, 281
  under feudalism, 294–7
  labour transformed by, 312–15
  revolution by, 358–61
property
  family property, 364–7
  as historical product, *17–18*, 94, 95
  See also private property
Protestantism, 170, 171
Proudon, Pierre Joseph, *23, 30*

rabble, 222–7
relations of production, *29*
religion, 80, 81, 84, 128, 130–3, 138–41, 148, 149
  Catholicism, 204, 205
  natural, 76, 77
  "of love," 126
  Protestantism, 170, 171
  voice of God in, 166–9
revolutionary class, 178–83
revolutions, 330, 331
  basis for, 282, 283
  Bruno Bauer on, 126
  communistic, 120–3
  by proletariat, 358–61
Roman Empire, 340, 341
  law of, 376, 377
  private property in, 372–5

"Sancho, Saint." *See* Bauer, Bruno
science, 272–5
self-consciousness, *5*, 34, 35, 126, 127, 194, 195
  Bruno Bauer on, 142, 143
  consciousness and, *21*, 130, 131
  Feuerbach on, 42, 43
  history and, 132, 133
  philosophers on, 134, 135
serfs, 218–21, 306–9
  become urban citizens, 312, 313
silver. *See* gold and silver
Sismondi, Jean Charles Léonard de, 346, 347
slavery, 338, 339, 366, 367
Smith, Adam, 268, 269
social activity, *17,* 68, 69
social classes, 52, 53, 116–21
  abolition of, 122, 123
  based in division of labour, 214, 215
  collective interests of members of, 314, 315
  common lives in, 302–5

division of labour and, 88–91
dominance and, 90, 91
dominant ideas tied to, 176–87
under feudalism, 294–7
as phases of development of man, 298, 299
social interaction
  means of, 116, 117
  modes of, 70, 71
state, *29,* 128, 130, 131
  commercial society structured as, 364, 365
  merchants and manufacturers protected by, 266, 267
  money raised for, 256–9
  private property and, 366–9, 372–7
Stirner, Max, *28,* 108, 142, 143, 162, 163, 326, 327
  Bruno Bauer on, 160, 161
  Hegel and, 172–7
  Hegelianism of, 188–93
  on history, 198, 199, 202–5
  on middle ages, 206, 207
substance, Feuerbach on, 40–3
supply and demand, 96, 97, 100, 101

tariffs, 262, 263, 272–5
taxation, 368, 369
"Theses on Feuerbach" (Marx), *4*
trade, 48, 49, 94, 95
  among cities, 232–7
  class of merchants for, 232, 233
  with colonies, 260, 261
  in eighteenth century, 266–9
  forms of, 282–5
  manufacturing for, 250, 251
  protective tariffs for, 262, 263, 272–5
  worldwide, 238, 239, 254–7
  in woven goods, 242–5

unions, 222, 223

vagabondage, 248, 249
Venedey, Jacob, 154, 155

wars, 338, 339
weaving and weavers, 242–5
women
  Engels on, *16*
  "woman question," *12*
workers. *See* proletariat
world market, 110, 111